Development Projects for a New Millennium

Anil Hira and Trevor Parfitt

Westport, Connecticut
London

Library of Congress Cataloging-in-Publication Data

Hira, Anil.
   Development projects for a new millennium / Anil Hira and Trevor Parfitt.
      p.   cm.
   Includes bibliographical references and index.
   ISBN 0–275–97502–9 (alk. paper) — ISBN 0–275–97503–7 (pbk. : alk. paper)
      1. Economic assistance—Developing countries.   2. Non-governmental
organizations—Developing countries.   3. Economic development.   I. Parfitt, Trevor W.,
1954–   II. Title.
   HC59.7.H487   2004
   338.9′009172′4—dc21   2003052899

British Library Cataloguing in Publication Data is available.

Library of Congress Catalog Card Number: 2003052899
ISBN: 0–275–97502–9
      0–275–97503–7 (pbk.)

First published in 2004

Praeger Publishers, 88 Post Road West, Westport, CT 06881
An imprint of Greenwood Publishing Group, Inc.
www.praeger.com

Printed in the United States of America

The paper used in this book complies with the
Permanent Paper Standard issued by the National
Information Standards Organization (Z39.48–1984).

10   9   8   7   6   5   4   3   2   1

Andy Hira would like to dedicate this book to Dean Cynthia Nelson, Tim Sullivan, and his co-author, who gave him his first chance to develop into a scholar.

Contents

Illustrations

Tables

Figures

Acknowledgments

This book comes out of a series of conversations that Trevor Parfitt and I began in 1997 regarding the lack of good, up-to-date, but critical books on development project management, as well as our passion for postmodernism. I made the recently graduated error then of pointing out the various problems with the existing literature, and so Trevor quite naturally told me to do something better. The initial research was funded by the American University in Cairo through a trip back to Washington. Preparing for detailed conversations on the subject with Mike McNamara gave me the opportunity to finally follow through on my unexpected commitment several years later. So here it is, at long last. On a practical level, we find that both in terms of development theory and actual experiments occurring in project management, there is an opportunity being missed to share information and ideas that could help increase aid effectiveness. As academics, we see our role in this book as providing a starting point for bringing into clearer analytical light the debates and practices in a way that development practitioners simply cannot afford to. In order to make the book user-friendly for students and practitioners as well as academics, we have sought to stick to the main points without extensive citation. We also provide a general bibliography at the end, with selected works relevant to each chapter subject. Our contacts and experience in the development community, both among practitioners and fellow academics, have been the primary sources of applied information, and we provide our own theoretical reflections. While we agree on both the general approach to the book and the particular issues that are raised, we should note here that the reader may notice nuanced differences in style and substance in the various chapters on which we took the lead. Trevor has done the yeoman's work of writing the most important chapters on current project management, participation, and environment, and I have written the introduction and chapters on evaluation, governance, and gender. We wish to thank first and foremost our students at the American University in Cairo, who helped to bring these issues forward through their own project management experiences. Particular thanks are due to Ms. Amina El Afifi and Mr. Ian Hargreaves, I.C.T. Facilitator at Manchester Central Library in the UK, both of whom provided invaluable assistance in formatting the tables in Trevor Parfitt's chapters. Trevor would also like to thank Craig Docherty for introducing him to the ideas of postmodernity all those years ago and Andy Hira for helping to apply that interest in the context of development. We would also like to highlight the helpful comments of colleagues Mike McNamara, Mónica Escudero, Kathleen Staudt, Duncan Knowler, James Busumtwi-Sam, Mike Howlett, Daniel Cohen, Bob Anderson, and Jane Jaquette, though the project was aided in various ways by numerous individuals over the years. Last but certainly not least, we would like to thank the editor, James Sabin, for his patience while we worked our way through the manuscript.

CHAPTER 1

Development Aid in the Post–Cold War Era

We continue to live in a world of crushing inequity and overwhelming poverty for a large part of our fellow human beings. Those of us in the First World live in a world of comforts, while many of our neighbors elsewhere live in a world of crushing day-to-day constraints. The principle idea behind development has been to bridge this gap; it is a simple idea with clear moral authority, yet, after 50 years of development aid, the 2–3 parallel worlds of comfort and misery continue. This book is designed to present in a manner accessible to students, practitioners, and researchers concrete steps to deal with the new situation of development after the end of the Cold War and in the new millennium.[1] Postmodernism, as we explain later in this chapter, has raised some serious questions about the very meaning of development as well as how it can be carried out,[2] but has never really been applied to project analysis.[3] We hope this book will be a first step in bringing together a new set of ideas, practices, opportunities, constraints, and problems suggested by postmodern theory that we believe can be applied to development projects. Our postmodern concerns are reflected in a number of exciting new initiatives in development project management[4] that we hope to share with the development community in this book. As academics, we aspire not only to bring critical analysis to the new reality, but also to help to push development project management forward in a way that is more satisfying to the participants in development projects, and that ultimately leads to longer-lasting and palpable impacts.

Before breaching the present confusion that surrounds development aid, we should briefly review the nature of aid. In the process, we will discuss the various definitions of aid, and how both the post–Cold War context and a new set of ideas has opened the way for a revolution in development thinking. We highlight the fact that aid has always been motivated and implemented with a variety of motives, both selfish and altruistic. Our idea is to find a way in which this mixture can be combined in a useful way. This chapter will lay the groundwork, then, for our explanation of how new ideas about aid might work with new practices in a better way for the participants of development projects.

INTRODUCTION: DECONSTRUCTING DEVELOPMENT AID[5]

Orientation: Different Types of Aid

There are at least 4 basic categories of types of aid:

1. Emergency food aid
2. Structural adjustment (macroeconomic policy-based and institution-building)
3. Infrastructure and large-capital project lending
4. Grassroots, micro-level project aid

This book focuses on institution-building from category 2 and all aspects of category 4, though we believe the implications of the various chapters, such as evaluation, are important for all types of projects. For the sake of brevity, we also focus on U.S. foreign policy, as we see this as the prime mover in the overall parameters of development policy.

The Genealogy of Development: A Quick Primer

When we think about development these days, it seems a commonplace pillar of international relations that has always existed. Actually, development of nations, which is what we have in mind here, as an idea, is *only about 50 years old.* Certainly the ideas of developing certain regions or one's own political entity are common to any political enterprise, but the idea of aiding another region to progressively change one's economic, political, and/or social systems is really a product of the post–World War II era.

Much of the relationship in years prior to World War II was either between colonizers and colonies or in the form of industrialized countries seeking to secure their companies' investments in the developing world. In fact, we might even think of the postwar period as one in which development and the notion of the developing world was born, on the pragmatism and ideals of American foreign policy in regard to Western Europe. The guiding motivation was a desire to avoid what were seen as the mistakes of World War I that supposedly led to the conditions leading to World War II. This diagnosis included a belief that widespread economic hardship in defeated Germany after World War I aided the German motivation to seek war as a means of redress. The hardship was caused, in the American view, in good part from the reparations and lack of international financial stability following World War I. More importantly, the American foreign-policy community believed that the isolationist policy of America during the better part of World War I in regard to European conflicts was no longer sustainable now that the United States had emerged as the strongest power.

The U.S. government was determined to make a difference in Europe to help stabilize international relations in military and political terms and began to see economic unhappiness as a potential source of military conflict. Bearing in mind the United States' refusal to join the League of Nations, the United Nations was seen as a key actor for discouraging military action as a solution for countries unhappy with their states of affairs. Unfortunately, the emergence of strong ideological and national interest differences with the former ally, the Soviet Union, precluded any strong confidence in the United Nations as an instrument of power. The Bretton Woods Conference set the stage for the new international financial structure, with the International Monetary Fund as the main coordinator of monetary adjustments. The key institution for our purposes came out of the European Bank for Reconstruction and Development, which later became the International Bank for Reconstruction and Development (IBRD), or World Bank, as it is commonly known. This institution was set up following the exemplar of the famous Marshall Plan by the United States to help ravaged European countries to reconstruct their economies.[6] Moreover, given the lessons of World War I, as well as the now-looming threat of Communism through the foreign policy of the Soviet Union, the United States extended its reconstruction aid to the losers of World War II, namely Germany and Italy. European powers also moved to aid their colonies, initially to reconstruct their commercial empires and to reward them for wartime support.

As the Soviet Union began to consolidate its buffer zone from Western Europe by installing puppet governments in Eastern Europe, the idea of a Cold War that could be fought through economic as well as military aid became established in the U.S. and, later, the Western European mindsets. Aid has been transferred in two forms, economic and military. For our purposes, we shall focus on economic aid, since that aid is apparently more concerned with development. Moreover, as the extension of the Cold War "conflict by proxy" spread to areas in the developing world, such as Cuba in 1960, the idea, still unproven, gradually spread among the donor countries that economic aid would buy allies (whether democratic or not), thus reducing the threat of Communism. The conversion of China to Communism in 1949, in particular, led the United States to consider economic aid a key component of their strategy to slow Communism's spread. The thinking was related to the commonsense idea that populations who were frustrated by their low material standards of living would naturally be more prone to calls for revolution by Communist organizers. Thus the game was set for more than 40 years, with Communism and Soviet interests countering economic liberalism and the United States. While in rhetoric the United States did also see democracy as part of the ideological struggle, in practice the U.S. government frequently supported authoritarian and oppressive regimes, as long as they were anti-Communist. What, you may ask, about multinational aid as funneled through international organizations? While the symbolic independence of international organizations gives them important leeway, as we shall see from Table 3, these organizations are largely dependent for resources upon the United States, Western Europe, and Japan (First World). They have naturally been quite responsive to their primary donors' concerns.

Within the overall context of Cold War relations, there were distinct periods of development practice. The large-capital and infrastructure project emphasis of the 1950s and early 1960s were supplemented in the late 1960s with a new emphasis on providing basic human needs, or poverty alleviation, that has continued through the present. The 1980s brought in a strong call for debt relief among developing world countries, but in practice led the way to structural adjustment lending, meaning that capital for new loan payments was forthcoming, as long as neoliberal (or market-liberalizing) policies were adopted. Despite these changes in emphasis, the bottom line is that aid was, and has always been, overwhelmingly determined by its donors' key interests. Aid is, and always has been, "tied." During the Cold War, the premise that the hungry were more prone to Communism, not some notion of altruism, led the way for the changes in development emphasis toward more grassroots poverty alleviation.

This chapter of international relations ended in 1989, when the Soviet Union, for a variety of reasons that are highly disputable, began to abandon Communism as well as its long-standing foreign policy of consolidation and expansion of power. The crisis in the Soviet Union opened the way for newly independent governments in Eastern Europe and in Central Asia. The transformation was accompanied by the equally interesting move toward a market economy, albeit under the leadership of the Communist Party under new leadership in China. For the developing world, the current scenario is thus completely transformed. We turn now to attempting to sketch out this brave new world in which development practitioners find themselves.

THE CONTEXT OF AID IN A POST–COLD WAR ERA

We can now ask the question, if development aid was a product of the Cold War by proxy, how does the end of the Cold War change the reasons, amount, and allocations of aid? If the primary reason for aid was to shore up either Communist or anti-Communist regimes, what foreign policy reasons can be given for continuing foreign aid? The answers to these questions will help us to set the macro-level scene, which is vital to our overall task of describing

Table 1.1a
Top 20 Grant and Loan Recipients before and after the Cold War: Multilateral Assistance ($ millions)

ODA Grants Cold War 1975–89	Annual Average	Grants Post–Cold War 1990–95	Annual Average	Multilateral Loans CW 1975–89	Annual Average	Multil. Loans Post–CW 1990–95	Annual Average
India	191.4	Ethiopia	364.6	India	1290.0	India	2300.2
Pakistan	139.5	Sudan	220.9	Brazil	909.3	Mexico	2157.4
Bangladesh	129.1	Mozambique	215.4	Mexico	854.7	China	1966.7
Ethiopia	122.7	Bangladesh	212.3	Indonesia	832.1	Indonesia	1839.6
Sudan	107.4	India	210.2	Turkey	607.7	Pakistan	1302.2
Somalia	87.0	Malawi	161.9	South Korea	487.2	Argentina	1193.9
Egypt	80.2	China	152.3	Colombia	417.3	Brazil	1018.1
China	76.3	Pakistan	151.7	Pakistan	408.7	Turkey	813.2
Tanzania	57.1	Kenya	147.0	Philippines	394.9	Morocco	776.2
Indonesia	53.2	Rwanda	142.8	Egypt	376.1	Philippines	760.3
Vietnam	49.7	Tanzania	136.5	Bangladesh	366.0	Bangladesh	730.7
Thailand	48.8	Egypt	136.2	Argentina	344.8	Algeria	704.7
Mali	48.3	Angola	135.6	China	325.7	Colombia	576.5
Mozambique	48.2	Uganda	132.0	Morocco	308.5	Nigeria	522.4
Zaire	45.0	Poland	131.1	Thailand	293.4	Hungary	518.5
Senegal	43.1	Côte d'Ivoire	126.2	Chile	231.9	Peru	498.5
Uganda	41.1	Morocco	125.6	Nigeria	209.5	Tunisia	491.2
Niger	40.6	Jordan	121.0	Ecuador	162.9	Côte d'Ivoire	444.8
Yemen	39.3	Somalia	109.7	Côte d'Ivoire	162.6	Venezuela	444.7
Chad	39.1	Cameroon	101.2	Algeria	162.2	Zambia	442.6
Côte d'Ivoire	38.1	Burundi	98.9	Kenya	154.7	Russian Federation	425.2
TOTAL	2788.58	TOTAL	7250.152	TOTAL	13394.8	TOTAL	30370.6

Notes: Units are US$ millions
Source: Author's calculations from Charles C. Chang, Eduardo Fernandez-Arias, Luis Serven, "Measuring Aid Flows, A New Approach," World Bank, 1998.

how the actual practices of development projects are changing in response to new ideas and the new environment.

Where has aid historically gone, who were the major donors, and where is it going now? To answer this question, we should first note the sea change in aid with the end of the Cold War as demonstrated in Table 1. Since security threats are no longer nearly as important a concern to the First World as during the Cold War, public aid as a whole has declined, and private capital flows have become increasingly important. Simply put, the United States and its partners care less about the developing world because there is no longer a threat of Communism to win over the impoverished masses there.

Second, as aid has moved from an economic- and security-motivated strategy for the First World to an almost purely economic angle, bilateral and multilateral aid (through international organizations) as a percentage of GDP (gross domestic product) have both declined.[7] Tables 1.1a and 1.1b show that the size of aid loans far outweigh grants, and that loans go to middle-level

Table 1.1b
Top 20 Grant and Loan Recipients before and after the Cold War: Bilateral Assistance ($ millions)

Bilateral Grants Cold War	Annual Average	Bilateral Grants Post–Cold War	Annual Average	Bilateral Loans 1975-89	Annual Average	Bilateral Loans 1990-95	Annual Average
Egypt	820.5	Egypt	2824.7	Egypt	980.2	Indonesia	2785.7
Syria	716.8	Poland	1605.5	Indonesia	970.5	China	2553.3
India	579.0	Russian Federation	1195.5	India	788.7	Russian Federation	1582.6
Bangladesh	576.3	Bangladesh	876.5	Turkey	636.5	India	1375.8
Jordan	569.7	Tanzania	739.0	Brazil	630.7	Philippines	963.7
Tanzania	431.8	India	729.8	Pakistan	531.9	Algeria	824.5
Sudan	363.2	Mozambique	718.2	China	478.7	Pakistan	816.4
Indonesia	269.6	Turkey	694.5	Mexico	445.5	Mexico	708.4
Papua New Guinea	268.6	Indonesia	620.7	Algeria	430.9	Thailand	705.4
Pakistan	257.9	China	609.3	South Korea	424.2	Turkey	633.2
Kenya	247.7	Philippines	585.8	Morocco	389.3	Argentina	579.6
Yemen	247.5	Zambia	536.2	Poland	381.1	Egypt	573.8
Philippines	218.2	Kenya	520.5	Bangladesh	332.5	South Korea	482.2
Zaire	186.7	Senegal	491.3	Philippines	329.9	Malaysia	410.0
Mozambique	183.5	Ethiopia	478.8	Peru	319.2	Morocco	370.8
Ethiopia	178.7	Nicaragua	429.1	Nicaragua	280.8	Côte d'Ivoire	329.0
Morocco	175.5	Bolivia	415.2	Thailand	256.4	Tunisia	310.5
Somalia	172.8	Morocco	400.8	Sudan	246.0	Colombia	246.5
Senegal	168.6	Pakistan	396.9	Tunisia	222.7	Jordan	243.0
Sri Lanka	166.7	Somalia	370.8	Romania	171.0	Cameroon	231.4
Thailand	163.3	Côte d'Ivoire	343.6	Malaysia	170.9	Brazil	210.4
TOTAL	11512.9	TOTAL	28191.5	TOTAL	14096.2	TOTAL	21829.9

Notes: Units are US$ millions
Source: Author's calculations from Charles C. Chang, Eduardo Fernandez-Arias, Luis Serven, "Measuring Aid Flows, A New Approach," World Bank, 1998.

developing countries in which the United States and its European allies have economic and security interests (such as petroleum). After the Cold War, a large percentage of aid has been redirected to the former Soviet bloc, particularly at promising economic markets such as Russia and China.

This picture of how much almost all aid is tied to the dominant powers' international interests is reinforced when we consider the top donors and recipients of bilateral aid, as presented in Table 1.2.

Both bilateral and multilateral aid still serve very important purposes in the international schemes of the First World after the Cold War. First, they serve to buffer the international financial system from crisis. Therefore, in recent years, loans have increased to East Asian countries to deal with the financial meltdown that began there in the mid-1990s. Second, multilateral organizations play the *gatekeeper* role for international finance, which we will show is

Table 1.2
Top Donors and Recipients of Bilateral Aid, 1999

Top 5 Recipients of Net ODA by Source Country, 1999

Source Country

	France		Germany		Japan	
Total LDCs	4124.7		3277.6		10475.8	
Top 5	*Recipients*	*Amount*	*Recipients*	*Amount*	*Recipients*	*Amount*
1	French Polynesia	352.7	China	304.6	Indonesia	1605.8
2	New Caledonia	313.9	Yugoslavia	119.1	China	1226
3	Egypt	254.1	Pakistan	83.4	Thailand	880.3
4	Senegal	226.4	Tanzania	66.6	Vietnam	680
5	Morocco	223.7	Bosnia & Hz	65	India	634

	Netherlands		United Kingdom		United States	
Total LDCs	2161.6		2248.6		6847.9	
Top 5	*Recipients*	*Amount*	*Recipients*	*Amount*	*Recipients*	*Amount*
1	Neth. Antilles	126.2	India	131.7	Israel*	2253
2	Bosnia & Hz.	77.0	Bangladesh	114.9	Egypt	666.8
3	Indonesia	71.9	Uganda	96.4	Bosnia & Hz.	218.9
4	Yugoslavia	63.1	Ghana	91.8	Indonesia	207
5	Tanzania	55.2	Tanzania	88.6	Colombia	183.8

Other Donors	Total LDCs
Australia	729.8
Austria	343.9
Belgium	436.7
Canada	1171.9
Denmark	1025.7
Italy	450.6
Norway	1006.7
Spain	829.4
Sweden	1146.3
Switzerland	719.1

Notes: Units are US$ millions; Countries with ≥$2,000 of ODA; Total includes only countries OECD classifies as less developed countries; i.e., more advanced and former Soviet bloc states are not included.

*Israel figure is for 1996

Source: OECD, *Geographical distribution of financial flows to less developed countries, 1995–99* (Paris: OECD, 2000).

the big player in development these days. Thus, the amount of loans from the International Monetary Fund (IMF) is not nearly as important as the rhetoric of critics of the IMF might suggest. Rather, the key is that IMF disapproval of a country's policies acts as a signal for all the private investment to stay, increase, or flee the country. Thus, the IMF acts as the unifying club for the private capital markets of the First World. Third, the World Bank's role is particularly magnified because of its sectoral expertise. Since most developing-world countries lack adequate technological and managerial expertise for large infrastructure and market reform operations, they ask for World Bank help on those projects. This means the World Bank has an enormous influence in shaping the key economic sectors of a country. Notwithstanding the rhetoric of independence of these agencies, all of their influences are conducted in the primary interest of the First World countries, as we realistically should expect, given that they are the primary financiers.

In terms of multilateral aid, we have to consider the dominance of the "big 3" in aid: the IMF, the World Bank, and the United Nations (UN). The fact of the matter is that that each of these organizations is an instrument for the interests of the First World, and primarily for the United States, as demonstrated in Table 1.3.[8]

Since the voting control noted above drastically *understates* the actual influence of the First World through the gatekeeper function, apologists may counter that, despite the influence of the major developed countries, these international organizations really do have some independence of action. While the UN is a highly diversified organization, we should not forget that it still depends largely on the developed countries for most of its finances. When the United States decided in the early 1990s to isolate UNESCO, for example, that arm of the UN was virtually paralyzed. The present sanctimony of the development community now has a firm base in the UN peacekeeping function. Yet we must again question the wisdom of such naïve optimism. In every case, the UN's peacekeeping missions are done at the behest and in the interests of the dominant global powers—the United States, Europe, and Japan. The UN's failure in Somalia and Lebanon, its present mission in Afghanistan, and, more importantly, the lack of concern about Sierra Leone, Algeria, the crisis in Rwanda, and its marginalization in the outcome of the invasion and reconstruction of Iraq all demonstrate that whatever the good intentions or symbolism of its role in the post–Cold War period, the reality is that it is intimately tied to U.S. foreign-policy interests and unable to act independently.

We can provide further evidence of our extreme doubt about the optimistic point of view by looking at *where* the World Bank placed resources (both loans and assistance) in 2000.

What we see from Table 1.4 is that international aid *does not go to the most impoverished*.[9] Rather, aid goes to those middle-level developing countries with the greatest market growth potential, places where First World exporters might have expansion. Therefore, the aim of international organizations can

Table 1.3
Control of International Organizations by Developed Countries

IMF Country	Voting %	World Bank Country	Voting %	UN Country	% assessment
United States	17.16	United States	16.49	US	22
Japan	6.16	Japan	7.91	Japan	19.63
Germany	6.02	Germany	4.52	Germany	9.83
France	4.97	France	4.33	France	6.5
United Kingdom	4.97	United Kingdom	4.33	UK	5.57
Italy	3.27	Canada	2.8	Italy	5.09
Canada	2.95	Italy	2.8	Sub-total	68.62
Netherlands	2.39	Netherlands	2.22		
Belgium	2.14	Belgium	1.82		
Switzerland	1.61	Switzerland	1.67		
Australia	1.51	Australia	1.54		
Spain	1.42	Spain	1.49		
Sweden	1.12	Sweden	0.95		
Sub-total	55.69	Sub-total	52.87		

We should note that the United States has been in arrears in terms of its UN debt for some time now. The resulting crisis within the organization speaks to its dependence on the United States for support. By assessment, we mean the amount owed to the UN each year.

Sources: IMF, *2000 Annual Report* (Washington, D.C.: IMF); World Bank, *Annual Report 2000*, (Washington, D.C.: World Bank); http://www.globalpolicy.org/ for UN breakdown.

generally be summarized as leveraging needed aid and private capital through its gatekeeper functions in return for market-opening reforms, which benefit First World companies and consumers. The two notable exceptions above are Pakistan and the Philippines. These can be explained by U.S. security interests. Pakistan has a unique security role that it plays for the United States in terms of U.S. interests in the petroleum-rich, but largely Muslim, Middle East, and in distracting the attention and resources of India. Despite the fact that the United States has given up its security bases there, the Philippines continues to play a very important role as a gateway to East Asia and the growing power of China. Both are fighting an Islamic insurgency and thus at the center of the new concern about terrorism.

In the United States, the U.S. Agency for International Development (AID), has experienced budget cutbacks and a change in priorities, a reflection of the diminished interest of the U.S. Congress in development assistance. AID has now taken a junior role to the lead of the Department of State, and there have even been conversations about phasing it out altogether. In addition, AID is

Table 1.4
Top World Bank Recipients in 2000

Country	Total
Argentina	17,771.8
Brazil	28,702.8
China	34,725.5
India	53,790.2
Indonesia	28,244.5
South Korea	15,757.8
Mexico	31,178.8
Pakistan	12,082.3
Philippines	11,288.1
Russian Fed.	11,811.5
Turkey	15,718.7

Notes: Units are US$ millions; total of IBRD loans and IDA credits
Source: World Bank, *Annual Report 2000* (Washington, D.C.: World Bank), Appendix 13.

run differently. There is a new emphasis on subcontracting out work, and, most recently, a new management system for projects that promotes management by objectives and attempts to demonstrate measurable successes. As we see from the budget priorities in Figure 1.1, USAID is in good part tying its organizational future to its ability to help pave the way for market reforms. Those market reforms in turn mean new opportunities for U.S. businesses, which could be a powerful constituency (so AID and its counterparts hope) for the continuation of U.S. aid.

European Aid Trends

A survey of European aid donors reveals that they are driven by similar concerns for strategic and economic advantage.[10] An additional factor in examining the activities of donors such as the United Kingdom and France is that they were major colonial powers and often their aid is directed toward their ex-colonies in the attempt to maintain clientelistic relations with them. Thus, Table 1.2 reveals that the five largest recipients of UK aid were once British colonies, while the five largest recipients of French aid are all nations that France once had imperial interests in, even if they were not all formally colonized. The strategic and economic interests underlying much European aid are particularly evident if one examines the trends in the targeting of European Union (EU) aid. The EU has emerged as a major aid donor since

Figure 1.1
Changing Priorities of USAID, 1961 and 2000

1961: President Kennedy's justification for a new aid program

1. Current foreign aid programs were unsatisfactory and ill-suited to meet the U.S.'s world challenges.
2. "The economic collapse of developing countries 'would be disastrous to our national security, harmful to our comparative prosperity, and offensive to our conscience. . . ."
3. The 1960s presented an historical opportunity for less-developed nations to move to self-sustained economic growth.

The program was based upon "country-by-country planning and a commitment of resources on a multi-year, programmed basis." The focus was to achieve economic growth and democratic stability to combat the spread of communism and instability arising from poverty.

2000 Priorities, from the 2000 Accountability Report
(budgeted amounts for FY2000 in parentheses in US$)

1. Encourage broad-based economic growth and agricultural development ($3.3b)
2. Strengthen democracy and good governance ($349.6m)
3. Build human capacity through education and training ($125.5m)
4. Stabilize world population and protect human health ($1.4b)
5. Protect the environment for long-term sustainability ($448.5m)
6. Promote humanitarian assistance ($1b)

The program has regional and functional bureaus. USAID follows a "managing for results" method of strategic planning, with a renewed emphasis on assessing performance through the development of performance data.

Sources: USAID Web site (http://www.usaid.gov/)—"A History of Foreign Assistance" for 1961 priorities, and "USAID FY 2000 Accountability Report," retrieved May 1, 2001. b = billions; m = millions.

its foundation in 1957. In the 1990s it was the fifth-largest aid donor, providing 7.3 billion ECU (European Currency Units, which generally are of a similar value to the U.S. dollar) in 1995, which amounted to 10.5% of all aid disbursed by OECD states.[11] Initially its main efforts complemented the post-imperial interests of its member states in that most of its aid was directed to their ex-colonies in Africa, the Caribbean, and the Pacific (the ACP states) through the Yaounde Conventions and then the Lomé Conventions. However, in recent years the proportion of EU assistance flowing to the ACP states has declined as other concerns have emerged that have diverted EU aid to other areas. Most notably the fall of Communism and the conversion of Eastern Europe to capitalism has led to an increase of EU aid to these post-Communist states in the attempt to bolster Western European interests in the area. The 1990s also saw the emergence of the Euromed initiative through which the EU has enhanced its aid to neighboring states in the Mediterranean. This is in good part a response to increasing European concerns at high levels of illegal migration into the European Union, particularly from North Africa. A major element of Euromed involves the North African states accepting a large measure of the responsibility for prevention of such migration, their incentive being enhanced levels of aid and some limited trade concessions on the European market.[12] All of this is indicative that EU aid targeting is driven more by Europe's changing foreign-policy concerns than by any concern with the plight of the developing world poor.

Why Aid Is Losing Importance

More importantly, aid has become dwarfed by the amounts of private capital investment, which is now viewed as the key vehicle for development, as illustrated in Table 1.5. Parallel to this development is the revolution in ideas since the 1980s in thinking about the role of the state. The strong consensus now is that states all over the world are inherently inefficient at running productive enterprises and that the private sector, in competitive conditions, is the actor that will bring development. This has led to the wave of privatizations, regulatory reforms, and trade and investment liberalizations that have occurred around the world in the last 10 years. The development of regional trade blocs like the European Common Market only accelerates these developments.

Table 1.5 shows us that not only have overall levels of capital increased steadily over time, but also foreign direct investment (generally, buying companies, plant, property, or equipment) and portfolio equity (generally, purchases of stocks) investment from the First World have come to occupy an

Table 1.5
Proportions of Aid vs. Private Capital to Developing Countries (total of 100% of all capital flows)

	1970	1980	1990	1998	1999
Long-term debt (private)	62.7%	78.8%	44.1%	32.9%	15.4%
FDI (net) (private)	20.0%	5.3%	24.5%	53.7%	66.0%
Portfolio (private)	0.0%	0.0%	2.8%	4.9%	9.5%
Grants (aid)	17.3%	15.8%	28.6%	8.5%	9.1%

Notes: Grants excludes technical cooperation; FDI = net foreign direct investment; Portfolio = portfolio equity capital
Source: World Bank, *Global Development Finance 2000,* Summary Table—"Aggregate Net Resource Flows and Net Transfers (Long-Term)."

increasing role, while aid has dropped precipitously. We should also note that the flows of capital follow the pattern we have sketched out for aid—they tend to go from First World investors to middle-level developing countries or one of the few low income markets with huge potential, namely, Brazil, China, India, and Indonesia. As a result, the most needy region, Africa, tends to be the most proportionately neglected, both in aid and in capital flows.

In sum, much of development is now considered to occur outside of aid per se. *Aid has always been, and remains, closely tied to developed world interests.* Many in the international community have lost faith in diminishing direct-aid flows to create development. During the Cold War, poverty alleviation took place as a part of the general strategy to fight Communism—that motivation no longer exists. Developing world governments, in turn, have had a major change in the way they think about their relationship with the First World. Many developing world governments have come to embrace international economic ties, including direct and portfolio foreign investment as a necessary vehicle for improving their country's standard of living. Most developing world governments see some form of economic market integration with the developed world as a desirable goal, as it solidifies market access for their products and shores up the flow of scarce capital to their industries and services. Even where there may be remnants of ideological or nationalist resistance, the bottom line is, given the weakness of taxation systems, huge external debts, and the drying up of foreign aid from both the West and the Soviet bloc, developing countries have little choice but to turn to the world market for capital. What we see, then, is a subservience of public aid to private capital. In fact, we discuss the new agendas of the 1990s, including governance, institutional reform, and civil society in a later chapter. Let us acknowledge here that the public-private convergence described above helps to explain the present emphasis on the new concept of governance, which we explore later. Since overall aid is shrinking, and economic interests are now more important than security interests, governance, especially of market regulation and investment assurance, naturally has become a key aspect of reform for aid donors, including the World Bank and the Inter-American Development Bank.

HAS AID CHANGED SINCE 9/11?

Our data and the context sketched above cover development over a long period of 50 years. However, since the terrorist attack on the World Trade Center in New York on September 11, 2001, a number of analysts believe that the context for international aid has once again changed. In March 2002, President Bush announced a pledge to increase aid by 50% over the next three years through his Millennium Challenge (MCA) in which he announced the three new principles of just rule, investing in people, and encouraging economic freedom. The Bush administration also suggested that the new initiative would be funded through grants, rather than loans, due to skepticism about recipients' ability to pay back loans. The giving of MCA monies is tied, not surprisingly, to market-friendly reforms and good governance. The second major initiative relates to preventing and treating AIDS in Africa, for which there have been notable increases in funding. The Bush administration in general has increased the levels of aid funding as part of its strategy to fight terrorism. However, most of this money is tied to security interests, rather than any attempt to directly deal with the economic misery in good part behind terrorism! Moreover, while the multilateral New Partnership for African Development initiative in 2002 suggested major increases in poverty-reduction aid to Africa, most of the grandiose pledges by a wide variety of developed countries have yet to be fulfilled in actual monies disbursed. Indeed, an analysis of official development assistance statistics of the OECD by the author reveals no real difference in the percentage of GDP given as official development assistance between 2000–2002, when viewed in historical perspective. The Scandinavian countries, the Netherlands, and Luxembourg remain the only countries giving official development assistance at the self-prescribed 0.7% of GDP. An analysis of the actual amounts of U.S. aid allocated reveals little significant change in spending priorities, with the exception of increases in health, as shown in Table 1.6.

Continuing massive U.S. and European subsidies, including the dumping of agricultural products through PL 480, reveal the hypocrisy of the new aid message. And what of the new partnership with Africa and fight against poverty? Table 1.7 reveals that the real priorities for U.S. economic aid are closely tied to security interests and the new war on terrorism.

Instead of a new partnership with the developing world, what we see analytically is that only HIV/AIDS, with strong domestic constituencies in the United States and Europe, including both victims and pharmaceutical companies, has achieved new attention in terms of resources. We can also suggest that new security interests, such as strife-ridden Colombia and post-invasion Iraq and Afghanistan, require new funding, yet we have demonstrated there is scant evidence of any significant increase in donor commitment.[13] It is likely, therefore, that countries and priorities not directly of interest to the war on terror will actually continue to see declines. Given this dismal picture on the foreseeable opportunities for major increases in aid, we now should turn to the more important possibilities for improvement through the way that aid is delivered. We turn now to a brief introduction to this theme of our book.

NEW CONCEPTS IN AID DELIVERY

Hope lies in the possibility for change. An important change is taking place in how aid is delivered. As direct aid as a source of poverty alleviation has diminished, new actors have risen to take its place. While NGOs' (nongovernmental organizations) sheer aid volume still pales in comparison to bilat-

Table 1.6
U.S. Aid by Function, before and after Sept. 11, 2001

	2000	% by function	2002	% by function	$ amount Difference 2002-2001	% Difference 2002-2000
Total Military/Security	6122	31.2%	6339	29.8%	217	-1.5%
Total Economic Assistance	4923	25.1%	5676	26.7%	753	1.5%
Total International Organizations	2584	13.2%	2249	10.6%	-335	-2.6%
Total Former Soviet Union	1419	7.2%	1579	7.4%	160	0.2%
Total Narcotics	1323	6.8%	1029	4.8%	-294	-1.9%
Total Trade Exp.s	835	4.3%	648	3.0%	-187	-1.2%
Agriculture - P.L. 480	800	4.1%	959	4.5%	159	0.4%
Total Health	724	3.7%	1568	7.4%	844	3.7%
Total Migration/Refugees	635	3.2%	820	3.9%	185	0.6%
International Disaster Assistance	227	1.2%	422	2.0%	195	0.8%
sum total	19592		21289		1697	

Notes: $US millions, by fiscal year, actual expenditures.

—Does not include expenditures by Department of Defense or other security agencies.

—Trade includes Export-Import Bank (net), OPIC (net), Trade and Development Agency, International Trade Commission, and other programs.

—Economic includes development assistance, transition initiatives, USAID expenditures, Economic Support Fund, Peace Corps, Inter-American Foundation, African Development Foundation, treasury technical assistance, and debt restructuring.

—Military/Security includes nonproliferation, antiterrorism, and demining; international military education; foreign military financing; peacekeeping; and international broadcasting.

Source: Department of State, International Affairs Budget Requests.

Table 1.7
Top U.S. Recipients of USAID Funding, before and after Sept. 11, 2001

	2000		2002
Israel	949,056	Egypt	891,271
Egypt	741,437	Israel	720,000
Russia	196,687	Pakistan	626,192
Ethiopia	178,874	West Bank/Gaza	334,206
Ukraine	170,851	Jordan	234,805
India	168,082	Turkey	199,908
Kosovo	155,273	Afghanistan	193,597
Jordan	149,500	India	177,493
Colombia	130,805	Ukraine	173,822
West Bank/Gaza	121,387	Russia	153,099
Indonesia	107,665	Indonesia	124,496
Peru	106,105	Kosovo	118,123
Georgia	97,105	Serbia	103,809
Bosnia-Herzegovina	86,171	Uzbekistan	99,716

Note: Colombia is the estimated third-largest recipient of aid if military aid is included. *Source:* Calculated by author from USAID budget reports found at http://www.usaid. gov/policy/budget, retrieved July 8, 2003. Figures are actual obligations (expenditures rather than estimates) and do not include any military or security assistance.

eral and multinational aid, they have become important players in particular countries and particular sectors. They play important roles, though their motives are not so transparently altruistic. They are also in good part responsive to the motivations of their resource providers and susceptible to pressure from their home (or donor base) and their target countries' governments. In some ways, their endorsement by the large multilateral and bilateral aid agencies seems to cover the agencies' own inadequacies and criticism received in terms of the failure to alleviate crushing poverty. Still, NGOs bring important expertise, are agile development actors on the field level, and have different priorities than donor agencies. For example, NGOs have been at the forefront of placing environmental, grassroots, and female development issues to the international discourse on development priorities. The role of NGOs has been discussed quite a bit in recent academic literature, particularly in regard to their relationships with host governments and multilateral organizations, and we shall make further comments later in the chapter.

Last, but not least, we find that development projects have changed qualitatively in the way they have been administered since the end of the Cold War. That is, bearing in mind the new political economy of development aid that we have sketched above, there is a *revolution in the thinking about what makes development projects effective over the long run.* To a large extent, this revolution in thinking was spurred on first by NGOs, but now has been adopted to some extent by bilateral and multilateral donor agencies. Before we discuss the new role of NGOs in development, we must first discuss the concept of sustainability, which is one of the guiding values of the transformation in development practices.

Sustainability: What It Means, What It Entails, and How It Can Be Accomplished

Like all buzzwords of the day, sustainability seems to have a definition that varies, depending on the particular development context in which it is used. For our purposes, we can define sustainability as engaging in development practices that have a long-term potential for continuation and growth. While that sounds general, it captures the various ways in which sustainability has been used. Those include financial, environmental, political, organizational, and what we might call participatory sustainability.

One of the nagging problems of development projects that we will discuss in the next chapter is that the funding cycle for projects seems to be a one-shot affair. Therefore, projects are seen by donors as things that can be accomplished in short order, with high capital and training expense, in a finite period of time. Unfortunately, the reality is that most projects do not have the kinds of lasting impacts expected because there are no provisions for long-term maintenance costs. If we begin with the simple fact that an aid project, by definition, is *dependent* upon external sources for its existence, we can begin to unravel the lack of sustainable (long-term) results from projects. The fundamental characteristic of projects is that they tend to live, die, or change at the whim of the donor agency. Donor agencies, in turn, are subject to their own domestic political machinations, including frequent changes in annual budgetary allocations and almost constantly shifting aid priorities. As a result, they are quite naturally unwilling to make any long-term financial commitments toward development projects generally. Therefore, development projects must produce visible results in quite short spurts of time, which of course goes against the brute reality that long-term and interconnected factors hold back development. Moreover, once the project is over, it is difficult to evaluate the long-term effects, if any, of projects. Furthermore, the volatility of funding puts the maintenance costs for ongoing projects, such as roads, in constant jeopardy.

A second aspect that has received considerable attention in the last few years is environmental sustainability. While we devote a chapter to this subject later in the book, for the moment let us underscore its importance in changing the development paradigms. By environmental sustainability, we refer to the idea that development should be in relative harmony with the environment. The value of environmental sustainability seems on the surface to lead to choices between the environment and growth. We argue that this is a false dichotomy. If we look at the future benefits of productive versus fallow land, we could argue that sacrificing some very short-term growth could mean much greater benefits in the long term. Of course, this means that the enormous pressure on land productivity, created by poverty, must be alleviated in other ways.

A third category of sustainability that is recognized, but largely ignored, by aid agencies is political sustainability. By political sustainability, we mean the support of central and local governments, interest groups, and power brokers. Aid agencies, particularly multilateral ones, prohibit themselves from taking open political stances on development. This dates back to the founding of these organizations by First World governments to pursue their interests and values, including the principle of sovereignty and not meddling in internal affairs. Developing countries' governments also argue that aid agencies should not meddle with local decision-making. The reality is quite different from this rhetorical game. Who can imagine any development project not having political implications? To begin with, development projects are always tied to the donor country and organization's political aims, getting down to require-ments that materials be bought from suppliers of the same country. The cen-tral government of a developing country also has to permit donor agencies to act in their territory, according to their own political aims. Different agencies and/or individuals within the government will have different aims. Last, but not least, regional and local authorities will want both a piece of the action in terms of financial benefits of the project as well as some say over the types of projects and the ways that projects are implemented in their area. There-fore, the political context of development projects seems to be guided by a mix of negotiations between the central government and donor agencies be-hind closed doors and a series of artificial restraints in which aid donors at-tempt to limit the scope of their actions. A cynical view would predict that the powerful will always triumph over the weak, and therefore that develop-ment projects are almost never aimed at the truly poor (an argument that seems to carry weight in terms of many kinds of government assistance as well). However, in politics, there are always possibilities for counterweights and for particular attempts at enlightened policies and leadership. Therefore, a central or regional government that saw the possibilities for both increases in agricultural production as well as political support from poorer farmers (or urban dwellers who want cheaper food), might steer a road project into a location that better benefits poorer and less powerful constituents, or at least attempt some type of compromise route. These types of compromises become especially complex when we begin to discuss issues that are controversial among some of the interested political parties, such as projects that allow women to become more independent in some more traditional areas of the developing world. In sum, successful development projects over the long run require the backing of a strong and supportive political coalition.

Organizational sustainability is our fourth important category. Every development project involves the creation of some type of administrative apparatus. The typical development project, especially when involving larger expenses or areas, has been conducted by the donor agency, which brings in the capital, the technicians, and manages the project with its own development experts. Once this team of resources and experts leaves, the project is expected to be carried out by locals who will take over the project. Unfortunately, all too often, not only the financial wherewithal, but also the actual management team, seems to disappear once the project is over. Moreover, we find that there is very little coordination among development agencies, even when they are conducting similar projects. This lack of a learning curve, both within the donor community and among the local population, is something we will discuss more in our chapter on evaluation. The lack of organizational sustainability is particularly disappointing given the steep learning curve that project managers often experience, and the dearth of technical expertise in developing countries. In general, taking basic steps such as training local managers and technicians is often a secondary, at best, aspect of any development project. Unfortunately, the Confucian proverb that it is better to teach a man to fish than to give him fish is rarely, if ever, followed in development projects for the political reasons we mentioned. We discuss how development organizations can be made more sustainable in our chapter on decentralization and organizational reform.

We should also not forget that all-too-often overlooked aspect of most development projects—they involve people! If we take a step back from the daily crises of project management, we should see that, as Dennis Rondinelli once pointed out, every development project is like an experiment. It is an experiment in two senses. In one sense, a development project is often the first attempt to create something new—a new irrigation canal, a new power plant—that has not existed before. Since it is new to the particular area, the local conditions are going to be different from anywhere else. Even assuming that the techniques and administration of the project have been worked out elsewhere, a rare case given the other problems we have noted above, they will have to be adopted to a new situation in space and time. Second, and perhaps more important, any development project requires the participation of the local population. All too often development projects have been designed without considering sustainability from the point of view of support of the recipient group itself! Since every group is made up of different individuals, every development project will not only change over time and space, but also need to be adapted to the particular group on which it is focused. Particular attention has been posed to the problems in incorporating gender considerations into development projects. We talk about the theory and practice of participatory techniques and of gender in development projects in subsequent chapters.

Last but not least, despite all the talk, perhaps the most dismaying aspect of development projects, even beyond the self-interested and paternalistic nature of aid itself, is the fact that both learning and coordination are so lacking. While it is a most ubiquitous characteristic of our own experience that efficiency of resource utilization is as, if not more, important, than the level of resources, there seems to be no recognition of this in aid. Unfortunately, aid has always operated like an extremely dysfunctional family. What we find is that there is almost no agreement in practice among the different players in development about long-term goals, priorities, roles, or how limited resources could be best used in the short term. Even more depressing is the stunning lack of meaningful evaluation of the use of resources and coordination of donor agencies, despite the unavoidable recognition that these are basic obstacles. Efficiency of aid is even disrupted by an unwillingness by the various agencies and NGOs to engage in some form of basic information-sharing. We seem to find instead a tone of competitiveness among agencies and NGOs to capture project turf that will make the biggest splash for their constituents.[14] Rather than shake our heads in denial, we offer a number of practical suggestions about how to alleviate this situation in our chapter on evaluation. We turn now to a closer look at some of the new actors in development, namely NGOs and social movements.

The Rise of NGOs and Social Movements as New Agents of Development

Commentary on the Rise of NGOs

Development practice and study go through distinct fads, each promising the solution for all development problems. Of course, most solutions have centered on the basic idea that development means recreating First World living, political, economic, and social situations in the developing world. Oddly, enough, both leftist and rightist solutions share these same goals. For now, let us note that the latest wrinkle in the development discourse is the rise of the NGO (nongovernmental organizations) as the newest vehicle for world development along these lines. NGOs could technically be a wide variety of organizations, from multilateral development organizations to charity relief ones, but in common development parlance the term is most often used to refer to small nonprofit organizations that are involved in grassroots development projects.

The fad to look at NGOs as the latest development savior can be traced in part to the rise of the environmental, gender-equality, and basic human-needs movements that swept the First World countries in the 1970s, and more recently with the idea of building "civil society." Civil society is an ambiguous concept, but at least in development-project practice, it refers to the idea that impoverished people must be become active participants on the local and national level politics of their countries for development to progress. The frustrations with the continuing problems of inequality and lack of development, in combination with the declining interest in aid on the part of developed-world governments as we have documented above, led to the emphasis on NGOs as an alternative vehicle for development. The idea is that NGOs can perform basic human-needs operations on a grassroots level in a much more effective way than large aid organizations, and in a way that supposedly is not compromised by the home government's agenda. NGOs tend to be run by enthusiastic staffers and volunteers who develop grassroots experience. The tightness of the NGO because of its personnel's zeal and the small size of the organization, in combination with the field experience, means NGOs can be more flexible and responsive to actual situations on the ground. The idea that NGOs are better equipped for grassroots, niche or specialized operations, and smaller-scale development projects really took off in the 1990s, when the World Bank and other major agencies began to openly incorporate them into their project plans as subcontractors and partners. The exact numbers are hard to gauge, but there is no doubt that NGOs have continued to mushroom, both in sheer numbers and in the scope and extent of activities with which they are involved.

Why have NGOs expanded so much? The bottom line is that once they were embraced by the mainstream development agencies, a huge flow of re-sources followed to fund their activities. This development is all the more surprising, given the historically strong emphasis on technical and hierarchical planning in the multilateral and bilateral agencies, and strong distrust and skepticism by the main agents of development, the host governments. Thus, we have an altogether unpredictable alliance between NGOs, multilateral and bilateral development agencies that provide a large portion of the funding, and host governments.

In this alliance, NGOs provide cover for the traditional aid agencies to claim that they are reaching and responsive to the grass roots, the most im-poverished of the poor, in developing countries. Second, NGOs provide heavily indebted host governments cover from domestic and international critics who point to diminishing safety-net expenditures as well as a long-lasting bias toward large macro-infrastructural projects, as opposed to poverty alleviation or redistributive ones. NGOs themselves are engaged in a com-petition with each other for funding resources; as a result, like the aid agencies themselves, they increasingly become "indicator" and "demonstrable results" oriented. Moreover, NGOs and their projects are particularly vulnerable to the problems of (lack of) sustainability discussed earlier, given their generally small size, uneven funding bases, and frequent staff turnover. We discuss this problem further in our chapter on evaluation. This is not to say that good, honest, and palpable work is not being done in development by each of the main actors. NGOs seem to be particularly adept at handling emergency relief operations, but their efficacy in other areas is questionable. The unspoken pact among these actors does break down from time to time, most often when

NGOs step into territory deemed "too political" by host governments that permit them to operate. Our main point here is that the political nature of the relationships and resource flows can have perverse and negative effects on the efficacy of the aid efforts.

An interesting new twist in the development discourse is the rise of a discussion among experts to increase NGO accountability and "representativeness." NGOs suffer from the same lack of transparency, accountability, actual (as opposed to window-dressed) results, and learning as all other development agencies with which we are familiar. Quite ironically, NGOs themselves are being rightly accused of being out of touch both politically and in fact with their clients, the actual aid recipients. As a result, there are a number of calls for greater representation of locals in NGO operations, in line with an increase in direct funding for Southern or developing world-centered NGOs. It remains to be seen if Southern NGOs are any less prone to the political strings attached to resource dependency than their Northern counterparts. Moreover, Southern NGOs tend to be populated by well-educated middle-class activists, which is perhaps a step better, but not really a solution to the problem of lack of representativeness in the traditional Northern NGOs. This brings us to the basic conundrum for NGOs' newly enhanced role in development: Resources are needed to make a significant impact on poverty, but in order to get resources, both political agendas and organizational representativeness are curtailed. For our purposes here, we will focus on how the new ideas in development are changing NGO practices, keeping in mind the political-economy context we have just sketched.

New Theories on How to Organize Society: Social Capital, Civil Society, and Social Movements

There is a growing set of ideas that promote the idea that better-organized and mobilized societies, particularly at the grass roots, have positive benefits for the whole nation.[15] The theoretical variations along these lines can be grouped into social capital, civil society, and new social movements, and each has important implications for development project management.

As the name implies, social capital tries to transfer social ideas into economic jargon, for the obvious reason that this increases the marketability and persuasiveness of the idea. Robert Putnam's seminal work in *Making Democracy Work* and James Coleman's earlier work are largely responsible for much of the flourishing of this idea. In his book, Putnam traces differences in quality of life in northern and southern Italy to the degree of organization and participation at the local level. The acclaim that the book received thus justified an oNGOing wave of scholarship that identifies "social capital," meaning the degree to which a society is organized, with positive implications for local and national welfare. Thus, social capital is like its somewhat older cousin, "human capital," which referred to the benefits of good health and education for productivity. Unlike the civil-society and social-movements ideas, social capital focuses on the individual level. Thus civic associations and social networks are seen as important vehicles for individuals to push forward their desires. Social capital has myriad forms and functions, depending on the author one consults, but the implications are clear—taking care of fellow humans is a worthwhile investment!

The civil-society approaches are very similar in their general orientation to social-capital theories. While not as directly interested in the productivity implications of social organization, civil-society approaches seem to agree that organizing at the local level is a necessary and neglected aspect of development. Civil-society approaches seem to presume that democracy is the best form of government. They look to the development of the developed-world nations such as England and the United States as places where local government flourished, as de Tocqueville once pointed out. Their conclusion is that the lack of such civic associations and local organizations explains a lot of the overall weakness of developing societies.[16]

Perhaps the most interesting aspect about the new social theories of development is their political implications for development projects. It seems odd to think that aid agencies, which can work only with the permission of the sovereign local government, are now often engaged in projects to organize people who may be quite opposed to that very government. Development agencies seem to be dealing with this basic contradiction by tailoring social projects toward nonpolitical aspects. In particular, many World Bank projects cleverly use the language of the social-capital and civil-society literatures, while limiting organizational efforts to purely economic and technical cooperation and organization on the local level.[17] These projects have been a mainstay of much of the new rush of development aid to Eastern Europe. No matter how you look at organizational efforts, *the bottom line is that better social organization is most likely to have one major effect—increasing demands on, and responses from, the government.* Depending on how the government responds, we believe this could be a big step forward in the development context.

On the other hand, we hasten to add that the participatory and civil-society approaches were adopted by aid organizations during the early 1990s, in the wake of a plethora of criticism directed at them because of the inequitable and harsh economic conditions of structural-adjustment programs. *As we saw with NGOs, it seems all too clear that aid organizations see adoption of civil-society approaches not only as a useful component of development in and of itself, but also as another method for co-opting (and thus silencing) critics.* Since the economic conditions, particularly in the area of debt, continue to require economic austerity in developing countries, *the promotion of civil society rings somewhat hollow when the state is simultaneously retreating from social-welfare obligations.* Without state cultivation of civic organizations and social capital, how can we expect them to fulfill their expected role of developing individuals and organizations to become an important actor in developing societies?

Developing civil society in the developing world requires a much higher level of sophistication than is presumed by the first generation of projects. Many developing-world countries are rife with class, regional, ethnic, and other deep divisions related to their colonial and postcolonial history. The result is that the easy optimism that a better-organized local population will have a national vision and organize for national benefits is quite a leap in reality. The civil-society approaches seem to have a Western bias, in other words, in terms of the general model, including goals and starting conditions, by which proponents characterize social relations in any society.

A last set of new ideas is called the new social-movements literature. Social movements are generally thought of as groups of concerned people who organized themselves for aims that do not fall along the traditional lines of economic or political interests. Moreover, new social movements are considered to be spontaneous organizations, that is self-organized by the group, with high levels of participation and a strongly democratic decision-making structure. Much of the social-movements literature identifies certain new issues around which new organizations have sprung up, such as environmental preservation, women's rights, and indigenous people's rights. These social movements are supposed to bear, in theory, similarities to the movements that sprung up in Western Europe after World War II. Social movements are not organized along political-party, social-welfare, or other conventional political organization lines. In fact, it is the neglect of these key issues by the current political structure that gives rise to the social movements in the first place. Social movements are therefore thought to be set up in opposition to conventional politics and particularly, by implication, in juxtaposition to the state, which is the main target for reclamation.

While social-movement theory is rich in its variety and innovative in theory, we cannot help but notice that the practice in the developing world does not seem to fit the theory. In other words, we see European and American foundations and movements donating resources and organization to developing country movements, thus shaping their agendas, identities, and *modus operandi* along the lines of their own aspirations and experience. Though this may have important benefits, the close ties might also limit the levels of concerns and the types of organizations that will be encouraged in the developing world. Another interesting question is to what extent social movements tend to become conventional in their politics over time. When we look at the Green Party in Germany, we see an environmental movement that now seems to act like a conventional political party, albeit with new concerns. This not only raises interesting theoretical questions about social movements, but it also raises the question of whether new social movements are really "new" in organization or simply in raising neglected (often economic) issues in the developing world. A final issue is whether new social movements can become transnational, in which local populations can unite in a common cause against their own governments. This seems to be precisely the case with the proliferation of movements' Web pages on the Internet, but so far seems to be limited to the previously noted North-South patronage and to information sharing. Nonetheless, whether or not they are new or innovative, organizations such as the Zapatistas in southern Mexico are bringing a proliferation of issues to the political table to be addressed, which is very encouraging for development.

Whether organizations or movements pattern themselves in opposition to conventional politics as presupposed by the social-movements literature; as part of the development of well-functioning democracy, as in the civil-society literature; or as integral to individual-level resources with external spillover effects for the society as a whole, as in social capital; new forms of social organization are certainly transforming development. Some organizations, such as the Zapatistas in Mexico and the MST (landless movement) in Brazil, that have had strong levels of success in terms of political awareness seem to cut across both conventional and innovative organizational lines and address a number of related issues for the constituencies they represent, *despite* the fact that they are very much an internationally funded phenomenon. These particular organizations seem to be successful in their challenges precisely because they have such strong local roots, what we might call "authenticity." While this requires more investigation, if our instincts are right, the chances for successful challengers to transform conventional political and economic structures depend more on being true to internal conditions than on outside help or inspiration. This reinforces our general theme in this volume that for development to occur, people must be helped to empower themselves in the way they see fit, true to the local context. For genuine participation, the presumptions of the new social theories, centered on the idea that all societies should have Western-style social, economic, and political organization, must be thrown out. The inevitable resulting tension, for example, between Islamist social movements and organizations and Western-sponsored ones, reflects the ambiguous terrain that all developing societies are facing in redefining themselves after colonialism. It is a good space, one to be cultivated and worked out, not suppressed, for these societies to reach a stable identity and reasonable consensus.

We believe that postmodern ideas, as well as the new context of social organization, reinforce these conclusions. Postmodern ideas also help us to put such efforts at social organization in better perspective in terms of the limitations implicit in their assumptions.

POSTMODERNISM AS A SOURCE OF NEW IDEAS ABOUT DEVELOPMENT

Postmodernism is such a common term in academia these days that scarcely anyone really questions what it means. Like a lot of other social-science terms, its definition seems to vary depending on the context in which it is used. We can give a general introduction for students and practitioners of development here. Postmodernism is a set of ideas that have grown in popularity in the last two decades, but whose seeds are World Wars I and II and the development of the nuclear era from the 1950s. Those two singular developments led to a whole new direction for Western culture, including abstract art, since they created a strong sense of doubt about the deeply embedded idea that progress, in both a scientific and humanitarian sense, was clearly attainable. The sense of fear during the Cold War, which was the height of tensions between the United States and the USSR, led to all sorts of doubts about the ultimate rationality of man and his ability to beneficially use steadily accumulating scientific knowledge. In other words, given the policies of mutually assured destruction, as well as the seeming futility of the Vietnam War, many wondered if their representatives might actually start a possibly earth-destroying war. On the philosophical and artistic side, thinkers such as Michel Foucault and Alain Touraine began popularizing (at least in academic circles) basic questions about whether there really was a universally testable mean of knowing the truth and gaining knowledge, and whether Western civilization really was leading to a steadily more progressive society. The development of postmodern thought has most clearly been linked so far to studies of culture, and so the techniques of analysis related to it, such as "deconstruction," have largely been applied to literature and media. Postmodernism is a ubiquitous part of modern film, music, and literature, but the development community seems slow to grasp its implications. We argue here that the ideas of postmodernism are applicable to development projects as well, with clear implications for techniques and practices.

In terms of development projects, we should first restate that a core premise of postmodernism is the questioning of the idea of progress. Thus, postmodernists would point out that "development" is a loaded term. This might seem a strange line of enquiry at first blush for students and practitioners, but we think it is a very useful exercise to question the basic assumptions and concepts that we take for granted in development. We might think, for example, that no one can be against general economic modernization, the raising of living standards, and increasing democratization. However, what postmodernism tells us is that there is an imposition at work in these kinds of suppositions. What we are suggesting when we talk about development for the developing world is a certain kind of development, with the idea that the developing world will begin to replicate the political, economic, and social situation of the First World. In political terms, it seems hard to argue against democratization. But, if we consider the common situation of many countries in which there are important subgroup minorities, a Western-style democracy may not be the most suitable vehicle. A quick look at Nigeria's on-and-off civil wars among ethnic factions tells even the beginning student of politics that a straight-up, majority-vote political system will not lead to consensus in that deeply divided country. Second, we have seen that even democratically elected governments, such as those of Alan Garcia and Alberto Fujimori in Peru, do not seem to follow the same kinds of implicit rules or have the same kinds of outcomes as more developed democracies. Even democratically elected governments seem to struggle in the developing world.

In economic terms, the ideas of increasing the standard of living seem irrefutable given the global wave of consumerism sweeping the globe. A postmodernist analysis tells us that such an assumption may not be universally shared. For example, the international controversy surrounding the costs of AIDS drugs brings into question the blind acceptance of developed-world standards regarding intellectual-property rights. More importantly, the developing world has not been able to follow that easy development path that economists and policy makers expected to happen automatically in the 1950s. Instead, while there has been a steady rise of overall statistical well-being in absolute terms, the relative gap both within the developing world and between the developing and developed world has actually grown. When we consider the East Asian tigers, and their recent downturn, it seems clear that no simple free-market, free-trade model will ensure equitable and sustained growth in the developing world.

In social terms, developing-world countries may not only be dealing with strong minorities, but they also may have a different sense of social values. In some areas of the world, notably the Middle East and Asia, for example, there is a much stronger sense of family or group values than in the West. We walk a thin line in terms of social modernization and postmodernist values in this volume. While we do advocate empowerment in the sense of increasing women's participation, for example, we suggest that societies should have some room for deliberation and discussion about social change. The population should have some room for maneuver about the actual definition and goals of development as well as the rate and nature of change envisioned. Instead, many developing countries feel besieged by cultural influences from abroad, including ubiquitous foreign advertising and cultural media, and under the gun and guidance of the well-meaning developed-world aid community. We would argue that the preservation of cultural diversity and some degree of autonomy for groups from developed-world culture are as important as the need for change in those societies.

In sum, by bringing up the question of what development means, postmodernism actually *liberates* us from the bonds of thinking that the only way of progress is one that creates societies like the United States. We acknowledge inspiration from two main thinkers whose concepts appear in our interpretive perspective throughout the book. From Antonio Gramsci, we borrow the concept of "cultural hegemony," or the idea that in the cultural sphere, as in the economic one, there tends to be a strong domination of values that reflect unequal power relations. Another particularly important concept from Gramsci is the idea of legitimation, that is, that an important source of the underlying props that sustain the inherent inequalities of a cultural hegemony, is the dominant ideology and values taught to justify it. Those values may be inculcated (e.g., "every person in the United States has equal opportunity to succeed"), but to the extent that they contradict reality, they can be exposed. This is where Foucault's seminal work is helpful. From Michel Foucault, we borrow the emphasis that power relations occur not just in overt forms of physical domination, but also in covert forms, including language, conceptualization, and modes and channels of discourse. Foucault and other postmodernists give us the important tools of deconstruction, genealogy, archaeology, and semiotics that guide our analysis. Detailed explanations of these techniques are not the subject of this book, but are readily found elsewhere. The essence of deconstruction, however, is to understand the underlying foundations, relations, and contradictions within a discourse or conversation, by examining the relations among the power, concepts, ideologies, and language. Foucault also gives us the precious concept of *résistance*, that is, the idea that the discourse itself can be challenged and its underlying contradictions exposed. Not only language, but symbols and icons are particularly important to understanding these new conceptualizations of power. Symbols bring people together, for better or worse (e.g., Ché Guevara T-shirts). The construction of paradigmatic heroes, such as the reification of the Grameen Bank, feed into our need to simplify problems, and come up with all-encompassing solutions. Postmodernism allows us to peel away this level of reality and attempt to look at the complex, if at times depressing, matrix of causes, factors, and power struggles beneath.

Yet, to our knowledge, there are few attempts to leap from these critical theoretical insights into practical questions, especially those regarding development projects. In terms of development projects, we postulate postmodernism leads us to rethink the imposition of a certain idea of development and to engender a definition that is more "authentic" in the sense that it is elicited from, and in alignment with, the desires of the local population. As we mentioned, this can lead to difficult situations, for example in societies with traditions of repressive roles for women, but we believe in such situations it is still better to have a dialogue than to impose Western cultural values on the local population. In the end, the society that freely chooses women's liberation will be much more likely to embed such values in its culture than the one which feels threatened if it does not comply. We should turn to persuasion as the primary mode of discourse in development for the values we hold dear, such as women's human rights.

In other words, we would like to see more of an emphasis on development as a way of helping our brothers and sisters to realize their own goals, rather than on development as a way of imposing our own reality upon others. We see already the beginnings of a shift in development practices from something that is *paternalistically done* to "recipients" to one in which the "donor" and "participant" are partners, with a mutual respect for each other's point of view. Thus, the donor's role, as we see it, should be to act as a cooperative partner in helping to empower participants to reach goals created by mutual agreement. Secondarily, we see that the need for participation in projects goes hand in hand with the movement in development toward development that is more sustainable. In a way, postmodernism tells us that the "donor" in an aid project is involved in an active transformation of him/herself as much as the participant.

In the next chapter, we shall review the traditional methods of development project management and break down the basic problems with them. We will then turn in the rest of the book to a series of practices currently used in the field that fit into a postmodern empowerment and sustainability strategy in development project management.

CHAPTER 2

The Project Approach to Development: A Blunted Edge?

About 20 years ago J. Price Gittinger of the World Bank pronounced that the project is the cutting edge of development.[1] Indeed, it would probably be fair to say that the project has been the dominant form that development aid has taken over much of the postwar period. Even though the project form has come under challenge from program and sectoral approaches in recent years, it seems likely that a significant proportion of aid will continue to be given as projects. In this chapter we shall examine the merits of the project approach together with its demerits. A central theme that will emerge in our analysis concerns a contradiction that lies at the heart of this approach. In essence this is the contradiction between the imperative toward control that is implicit in the planning process and the radical uncertainty that characterizes the environments where developers seek to engender their controlled changes (i.e., projects). It will be useful to commence this analysis by examining the question of what a project is.

WHAT IS A PROJECT?

In yet another volume by two authors associated with the World Bank, Tolbert and Baum answer this question in the following terms:

The project concept essentially provides a disciplined and systematic approach to analysing and managing a set of investment activities. However diverse the specific activities they embrace, projects are likely to include several or all of the following elements, although in varying proportions and with different emphases:

- Capital investment in civil works, equipment, or both (the so-called bricks and mortar of the project)
- Provision of services for design and engineering, supervision of construction, and improvement of operations and maintenance
- Strengthening of local institutions concerned with implementing and of operating the project, including the training of local managers and staff
- Improvement in policies—such as those on pricing, subsidies, and cost recovery— that affect project performance and the relationship of the project both to the sector in which it falls and to broader national objectives
- A plan for implementing the above activities to achieve the project's objectives within a given time

These common elements suggest a way to define a project that captures its essential features . . . a project is taken to be a discrete package of investments, policy measures, and institutional and other actions designed to achieve a specific development objective (or set of objectives) within a designated period.[2]

This definition of a project shows two things about the project form. First, that it is supposed to be a way of efficiently organizing investment in developing countries to maximize its effects or returns within a set time frame. Second, even the simplest project is likely to be complex to design and implement, involving timely provision of investment and other inputs, institutional and policy interventions, and organization of the disparate activities of those involved in the project to ensure that they bring about its intended outcome. It is worth noting that this is a relatively basic definition in that it does not even bring into play questions such as how to sustain the project after the sponsoring aid agency has withdrawn its support, or how to enhance sustainability by encouraging the active participation of the project recipients. Even so, it illustrates the contention that projects represent an attempt to achieve desired outcomes through an exertion of control over the complex circumstances likely to pertain in a development situation.

Gittinger indicates the extent of this complexity when he examines the various issues that will have to be addressed during the process of project preparation (agrarian projects in this particular case). He writes as follows about how the institutional setting of the project must be taken into account:

The sociocultural patterns and institutions of those the project will serve must be considered. Does the project design take into account the customs and culture of the farmers who will participate? Will the project involve disruption of the ways in which the farmers are accustomed to working? If it does, what provisions are made to help them shift to new patterns? What communication systems exist to bring farmers new information and teach them new skills? Changing customary procedures is usually slow. Has enough time been allowed for farmers to accept the new procedures, or is the project plan overly optimistic about rates of acceptance?

To have a chance of being carried out, a project must relate properly to the institutional structure of the country and region. What will be the arrangements for land tenure? What size holding will be encouraged? Does the project incorporate local institutions and use them to further the project? How will the administrative organization of the project relate to existing agencies? Is there to be a separate project authority? What will be its links to the relevant operating ministries? Will the staff be able to work with existing agencies or will there be institutional jealousies?[3]

It can be seen that the project planner must make a large number of judgments about multifarious issues, many of which may be characterized by a dearth of information. For example, little may be known of the social structure and farming practices of more remote communities. Moreover, these questions only deal with one aspect of the project, its institutional context. Gittinger poses similarly extensive lists of questions that project analysts must answer about projects' technical requirements, as well as their social, commercial, financial, and economic aspects. As in the case of the institutional questions, some of them are difficult to answer because of their intrinsic complexity or due to lack of information. An additional layer of complexity emerges from Gittinger's observation that answers to questions about one aspect of the project are likely to have a bearing on other aspects of the project.[4] For example, the answer to a question about a community's traditional farming practices is likely to have a bearing on the question as to which technical package may be most appropriate for that community. Yet more complexity arises from the inevitability of change in the project's external environment. Climatic change may have an effect on an agricultural project's prospects for success. Similarly, social upheaval is likely to have a destabilizing effect on projects in the area. Changes in national economic fortune are very likely to affect projects, perhaps by changing the prices of inputs, or the profitability of project outputs. Given this picture of enormous complexity, it hardly comes as a surprise when Gittinger observes, "When a project analysis has failed to anticipate the outcome of a project investment, a common reason appears to have been simply poor preparation of the analysis."[5] Perhaps the salient question concerns how feasible it is to actually produce an analysis that can take adequate account of all the variables involved in designing a project.

All of this is indicative that the project approach is characterized by the aforementioned contradiction between the need for control in order to plan effectively and the radical uncertainty and complexity of the development context. Dennis Rondinelli focused on this contradiction in his volume of 1983, *Development Projects as Policy Experiments*. He asserted:

Ironically, politicians and administrators embraced control-oriented planning and management techniques that were either ineffective or inherently incapable of reducing uncertainty at a time when the recognition that development was an uncertain process was becoming widespread.[6]

In subsequent sections we shall examine some of these techniques with a view to drawing out their implications for project effectiveness and their appropriateness for dealing with situations of uncertainty.

THE PROJECT CYCLE

One of the central ways that project work is rendered manageable is through dividing it up into successive phases collectively known as the "project cycle." Any project can be conceived of as passing through a number of stages of development, each of which is characterized by performance of a particular aspect of project work. There is no single accepted model of the project cycle, with some agencies and analysts referring to a five-stage cycle, while others specify six stages. Baum and Tolbert describe the World Bank cycle as follows:

- *Identification.* The first phase of the cycle is concerned with identifying project ideas that appear to represent a high-priority use of the country's resources to achieve an important development objective. Such project ideas should meet an initial test of feasibility; that is, there should be some assurance that technical and institutional solutions—at costs commensurate with the expected benefits—will be found and suitable policies adopted.

- *Preparation.* Once a project idea has passed the identification test, it must be advanced to the point at which a firm decision can be made whether or not to proceed with it. This requires a progressive refinement of the design of the project in all its dimensions—technical, economic, financial, social, institutional, and so on.

- *Appraisal.* Before approving a loan, external agencies normally require a formal process of appraisal to assess the overall soundness of the project and its readiness for implementation. For an internally generated and financed investment, the extent of formal appraisal varies widely in accordance with government practice. Some explicit appraisal, however, is a necessary, or at least a desirable, part of the decision-making process before funds are committed.

- *Implementation.* The implementation stage covers the actual development or construction of the project, up to the point at which it becomes fully operational. It includes monitoring of all aspects of the work or activity as it proceeds and supervision by oversight agencies within the country or by external lenders.

- *Evaluation.* The ex post evaluation of a completed project seeks to determine whether the objectives have been achieved and to draw lessons from experience with the project that can be applied to similar projects in the future. Although some lending agencies such as the World Bank routinely require an ex post evaluation of all projects that they finance, few developing countries have established a comprehensive system for evaluating the results of their project investment portfolio.[7]

It is generally recognized that there is considerable overlap between the different stages of the project cycle, notably between the starting phases of project identification and preparation. It would also be fair to say that more emphasis is put on some phases of the cycle than others. As we shall see in a separate chapter the evaluation phase is generally underemphasized, arguably at the expense of project effectiveness. However, it can also be seen that the project cycle represents a useful intellectual construct for classifying different elements of project work and organizing them into manageable, discrete elements, thus securing the efficiency gains associated with division of labor. We might also argue that this is suggestive of a disadvantage in that this view of the project as being composed of discrete elements may lead to a loss of focus on the macro-level, that of the project as a whole. The danger is that project personnel will focus on their own narrow tasks at the expense of overall project effectiveness. It might be argued that this is what has happened to the evaluation stage, with many agencies focusing on what they perceived as the vital questions of appraisal and implementation (actually getting the project working on the ground), forgetting the need to record and learn lessons from their errors or successes.

An associated problem arising from the project cycle is that it might be seen as leading to a view of projects as temporally finite phenomena. Most projects are designed to last for a few years during which the project cycle runs its course. When the cycle is finished the project is seen as having reached its conclusion. However, the central purpose of projects is that they are supposed to make a lasting impact. A health project may only be designed to operate for three years, but it is expected that the project will continue to deliver benefits after all of its aid-financed activities have been concluded. In fact various observers have commented that in all too many instances projects collapse and cease to deliver any benefits after they have reached their conclusion, that is, after the aid has stopped. It is true that over the last few decades development agencies and commentators have become increasingly aware of the need to create the conditions for sustainability. Even so, it might well be argued that the tendency for projects to collapse after their official conclusion is related to a vision of the project cycle that presents projects as temporary phenomena that have a clear point of termination. This can be seen as contributing to a mind-set amongst project analysts and personnel in which the emphasis is put on projects as temporary interventions and the need for sustainability is undervalued.

Particularly worthy of note is the way in which Baum and Tolbert define the "initial test of feasibility" that they see as a central part of the identification stage of the project cycle. Their terminology that "there should be some assurance that technical and institutional solutions—at costs commensurate with the expected benefits—will be found and suitable policies adopted" is redolent of the language of rational maximization of utilities. It is indicative of the influence of the synoptic model of rational decision-making in project design. The synoptic model may be represented as a three-stage process, consisting of first, problem definition; second, assessment of alternative solutions; and third, adoption of the most efficient solution to the problem. On the face of it this seems like an eminently sensible way of setting about solving any sort of problem, inclusive of development problems. Indeed, there is something to be said for emphasizing criteria of efficiency in a development situation that may well be characterized by resource shortage.

However, many policy analysts have identified a variety of problems associated with the synoptic approach. First, it incorporates an assumption that all relevant data is available to the problem analysts, that they have perfect information. This is at the very least a situation that is unlikely to pertain to any real-life policy situation. Indeed, it is particularly unlikely to be the case in development situations where, as we have already noted, information tends to be in short supply. This initial shortcoming feeds into problems that arise with the assessment of alternative solutions. If information is imperfect, the problem analysts, in our case project analysts, cannot be sure that they have accurately identified all of the potential solutions to the problem at hand, and this means that they cannot be sure to identify the most efficient solution. In other words, they may conduct a painstaking investigation into a development problem, investigating various ways of solving it, but they are still unlikely to arrive at the optimal solution. However, the rationalistic trappings of the process, together with the aforementioned complexity of project design, tend to legitimate the outcome irrespective of whether it actually is the optimal solution or not.[8] This feeds into an attitude whereby the project plan adopted is equated to a blueprint.

Rondinelli points out that "(i)nternational assistance agencies and most governments of developing countries have attempted to plan and control development projects through complex design, selection and appraisal procedures"[9] (Rondinelli 1983, 65). He notes that agencies like the World Bank, UNDP, and IDA attempt to impose their control over projects through the design process, going so far as to specify quite minor details, as the following example shows:

In a loan for a rural development project in one African country . . . the World Bank Group's International Development Association (IDA) insisted on conditions that specified the number and type of wells and pumps to be used in irrigation systems, the structure of the organization that would finance loans by the nation's rural development bank, and the creation of a separate management unit to execute the project. IDA also insisted on centrally consolidated accounts for the rural development fund. It set guidelines for the types of administrative and technical personnel to be hired, and prescribed mechanisms for providing extension and credit services to farmers as well as procedures for performing cost-benefit analyses in subprojects. In addition, IDA established detailed duties and responsibilities for the project manager and outlined the contents of contracts for farmers participating in the subprojects.[10]

In going to such lengths to predetermine so many aspects of the project it is evident that IDA regarded the project plan as a blueprint that was meant to be followed quite rigidly, if not to the letter. Yet, as we have seen, no amount of rational planning can ensure that all the needed data will be collected to produce the optimal plan.

Nevertheless, as Rondinelli observed, aid agencies have sought to enhance mechanisms of planning control, even as evidence has mounted that such efforts are likely to be subverted by the uncertainty of the development environment. In the next section we shall turn our attention to the question of why development and government agencies have responded by attempting to tighten their control of the development process.

RATIONAL BUREAUCRACIES, IRRATIONAL OUTCOMES

We have already touched on some of the reasons why agencies try to exert control over development. In the first instance planning and classification are necessary to ensure an efficient use of resources in situations of resource scarcity. However, the agencies dealing with development are also predisposed toward an emphasis on control, which is largely to do with their nature as bureaucracies.

Any discussion of the nature of modern bureaucracy must inevitably start out from Max Weber's model of rational bureaucracy. Parsons aptly summarizes Weber's account of the emergence of the modern age as offering "a model of capitalism as a high form of rationality, and in which history displayed a process of rationalization and bureaucratic 'disenchantment.'" Parsons continues:

The main effect of capitalism was . . . its capacity to disseminate the pursuit of the kind of instrumental rationality, which was manifested in machines. In industrial society the organizational analogue of the machine was bureaucracy.[11]

This mechanistic quality is reflected in several characteristics of rational bureaucracy. First, it is rule-bound in that it proceeds according to a set of impersonal rules that bind all members of the bureau equally. These determine the areas of competence of the bureau and define how bureaucrats should perform their respective duties. Second, it is hierarchical, thus manifesting the instrumental gains to be made through division of labor. The bureau will consist of a number of hierarchical levels and the functions and duties of each level will be clearly defined and organized in such a way that they complement each other rather than conflicting and/or overlapping. Third, bureaucrats will be trained in order to ensure their efficiency, and they can be promoted on merit. Fourth, bureaucrats do not own their jobs, or any of the resources associated with it. This militates against any proclivity toward corruption or similar abuse of office. The provision of a salary to each official also helps to prevent such abuse. Finally, it is worth noting that continuity and consistency of operation are secured through the maintenance of records that can provide guidance as to precedent, or to the facts of any particular case.

While this by no means represents a complete account of Weber's theory of bureaucracy, it will suffice to demonstrate its advantages and drawbacks for a developmental situation. Advantages that can be attributed to the rational model of bureaucracy include precision, continuity, discipline, strictness, and reliability. Such a bureaucracy can be seen as efficient in the sense of being conducive to the economical organization of human and other resources in pursuit of certain defined goals according to set rules. It might be argued that this sounds quite appropriate for a developing society that wants to attain development objectives efficiently with minimal waste of resources. Certainly, many commentators are agreed that numerous postcolonial societies inherited bureaucracies that owed something to this model in the sense of being structured hierarchically and based on rules. Staudt argues that the "civil service structure left in place after colonialism emphasized law, order, and revenue collection in a highly centralized, control-oriented system"[12] (1991, 129), although she also notes that rationalism had been compromised in the colonial context by racist recruitment policies. Nevertheless, many developing states were left with professionalized bureaucracies.

However, to the extent that these organizations bore some resemblance to Weber's model of rational bureaucracy, doubts quickly arose as to their appropriateness in a developmental context. Questions concerning the efficiency of rational bureaucracy had already arisen with the work of Robert Merton, who pointed out that a rule-bound approach to administration could lead to goal displacement.[13] A focus on following rules could result in their becoming more important to bureaucrats than organizational goals. This tendency is likely to be reinforced by a career structure that encourages bureaucrats to pursue advancement through a strict observance of discipline and the rules of the bureau. The implications of this are fairly obvious. The broader aims of the bureau are displaced as bureaucrats seek promotion through playing safe and adhering rigidly to petty rules, which in themselves make little contribution to achievement of the bureau's mandate. By extension this is particularly retrograde for developmental bureaucracies that are supposed to oversee social change. An ethos of rule following and adherence to precedent is hardly conducive to change and innovation. Bernard Schaffer made this point in the following terms:

So, with the development agenda in mind, the following points can be made about the costs of bureaucracy. The bureaucratic model is not really an efficiency or output model. The emphasis is on repetition and reiteration rather than on innovation. Inevitable tensions of administration are solved by personality bureaucratisation and institutionalisation. The prime concern is not the product but the value of certainty. Certainty requires controls.[14]

Schaffer's emphasis is that the bureaucratic demand for a rule or a precedent to back up their actions leads officials to become rigid and inflexible in situations where they face conflicting or unprecedented demands. Such situations place pressures on them that they cannot readily respond to in institutions that value repetition over innovation. Their response tends to be to retreat further into the bureaucratic safety blanket of rule following and precedent, which leads in turn to further demands for certainty and control. Hence the uncertainties of the development process result in increasing emphasis on planning and control.

THE INFLUENCE OF CORRUPTION

Tendencies toward bureaucratic control and rigidity are further emphasized and complicated by the prevalence of corruption in many developing societies and its impact on administration. While corruption is a universal phenomenon, it is generally recognized that levels of corruption in many developing states tend to be higher than in developed countries. This was noted as early as the 1960s by Gunnar Myrdal, who wrote:

Corruption is part and parcel of the general condition in the underdeveloped countries of their being soft states. . . . Not only are politicians and administrators affected by the prevalence of corruption, but also business, and, in fact, the whole population.[15]

For Myrdal the high prevalence of corruption in the Third World was attributable to the under-institutionalization of political institutions in the developing states. Other theorists relate it to the salience of ethnocultural loyalties, combined with a chronic shortage of resources, a combination that has deleterious effects on the nature of governance. Fierce competition for control of resources tends to emerge amongst the various contending groups, and corruption is one of the central manifestations of such competition. Sometimes systematized corruption can run out of control going so far as to bring about state collapse. The voracious corruption of the Mobutu regime in Zaire, and of successive regimes in Liberia and Sierra Leone, can be seen as directly contributing to the breakdown of law and order in those countries. While such extremes are not universal, it would be fair to say that many developing states are characterized by comparatively high levels of corruption that permeate all levels of administration.

Our central concern here is not to analyze the origins of corruption or its broader political effects, but rather its implications for the project approach. Certainly, some countries are notorious with aid agencies and personnel for their corruption. For example, an agrarian consultant to the Sierra Leonean government in the 1980s informed one of the authors that the then government's affinity for agricultural interventions involving tractors had much to do with the fact that a kickback could easily be factored into such projects. Similarly, a European Union aid official working in Sierra Leone in the 1980s avowed that the main concern of the EU Delegation in Freetown was to try to ensure that the aid committed to that country was spent properly and not misallocated. By the 1990s this general perception, that a central obstacle to aid effectiveness in Africa was corruption, had percolated into the higher reaches of the EU bureaucracy. EU policy makers saw corruption and associated abuse of EU aid as one of the central reasons why the Lomé Convention had failed to bring about any substantial development throughout much of Africa.[16] This growing perception that much aid was being wasted played a major part in the gradual transformation of the Lomé Convention. In the 1970s the Lomé regime represented a relatively unconditional source of aid. However, by the late 1990s it had been changed into an aid regime characterized by multiple layers of economic and political conditionality and extended planning exercises. All these various forms of conditionality had been added in the effort to ensure that the EU maximized its control of aid with a view to limiting recipient state ability to misallocate or misappropriate funding.

This tendency can be illustrated with reference to the Stabex Fund set up by the EU in 1975 as part of the Lomé Convention. Stabex had been designed to compensate the African, Caribbean and Pacific (ACP) states for shortfalls in the receipts they received for their exports of certain (mainly agricultural) commodities to the European Union. In very simplified terms, the system worked as follows. In any given year of the Convention, a running average would be taken of a country's receipts for a particular commodity over the previous five years. If the country's receipts from that commodity fell a certain amount below the average, the country concerned could make a claim to Stabex for a transfer of the shortfall, that is, the difference between the receipts actually obtained and the average. In the early years of the Lomé regime this transfer took the form of a transfer of foreign exchange from the EU to the recipient state. The funding could then be used for budgetary support, or projects according to the preference of the ACP recipient, the only condition being that the EU should be given a report as to how the funding had been used. At the time this was a revolutionary and flexible system that could have been of considerable benefit to recipient states that stood to gain timely inputs of valuable foreign exchange from it.

Unfortunately, when the EU began to investigate exactly how Stabex funding had been used, they found a number of instances that they deemed illegitimate, one (not atypical) example being that of a state president who had spent the proceeds on a fleet of Mercedes Benz cars for himself and his cronies. Consequently, the EU decided to tighten up the system, introducing the practice of negotiating what they termed a "framework of mutual obligation" (MFO) with each Stabex recipient. This was effectively a contract stipulating what Stabex funding would be spent on and establishing a timetable for expenditure of the aid. In this way the EU won itself a voice in how the funding should be used and also the potential for a sanction in the event of any abuse of the aid. The new system made it possible to disburse Stabex funding in tranches, and so the detection of misuse of one tranche could lead to the withholding of later tranches. This may have helped to limit abuse of Stabex funds, but there were a number of costs associated with the new system. EU personnel commented negatively on the cumbersome process of having to negotiate MFOs with each recipient, a time-consuming procedure that put additional strains on the EU and ACP bureaucracies. These negotiations essentially meant the introduction of a new layer of planning as to how and when Stabex funds could be spent. Inevitably this introduced delays into a system that at least had had the merit of working quickly.[17] The salience of this case is in showing how donor concern about corruption leads to the introduction of new bureaucratic controls in the attempt to dictate how and when as much of the aid as possible will be spent. None of this is conducive to the flexibility needed to operate effectively in a development context.

If this constitutes evidence that corruption can prompt donor agencies to moves toward control and inflexibility, it can be argued that moderate corruption within recipient agencies is associated with increased formalism and goal displacement. So long as a bureaucracy has not reached a stage of extreme kleptocracy where all attempts at concealment have been abandoned, corrupt officials are prone to cover their tracks by a display of rigid observance of petty rules while actually engaging in corruption. Sometimes, the two behaviors will be combined, with officials specifying a battery of petty conditions that a client must satisfy in order to obtain a service (which should be given free in many cases), unless the client takes the hint and offers a gratuity to the official upon which the "rules" are waived. The headquarters of many branches of the Egyptian government bureaucracy, known as the Mogamma (this being the name of the monolithically ugly building in which it is housed in Cairo), is so notorious for such behaviors that it was lampooned in a popular Egyptian film called *Terrorism and Kebab*. Where such combinations of bureaucratic rigidity and corruption occur, they bring together the worst of all worlds for development work. The possibility for flexibility is virtually eliminated by a nitpicking bureaucracy while development projects and programs are further undermined by delays and losses of funds due to corrupt practices.

BUREAUCRATIC CONTROL AND PROJECT DESIGN

In the last two sections we have seen first that rational bureaucracy values precedent, predictability, and rule following. These qualities lead it to try and impose ever-greater levels of control in situations of complexity and uncertainty, which typify the development context. Second, the prevalence of corruption in many developing states reinforces this proclivity toward control amongst aid agencies that see their mandate as involving prevention of misuse of the funds they administer. In this section we shall examine how these tendencies are manifested in the project-design methodologies used by such agencies.

Many agencies recommend that the process of project formulation be commenced with the design of a problem tree. For example, the EU manual on Project Cycle Management states that the identification phase of project de-

Figure 2.1
Diagram of Problems (Example)

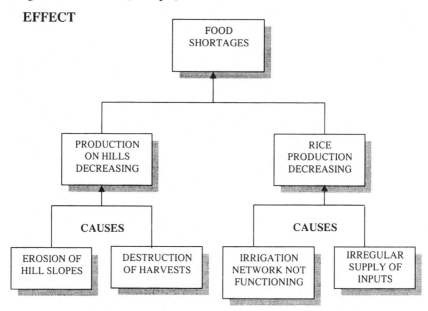

Taken from the Commission of the European Communities, *Manual: Project Cycle Management—Integrated Approach and Logical Framework* (Brussels, 1993), 19.

sign should start with such an exercise as shown in Figure 2.1. Analysis of a development problem in the form of such a diagram serves a number of purposes according to the EU. First, it clarifies the framework of the problem. Second, and arising out of such clarification, it enables project designers to develop an understanding of a broadly defined development problem as a hierarchy of problems that are related in a cause-effect relationship. Thus, the broad development problem of food shortages can be explained as the effect of a number of subsidiary problems or causes, such as decreasing food production on hills and decreasing rice production, which themselves have been caused by a variety of subsidiary problems. It can be seen how the process of tracing a broad or macro-level development problem to a set of lower-level causes sets the framework for a project. The explanation of food shortage in terms of declining production on hills together with falling rice production is indicative of a project that will be structured around hill and/or rice production. This also shows us how formulation of a problem tree can identify a suitable intervention point for a project. It is not immediately clear how to solve a problem of food shortage until one has traced that problem to its causes in hill and rice production, which are far more amenable to solution by a project.

Figure 2.2
Diagram of Objectives

END

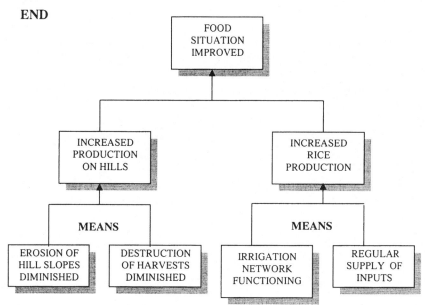

Taken from the Commission of the European Communities, *Manual: Project Cycle Management—Integrated Approach and Logical Framework* (Brussels, 1993), 20.

The latter point is acknowledged by the EU when it notes that the problem tree (what it terms a "diagram of problems") can quite simply be converted into a "diagram of objectives" as seen in Figure 2.2. The negative statements of problems in the problem tree are turned into statements of the positive achievements that a future project will bring about. Thus, "production on hills decreasing" becomes "increased production on hills." The problems that were identified as causing falling hill production are also rendered as achievements, "erosion of hill slopes" becoming "erosion of hill slopes diminished." In this way the problem tree's presentation of a development problem as a series of cause-and-effect relationships is turned into a means-and-end analysis of how the project will solve the problem. The EU manual even points out that the diagram of objectives can be disaggregated into an analysis of the different strategies a project might take to contribute to a solution of the development problem.[18] It can be seen from our example that two strategies can be identified to improve food production, one pertaining to production on hills, the other concerning enhancing rice production. The questions of whether or not a project will be focused on one out of a number of possible strategies, and which strategy that might be, will depend on a number of factors including availability of financial and other resources, together with managerial and strategic issues.

This examination of problem trees is indicative of some of the advantages and disadvantages of this mode of analysis. On the positive side it can be seen that a problem tree can be used to render a general, perhaps amorphous development problem (such as food shortages) into a better-defined problem (such as declining rice production) that can be more readily solved by a project. However, this process also has a negative aspect that was implicit in our criticisms of synoptic decision-making, this being the likelihood that imperfect information will lead to some significant aspect of the development problem being overlooked or ignored. This could lead to a misdirected project that does not deal with a fundamental aspect of the development problem that it is meant to alleviate. Some agencies show a certain awareness of this shortcoming. For example, the UNDP project-formulation manual recommends that completion of a problem tree should be followed by a brainstorming exercise to think up possible alternatives to the strategy indicated by the problem tree.[19] Clearly, this is meant to be a corrective to the reductionist tendencies of problem trees. However, it is only an optional recommendation, which undercuts any useful influence it might otherwise have had. Having already identified a project as a result of the problem tree, it is unlikely that bureaucrats will spend further resources on identifying new alternatives, an exercise that they will probably see as confusing an issue that they have already settled.

Indeed, problem trees can be seen as a bureaucratic technique for exerting an agency's power through its ability to define a problem and thus identify a solution, one that falls within its parameters of operation. If the problem tree represents an initial bureaucratic exertion of control, we shall see that subsequent stages of the project-formulation process deepen and extend this control to most aspects of the project under design. Such control usually takes the form of an attempt to plan and design the project down to the finest details.

This may be illustrated with reference to UNDP methodology, which requires that a project be planned right through from its main objective, or objectives (for example, increased rice production and/or decreased erosion of hill slopes), through medium-level outputs required to attain project objectives and an account of the activities required to produce the outputs. The detail in which this has to be done can be gauged from Figure 2.3, which gives an example culled from the UNDP project-design manual in common use throughout the 1990s. This example is based on an actual project to develop the capacities of the National Institute of Fashion Technology (NIFT) in India to mount courses and undertake research and consultancy that would be of use to the Indian textile industry. It can be seen that the process of working out the outputs and activities required to implement the project is similar to that involved in formulating a problem tree. That is, it involves utilization of a cause-effect/means-end logic in which one proceeds by working out the means/cause needed to achieve the end/effect required to produce

Figure 2.3
UNDP Project Formulation Framework (Excerpt). Section G: Major Elements

Fashion Institute

Immediate Objective	Success Criteria
To enhance the capabilities of the NIFT in the functional areas of training, applied research, and consultancy and information services to serve the Indian garment industry and trade.	By the end of the project: The NIFT will be able to offer annually three two-year diploma courses recognized by the Ministry of Technical Education. Each course will be able to accommodate 100 trainees; The NIFT will be able to carry out applied research - at least five studies annually – that responds to industry needs. Research methodology shall be at standard of professional market research; The NIFT will be able to provide problem-solving consultancy services and up-to-date, useful information in response to needs expressed by the garment industry and trade.

continued

project objectives and outputs. Thus, the project objective for NIFT, or its immediate objective in UNDP parlance, leads to the proposal of outputs that are designed to achieve said objective. In the first instance the project designer will work out just what achievement of the objective will involve by writing a set of success criteria. As can be seen from Figure 2.3, this involves elaborating in some detail what will constitute successful achievement. While the objective is stated as enhancing NIFT's capabilities in the areas of training, research, and consultancy/information services, the success criteria make it clear just what form this enhancement will take. So teaching enhancement will mean that the Institute can offer three two-year courses annually to a certain accepted standard, each of which will accommodate 100 trainees. On the basis of this, the project designer can then proceed to working out the outputs (causes or means) needed to bring about the situation described in the success criteria (the effect or end). For example, it can be seen that the criteria for teaching enhancement are directly related to output 2, which takes the form of new or revised training courses. Output 3 can be seen to be similarly related to the elements of the success criteria dealing with consultancy and information services. The first output's relation to the success criteria is less obvious in that operating systems and procedures are not directly mentioned in the criteria. However, the need for administrative improvements can fairly easily be inferred from the plans for changes in NIFT's services. Having worked out the outputs needed to produce the project objective, the manual suggests that the designer then embark on a similar process of elaborating the

Figure 2.3
Continued

Fashion Institute, continued

Output 1

New or revised operating systems/procedures
for NIFT programs

Success Criteria (optional for outputs)

New or revised operating systems and
procedures for NIFT programs in training,
applied research, consultancy and information
services will have been developed and tested.
In all program areas, procedures for needs
assessment, course or program development
implementation, evaluation, and regular
feedback from clientele groups will have been
established.

Activities for Output 1

Responsible party

1.1 Development of procedures for
assessment of training needs in
the garment industry

Consultant

1.2 Training needs assessment

NIFT staff, Consultants

1.3 Analysis of training needs

NIFT staff, Consultants

1.4 Planning development or adaptation
of programs in training to meet
identified needs

NIFT staff, Consultants

1.5 Development of procedures for needs
assessment in the areas of applied
research, consultancy, and information
services

Consultant

1.6 Needs assessment for applied research,
consultancy, information services

Consultant and NIFT staff

1.7 Analysis of needs

Consultant and NIFT staff

1.8 Program planning in applied research,
consultancy, and information services to
meet identified needs

Consultant and NIFT staff

1.9 Development and testing of a system for
regular collection and analysis of data from
NIFT's clientele on program operations
and emerging needs

Consultant and NIFT staff

1.10 Development of priorities and policies for
all programs

Consultant and NIFT Director

success criteria for each output.[20] However, this is hardly ever done in actual practice. The culminating element of this stage of the project-design process consists in working out each of the activities needed for the production of each output and specifying a member of project personnel whose responsibility that activity will be. Again, the latter task is something that is often ignored in practice. However, as Figure 2.3 illustrates, the activities for each output have to be worked out in some detail and listed in the order in which they are to be performed. Indeed, the process described here is that of designing a blueprint that specifies the main actions to be taken in a project, the order in which they are to be taken and the exact results that they should have. In addition to all of this, the UNDP manual stipulates the need for a thorough list of the inputs needed to mount the project, a detailed budget, and

Figure 2.3
Continued

Fashion Institute, continued

Output 2	Success Criteria
New or revised training courses (diploma and continuing education)	All diploma courses will have been revised or prepared and certified by the Ministry of Technical Education. Continuing-education courses will have been developed in response to industry needs.

Activities for Output 2	Responsible party
2.1 Assessment for NIFT staff training needs in curriculum development and training aids preparation	Consultant
2.2 Preparation of training for NIFT trainers in curriculum development	Consultant
2.3 Training for trainers in curriculum development	Consultant
2.4 Revision or preparation of diploma courses	NIFT staff and consultant
2.5 Training for NIFT staff in training methodology.	Consultant
2.6 Pilot implementation of diploma curricula	Consultant
2.7 Evaluation and revision of curricula, as necessary	NIFT staff and consultant
2.8 Preparation of continuing education (CE) courses based on industry needs	NIFT staff and consultant
2.9 Pilot implementation of CE courses	NIFT staff
2.10 Evaluation and revision of CE curricula, as necessary	NIFT staff and consultant

continued

an account of "project strategy," which should identify the different groupings involved in the project and their respective roles and responsibilities.

It should be clear from the foregoing description of the UNDP project-design methodology that as little as possible in the process is left to chance. The emphasis is on planning in as much detail as possible just how UNDP aid is to be spent in order to ensure that it is only used for approved purposes. The determination to maintain such control is continued throughout the life of a project, being manifested in the necessity for project implementers to submit annual project reports accounting for progress (or lack of it) over the year. The Cairo Office of UNDP has felt compelled to go even further in its

Figure 2.3
Continued

Fashion Institute, continued

Output 3

New programs in applied research,
consultancy and information services

Success Criteria

Applied research, consultancy and information
services programs will have been established and
are operated in response to industry needs. NIFT
will be able to carry out at least five applied research
consultancies at the standard of professional market
research.

Activities for Output 3

3.1 Assessment of training needs of NIFT
    staff in the areas of applied research,
    consultancy and information services
3.2 Preparation for training for staff on
    applied research, consultancy and
    information services
3.3 Training as per 3.2 above
3.4 Preparation of pilot programs
    in applied research, consultancy
    information services
3.5 Implementation of pilot programs
3.6 Review of operations and results of pilot
    programmes and revisions and additional
    training as necessary

Consultants

Consultants

Consultant
Consultant and NIFT staff

NIFT staff
Consultant and NIFT staff

Output 4

Upgraded facilities and equipment for NIFT
programs

Success Criteria

Facilities and equipment will be adequate for
NIFT programs

Activities for Output 4

4.1 Review of equipment and facility needs
    in accordance with the plans for the various
    NIFT functions
4.2 Procurement of equipment
4.3 Installation and test operation of equipment
4.4 Coordination of planning for new facilities
4.5 Construction of new facilities
4.6 Relocation to new facilities

Consultant, NIFT Director

NIFT Director
Equipment supplier
NIFT Director
Contractor
NIFT staff

Taken from UNDP, *How to Write a Project Document: A Manual for Designers of UDNP Projects* (New York: UNDP, 1991), 60–64.

efforts to impose accountability for the funds it administers. In addition to formulating objectives, outputs, success criteria and activities, project designers must now also write deliverables. Each output must have a specific, well-defined deliverable that will be produced within a given time. Failure carries the risk of suspension of aid. The reason given for this innovation is that UNDP workers and consultants in Egypt noticed a common tendency for projects to fall behind schedule. The obligation to produce deliverables was introduced to impose a discipline on aid recipients to properly use their aid and maintain a schedule. It might be argued that such concerns are under-standable given the sclerotic nature of much Egyptian bureaucracy (both governmental and private), which has given rise to considerable waste and misallocation of funding. Nor are they specific to the UNDP, which mirrors many agencies working in the developing world in its concern to ensure an effective use of its funds by means of exerting its control. Indeed, USAID has taken a similar line in placing an emphasis on a results-oriented approach.

The obvious disadvantage to such an approach is that it leaves little if any room for flexibility in project management, while doing nothing to enhance the abilities and capacities of local staff whose remit is subject to tight control. The UNDP manual stipulates that objectives and outputs should be as specific as possible so that everybody involved in the project is clear as to what they should produce and when.[21] The down side of this is that the consequent focus on these intermediate targets can result in goal displacement, with staff concentrating on their own responsibilities and losing sight of the overall project goal. Furthermore, the imposition of what tend to become rigid ob-jectives can become an obstacle in the way of managerial ability to improvise in the face of unanticipated developments that may affect the project. It seems likely that such innovations as deliverables will exacerbate these tendencies toward inflexibility. Indeed, the concept of designing a project right down to its activities and the specifics of its budget is antithetical to flexibility. Given that no planner can anticipate all the eventualities that might face a project in a context characterized by uncertainty and complexity, this approach can be seen as a major obstacle to project effectiveness. Additionally, it is impor-tant to note that the blueprint approach to project design leaves little effective role for participation by the project recipients, which can have negative im-plications for sustainability.

Advocates of the logical-framework approach to project design argue that their preferred method provides a corrective to many of the above problems. The EU manual that we referred to earlier points out that the identification exercise should involve as many project recipients and stakeholders as possi-ble. It also notes that the "logframe" takes the form of a flow chart and that this makes it easier to take an iterative approach in which the project design can be revisited in order to add in activities designed to promote sustainability. Figure 2.4 indicates that the logframe consists of four horizontal and four vertical columns. A look down the first vertical column is indicative that this first phase of filling in the logical framework is essentially the same task as that we just described for the UNDP. As with the problem tree, a means-end logic is used to work out a project purpose from the broader development objective, and then project outputs and activities are worked out from the project purpose. The EU defines this first vertical column as follows:

The first column sets out the intervention logic, which is the basic strategy underlying the project covering all the steps to be taken within the project framework in order to contribute to the overall objectives namely:

Figure 2.4
Logframe Planning Example, Northern Province, Bogo: Intervention Logic

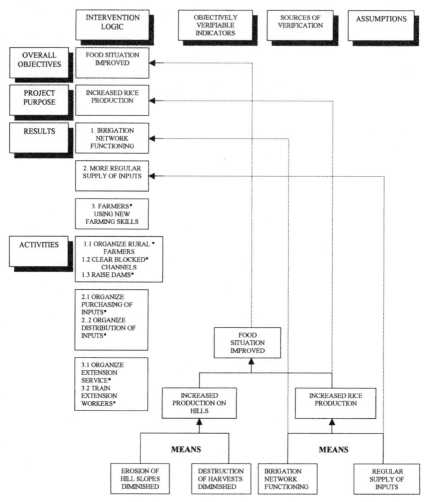

Taken from the Commission of the European Communities, *Manual: Project Cycle Management—Integrated Approach and Logical Framework* (Brussels, 1993), 27.

- The availability of means by which activities can be undertaken (2nd column, 4th row);
- Through these activities, results are achieved;
- Results achieve the project purpose;
- This project purpose contributes to the overall objective(s).[22]

As is indicated in Figure 2.4, the diagram of objectives in Figure 2.2 (which was also drawn from the EU Manual) can be used to fill in this intervention logic by transposing objectives from Figure 2.2 to the corresponding level in the intervention logic.

However, the logframe goes further than the UNDP methodology in that it takes greater account of the complexity and uncertainty of the development situation, which can lead to factors external to the project (often arising out of the local environment in which the project is implemented) causing problems or obstacles to project progress. This is done in the fourth vertical column dealing with "assumptions." The process of filling in this column involves modifying the cause-effect logic used thus far in our project-design methodologies to take into account the proposition that any statement suggesting that a cause will lead to a specific effect involves at least one assumption—that is, nothing will occur to prevent attainment of the anticipated effect. In other words, when we assert that a certain set of project activities will lead to a certain output, we are assuming that nothing will happen to upset such an expectation. The assumption column requires the project planners to give some thought to what might occur to set a project off course. For example, Figure 2.5 shows that the proposition that activities to train farmers will result in farmers adopting the techniques they have been taught involves a number of assumptions. It assumes first that adequate access roads exist so that extension workers can reach farmers to train them, and second that the extension workers can establish a useful dialogue with the farmers. It can be seen that such assumptions are made at every level of the intervention logic.

By forcing planners to think about the assumptions they are making, the logframe is more responsive to the specifics of the project environment than the UNDP approach. It encourages planners to think about potential difficulties arising from this environment and to make allowance for them. For example, where it is thought that motivation of farmers might be difficult, planners can think about incorporating activities to try and counter this problem, such as provision of incentives for the farmers and/or the extension workers. Thus, the logframe provides a space for planners to think about potential problems that might beset the project and make provision for them in advance. While this may be an improvement on the UNDP methodology described here, it still does not solve all the problems of the blueprint approach. Most notably it does not dispose of the problem of imperfect information, which makes it extremely unlikely that planners will be able to isolate every assumption that is made in proposing that certain activities will result in certain outcomes. Nor does it compensate for the fact that planners cannot be expected to anticipate every single problem that will beset their project. If anything, it forces them to behave as if they can foresee all potential difficulties and compensate for them in advance. In this sense the logframe falls into the same traps of inflexibility that characterize other blueprint methodologies.

If anything, the remaining two columns of the logframe underline the

Figure 2.5
Example, Northern Province, Bogo: Listing Assumptions

INTERVENTION LOGIC	OBJECTIVELY VERIFIABLE INDICATORS	SOURCES OF VERIFICATION	ASSUMPTIONS
OVERALL OBJECTIVES	FOOD SITUATION IMPROVED		
PROJECT PURPOSE	INCREASED RICE PRODUCTION		Increased rice production. Increased output on hills (vegetables).
RESULTS	1.IRRIGATION FUNCTIONING 2. MORE REGULAR SUPPLY OF INPUTS 3. FARMERS USING NEW FARMING SKILLS		No sabotage of irrigation system. Farmer associations maintain irrigation. Mechanized rice production. Sales cover production costs.
ACTIVITIES	1. ORGANIZE RURAL FARMERS 1.2 CLEAR BLOCKED CHANNELS 1.3 RAISE DAMS 1.4 TRAIN FARMERS IN NEW TECHNIQUES 2.1 ORGANIZE PURCHASE OF INPUTS 2.2 ORGANIZE INPUTS DISTRIBUTION 3.1 ORGANIZE EXTENSION SERVICE 3.2 TRAIN EXTENSION WORKERS		Access roads in good condition (see 2.1). Extension workers motivated by incentives (see 3.1). Extension workers able to establish dialogue with farmers.

Preconditions
Disputes between hill farmers and lowland farmers are settled.

Official approval of organization set-up.

Taken from the Commission of the European Communities, *Manual: Project Cycle Management—Integrated Approach and Logical Framework* (Brussels, 1993), 31.

method's basic nature as a blueprint. The second vertical column deals with objectively verifiable indicators, which the EU manual describes as follows:

Objectively verifiable indicators (OVIs) describe overall objectives, project purpose, and results into operationally measurable terms (quantity and quality, target group(s), time and place); they should give an adequate picture of the situation and be measurable in a consistent way at an acceptable cost.

Operational descriptions give insights into the overall objectives, project purpose and results, enabling us to:

- Check the pertinence and viability of the project purpose and results;
- Monitor progress toward achieving them.[23]

This indicates that the OVIs serve the same purpose as the equally specifically defined objectives and outputs of the UNDP methodology. As can be seen from Figure 2.6, project personnel will know that they have achieved the project result pertaining to more regular supply of project inputs when all project farmers have seedlings and 50 kg of fertilizer per hectare a month in advance of planting. In other words, the OVIs indicate what constitutes success and provide a yardstick so that project personnel know how close to (or distant they are from) attaining success. They fall very much in line with the blueprint model inasmuch as they set exact targets, which do not leave much room for flexibility. This tendency toward exactitude is reinforced by the need to confirm the OVIs by providing sources of verification (the third vertical column of the logframe), which must be specific and reliable.

All of this demonstrates that the project formulation methodologies endorsed by most development agencies are designed to exert control through planning out most aspects of the project in advance. Clearly this leaves little if any room for the flexibility (or participation) needed to deal with the uncertainties and complexities of development.

ALTERNATIVE PROJECT APPROACHES

We have already observed that Rondinelli emerged as one of the central critics of the latter approach to project design, and he is one of a few analysts to have broached the question of what might constitute a viable alternative. He has advocated what is generally summarized as an experimental approach to project design and implementation. His approach is termed experimental because he argues that projects should start with an experimental phase, which would be small-scale and designed with a view to learning about a development problem and how it might be dealt with. Such projects would not be regarded as magic bullets that would be expected to solve the problem in one shot. Their small scale would make failure a tolerable risk, which would help to create the conditions for the flexibility needed to bring about positive developmental change.

Figure 2.6
Example, Northern Province, Bogo: Adding Objective Indicators and Sources of Verification

	INTERVENTION LOGIC	OBJECTIVELY VERIFIABLE INDICATORS	SOURCES OF VERIFICATION
OVERALL OBJECTIVES	FOOD SITUATION IMPROVED	Food situation improved after 1997, 300 kg rice or 600 kg manioc consumed at same (indexed) price as in 1992	Survey by Ministry of Agriculture in 1998
PROJECT PURPOSE	INCREASED RICE PRODUCTION	Increase rice production per ha (+/-45% output sold) 94 95 96 97 10% 20% 30% 10%	Project report in 94/95/96/97
RESULTS	1. IRRIGATION NETWORK FUNCTIONING	From 1995 all fields adequately irrigated	Survey of peasant farmers 95/96/97
	2. MORE REGULAR SUPPLY OF INPUTS	A month before planting all peasant farmers have seedlings and 50 kg fertilizer per ha	Reports from extension services and project team
	3. FARMERS USING NEW FARMING SKILLS	Farmers apply the agricultural calendar and plant at right distance from 1996 onward	

Taken from the Commission of the European Communities, *Manual: Project Cycle Management—Integrated Approach and Logical Framework*, (Brussels, 1993), 41. Section showing first three vertical and horizontal columns of logical framework. Assumptions, Preconditions, and Activities would be as shown in Figure 2.5.

However, Rondinelli's proposals do not stop at this point. In fact, he suggests that projects should be planned and implemented through a four-phase process, consisting of the experimental stage, followed successively by a pilot, a demonstration, and a replication phase. As noted above, the experimental stage would be principally a learning experience, which would enable designers to learn about the characteristics of a problem in a particular area and to explore the variety of possible strategies for dealing with the problem. Experimental projects would also facilitate innovation in the following way:

Different techniques, combinations of inputs and organizational arrangements can be tested on a limited scale or in only a few places. If the experiments do not succeed, other approaches can be tried quickly without wasting large amounts of money or unduly embarrassing the government and the sponsoring organization. Small experimental failures may not threaten the survival of a larger program. In addition, experimentation sets in motion a learning process.[24]

Rondinelli uses the work of R. Cuca and C. S. Pierce on family-planning programs to note that experiments contributed to the development of a new methodology.

If this approach is to bear fruit, experimental projects need to be protected from the normal bureaucratic pressures examined above. First, personnel on such projects have to be given the time and freedom to try different strategies and not be penalized when some of them fail, characteristics that do not generally typify bureaucracy. Second, experimental projects may need special supplies and staff with special skills, which must not be subject to the bureaucratic delays that are normal in all too many countries. Third, personnel have to be protected from normal bureaucratic duties in order to ensure that they are properly motivated to do their work well. Finally, adequately qualified and skilled staff must be appointed if experimental projects are to have any worthwhile results.

Once an experimental project has given rise to an idea that has some promise a pilot project can be designed to test it further. Thus, innovations that have been successful in an experiment can be tested in other locations to see if they can be more generally applied. A pilot project may also take the form of a small-scale prototype for a large project to see if an idea works before committing the money to set up the full operation. Such projects must be flexible enough to allow for personnel to react to developments during implementation and to adapt the project to conditions on the ground. In this way pilot projects can generate data concerning how far innovations can be adapted to various environments and whether or not an idea for a major project is at all workable in practice.

If a project idea survives these two phases it can progress to the final two stages. The penultimate stage, that of the demonstration project, is designed to convince a potential group of project recipients that an innovation (being promoted by the project concerned) is worth their while adopting. For example, a demonstration project might be initiated with a view to convincing farmers in a particular region that a new package of production techniques will be of benefit to them. Hence, the project will assist a sample of the farmers in adopting the package, the aim being to demonstrate the success of the package to the others so that they will also want to adopt it. The experience of this will enable project designers to fine-tune their packages and approaches to take account of differential demands and preferences on the part of potential beneficiaries. This sets the scene for the final phase, that of full-scale production or service delivery projects, these being projects as we know them.

Rondinelli's proposals have the merit of allowing for experimentation and flexibility in the earlier stages of the process so that project designers can learn what will and will not work in which places. On the basis of such knowledge they will be better able to design workable projects. It might be argued that such projects would still be prone to the problems posed by unexpected events. However, Rondinelli sees the adoption of this four-phase approach to projects as being premised on the adoption of a more adaptive approach to administration, which would involve a more collegial approach to decision-making; mobilization of information across ranks (rather than down a hier-archy); adjusting tasks so that personnel will be more flexible; encouraging an administrative environment that rewards staff for effective performance of their responsibilities (rather than for obedience to their superiors); and in-creasing participation by staff and clients in decision-making.[25] All of these qualities would help to create a situation in which project personnel and ad-ministrators would be better able to take a more flexible and adaptable ap-proach to project implementation. However, they all stand in marked contrast to the present characteristics of many bureaucracies, including rigid hierarchy and definition of staff responsibilities, together with a focus on repetition, rule following and precedent.

Furthermore, we have to factor in the political pressures on aid-giving bu-reaucracies to account for the funding governments vote to them and to pro-duce specifically defined outputs. The political demands of both donor and recipient governments for concrete results apparently leave little room for experimentation and flexibility. Having noted this, it would seem that some aid agencies, notably Norway's NORAD, have moved toward acceptance of Rondinelli's principles.[26] Furthermore, in the next section we shall examine a recent move toward program-aid approaches that can accommodate elements of the flexibility advocated by Rondinelli.

Before moving on to these program approaches, it is worth noting another major alternative to the traditional school of thought in what is variously known as community, popular, or participatory development. Indeed, it emerges from Rondinelli's arguments that participation constitutes a major element of his suggested approach. Such is the importance of the participatory tradition within the field of development that it will be dealt with in a separate chapter.

FROM BLUEPRINTS TO SWAPS

Sector Wide Approaches (SWAPs) have arisen out of many of the problems we have examined above, but also due to a number of shortcomings in the project approach that we have not as yet dealt with. In the 1990s a number of aid donors became disillusioned with the project approach for many of the reasons given above. However, they identified additional problems with this approach, including duplication of effort, overloading of local capacity to co-ordinate donor contributions, and consequent waste of resources. Indeed, it has often been noted in various contexts that donors tend to duplicate each other's efforts, so that two or three donors may be running their own very similar projects in the same area. This can lead to a negative situation of competition between donors. In addition, recipient governments often lack the capacity to properly organize their investment programs and consequently tend to overcommit themselves to projects. Baum and Tolbert noted a pattern whereby aid recipients would tend to focus on winning the next project without giving too much consideration to how to meet their obligations for recurrent costs on projects that were already in progress. This could lead to a situation where a government would meet the costs of its new projects, but its older projects would almost invariably be underfunded.[27] Given that conditionality often includes a government commitment to meet certain counterpart costs, failure to produce scheduled government contributions could carry the risk of suspension of aid, which would undermine the viability of the project. More generally, Foster notes that "(i)f donor projects are not set within a coherent plan and budget, the result can add up to a development effort that is expensive to manage, and in which there is wasteful duplication, uneven coverage, inconsistent approaches, and poor sustainability of projects once donors withdraw."[28]

SWAPs represent an attempt to eliminate such problems by organizing the aid efforts of various donors on a sectoral basis in agreement with the recipient government. A number of agencies have moved toward embracing this approach, including USAID, the EU and various EU member states, and Canadian CIDA. The EU has defined SWAPs as follows:

The SWAP defines a way of working between donors and governments and should not be confused with any funding instruments. The SWAP is not a blueprint but an approach, a new way of doing business through a long-term partnership and a statement of the intended direction of change.[29]

This clearly reflects a growing disenchantment with the idea that development could be planned as a blueprint. SWAPs are essentially program approaches through which donors and recipient governments agree on the development strategy and objectives for a sector and then various types of support are made available to implement the strategy. However, a central aspect of this is that the process of policy-making for the sector is ongoing throughout implementation. The SWAP does not define a blueprint for the sector under consideration, whether it be health, education, or another field. Instead, donor-recipient cooperation is processual, "moving over time to deepen policy dialogue, to make the coverage of the sector more comprehensive, to bring more funds into coordinated arrangements and to develop common procedures based on those of governments'." The EU moves on to delineate the characteristics of SWAPs:

The defining features of a SWAP are that:

- Government takes responsibility for setting policies, priorities, and standards, which apply to all public activity in the sector including that financed by donors (the sector policy):

- All significant funding for the sector supports a single-sector policy and expenditure program (covering at least one year) under government leadership with participation of key stakeholders (the sector expenditure program):

- Partners adopt common approaches across the sector and rely on government procedures to disburse and account for all funds (the sector partnership):
- A SWAP does not equate to budget support or budget pooling arrangements such as "basket" funding although these are desirable funding modalities. This distinction is important and remains the source of confusion. At various stages of a sector program appropriate forms of assistance may include: technical assistance, an earmarked project, commodity support, pooling of funds and untied budget support. The hope is that as a SWAP evolves, and trust and confidence increase, donors will gradually move toward providing a greater part, if not all, of their support as untied budgetary assistance.[30]

The central points that emerge from this concern the leadership role that is supposed to be taken by the recipient government, the suggestion that there should be a participatory element with key stakeholders involved in the dialogue, and the fact that a wide variety of aid mechanisms can be used, including projects. With regard to the leadership role of government it is clear that a certain level of state capacity is implied here as well as commitment to the SWAP and its objectives. This implies that SWAPs will not be suitable for all states, a conclusion that is underlined by Foster's comment that "the lesson from the experience of trying to operate sector programs in hostile environments is not a positive one."[31]

The passage also indicates that the project form is not being entirely supplanted by SWAPs, despite the suggestion that well-advanced SWAPs would tend to move toward reliance on budgetary support. It might be argued that some environments that are unsuitable for a SWAP could still be suitable for projects. There is also some evidence that the SWAP presents a framework in which the more experimental approaches recommended by Rondinelli can be embraced. Foster refers to the development of a number of pilot projects in the health sector in Tanzania to test the viability of market-based approaches to health provision.[32]

One might ask how realistic it is to expect the governments of underdeveloped countries to take charge of SWAPs, especially considering that this move toward a programmatic approach to aid has occurred mainly at the behest of donor agencies. Brown et al. have examined a number of the SWAPs in implementation and point to three types of experience that have varying implications for "government ownership" of the programs. Perhaps the clearest example of a government taking the lead in a program concerns the Universal Primary Education initiative in Uganda. President Museveni committed himself to the program and the Ugandan Government took a lead in trying to mobilize the donor community. Most SWAPs do not fall into this category. Rather, they fall into the second category where certain domestic forces (such as change agents, ministers, senior officials) enter into an alliance with donors to persuade government to take on a program, or into a third category where the donors essentially force a program onto the recipient government. Most of the programs in the latter two categories tend to be problematic due to questionable government commitment. In cases where programs are dependent on a narrow base of allies they can suffer if those allies experience a reversal in their fortunes and influence. By contrast with this example, the Zambian health SWAP benefited from the patronage of a particular minister, but this was more than offset by the fact that other stakeholders felt they had been excluded and consequently opposed it. In those cases where donors have taken a lead there has been a tendency for negotiations to stall (as in the case of a Vietnamese health SWAP and a Tanzanian education SWAP), or to result in a flawed program as with the Ghanaian education SWAP, which is thought to have a fragmented approach to the sector.[33] It is for these reasons that Brown et al. argue that a broadly based negotiation of the program should take place in order to ensure adequate support, but that it should take place according to a timetable. They suggest that gaining support from the head of state and the legislature are key to rallying official acceptance of the program in the recipient state.[34]

One thing that undermines any contention that SWAPs are subject to government control and ownership is the continued effort of donors to exercise control by means of conditionality. Various types of conditionality occur at different levels of the SWAPs, notably IMF/World Bank structural-adjustment macroeconomic restrictions, which limit the parameters within which recipient governments can maneuver their commitments to the program. Brown et al. note that the World Bank seem "most inclined to include specific policy undertakings in financing agreements" as in the case of Bangladesh, where the "health and population credit is conditional on a range of both policy and implementation conditions, including implementing agreed reorganization of the Ministry, and implementation of an Action Plan with 22 key measures."[35]

The overall impression that is emerging here of a continuing top-down approach to aid is confirmed by the lack of evidence of participation in most of the SWAPs that have been implemented. Brown et al. observe:

There has been very little participation in the SWAP process within Government below senior level. In Mozambique, Uganda, Tanzania, Ethiopia, and other countries even dissemination of information about SWAPs to lower levels is very poor. Similarly, in Bangladesh there was little local involvement in the sector strategy outside the Central Ministries, and the concept of the SWAP was poorly understood in the field, although significant efforts were made to take the message out, and part of the problem may be that it was both complex and not fully believed.[36]

It is notable that this does not even refer to local participation by the targeted recipients of aid. Clearly, the introduction of SWAPs has not led to any modification of the bureaucratic hierarchies that dominate aid, either amongst the donors or the recipients. The two exceptions to this rule are the Ugandan poverty-eradication action plan, in which there is participatory planning at every level, including school, pilot districts, and civil-society involvement in monitoring the plan; and the Ghana health-sector plan, which involved the broad participation of health-sector staff at all levels, though not of local communities.[37]

This is likely to have a negative impact on the effectiveness of SWAPs for dealing with poverty. At time of writing there is little evidence of any impact on poverty as a result of SWAPs, but this may simply be because it is too early in the life of many programs for any decisive results to have emerged. What Brown et al. do note is that the "quality of poverty diagnosis is low at (the) program-design stage in most cases," but that the "review process is providing an opportunity to inject better analysis and feedback, e.g., from participatory poverty assessments and service-delivery surveys."[38] It remains to be seen if the results of such investigation actually are incorporated into the design and management processes for SWAPs, but it is worth noting that nobody is talking about directly involving the poor in the processes through which policies are made that affect them. In this sense, there seems to be little chance that SWAPs will subvert the top-down hierarchy through which only those at the head of development bureaucracies are involved in deciding what is in the best interest of people living in poverty. However, SWAPs do offer the chance for agencies and governments to use and organize a variety of different aid-delivery mechanisms (including the traditional project where appropriate) in a combination that can be nuanced to fit whatever problem is being dealt with. Thus, we can argue that they at least offer a more flexible modus operandi than projects for dealing with development problems, including poverty.

THE WASHINGTON CONSENSUS AND PROGRAM AID

As we have seen, the Washington institutions, the IMF and the World Bank, are most associated with their structural-adjustment programs, which largely address the macroeconomic level. It is commonplace to observe that these programs have earned the Bank and the Fund considerable disapprobation because of their effects on the poor. There has been much argument over how far SAPs actually disadvantage poor people, but it would be fair to say that over the period of the 1990s a degree of consensus has emerged to the effect that both the Bank and the Fund need to make a greater effort to integrate the needs of the poor into their shared policy agenda. This tendency has been a major factor in the emergence of the program approaches currently sponsored by the Bank and the Fund, the Comprehensive Development Frameworks (CDFs) and the Poverty Reduction Strategy Papers (PRSPs).

As an approach, the CDF bears quite a strong resemblance to that of

SWAPs, the essential difference being that whereas the latter is aimed at coordinating activities in a single sector, CDFs are aimed at producing national strategies integrating the various sectors. The approach has been described as follows:

The CDF seeks a better balance in policy-making by highlighting the interdependence of all elements of development—social, structural, human, governance, environmental, economic, and financial. It emphasizes partnerships among governments, donors, civil society, the private sector, and other development actors. Of particular importance is the stress on country ownership of the process, directing the development agenda, with bilateral and multilateral donors, each defining their support for their respective plans.[39]

As with SWAPs, there is an emphasis on country ownership of the program, coordination between donor and recipient institutions and involvement of civil and society and various stakeholders.

Since 1999 pilot CDFs were begun in a number of countries, including Bolivia, Côte d'Ivoire, Eritrea, Ethiopia, Ghana, Jordan, Kyrgyzstan, Morocco, Uganda, Vietnam, and the West Bank and Gaza. A report of May 2000 noted that the pace and depth of progress had been uneven, mainly because of the varying circumstances and capacities of the different countries, or due to unforeseen circumstances. These included political conflict as in Eritrea and Ethiopia, a coup in Côte d'Ivoire in 1999, and changes in political leadership in Jordan and Morocco. Such factors were seen as underlying variable progress. However, the report stressed the long-term nature of the CDF strategy, arguing that its success could only be gauged over the long term.[40]

It would probably be fair to say that CDFs have been largely subsumed under the PRSP strategy. PRSPs emerged out of the World Bank/IMF initiative agreed in 1996 for comprehensive debt relief to the Heavily Indebted Poor Countries (HIPC). The initial results of HIPC were generally agreed to be disappointing with very few countries able to meet the criteria for assistance. This led to an agreement at the World Bank/IMF Annual Meetings of 1999 to link debt relief under HIPC to the implementation of a poverty-reduction strategy in the debtor state. The World Bank describes the PRSP strategy as follows:

At the September 1999 Annual Meetings of the World Bank Group and IMF, Ministers endorsed the proposal that country-owned poverty reduction strategies should provide the basis of all World Bank and IMF concessional lending, and should guide the use of resources freed by debt relief under the enhanced HIPC Initiative. This strategy will be reflected in the Poverty Reduction Strategy Paper (PRSP) prepared by country authorities with broad participation of civil society.

The PRSP will, in effect, translate the Bank's Comprehensive Development Framework (CDF) principles into practical plans for action. The PRSP's aim is clear: to strengthen country ownership of poverty reduction strategies; to broaden the representation of civil society—particularly the poor themselves—in the design of such strategies; to improve coordination among development partners; and to focus the analytical, advisory, and financial resources of the international community on achieving results in reducing poverty.[41]

This means that countries seeking aid under the HIPC Initiative need to produce a Poverty Reduction Strategy Paper to qualify for assistance. They must have their poverty strategy in place when the decision to commit aid is taken, and it must be well into implementation by the time of disbursement.

It is also clear that the PRSPs are based on a similar programmatic model to the CDFs in that they are meant to be owned and driven by the debtor states, take an inclusive approach to civil society (including the poor), are based on coordination between the various donor agencies and recipient institutions, and aim at development over the long term. In addition they are supposed to be results-oriented, focused on aims that will help the poor, comprehensive in the sense that they take account of the multiple causes of poverty, and prioritized with a view to making implementation feasible.[42]

The Bank insists that there is no blueprint for formulating a PRSP, stipulating that each strategy should be determined by the specific needs of the country in question. However, it does suggest that "there are three key steps that typically characterize the development of effective poverty reduction." These are as follows:

1. **Develop a comprehensive understanding of poverty and its determinants.** Beginning with an understanding of who the poor are, where they live, and their main barriers of moving out of poverty is key. Further, the multidimensional nature of poverty (low income, poor health and education, gender, insecurity, powerlessness, etc.) needs to be carefully considered.

2. **Choose the mix of public actions that have the highest impact on poverty reduction.** A solid understanding of the nature and causes of poverty allows a foundation to select and prioritize macroeconomic, structural, and social policies based on their expected impact on achieving a country's poverty targets.

3. **Select and track outcome indicators.** An appropriate framework for selecting and tracking measures to indicate progress for chosen poverty outcomes is needed to test the effect of policies and programs and adjust as needed.[43]

All of this is suggestive of a serious reorientation of Bank and Fund methods to place poverty at the center of their approach to the HIPCs. First, the commitment to base any action on an understanding of the actual conditions of the poor is suggestive of a move toward a more nuanced policy of tailoring activities to the particular context. In the past, the Washington institutions have both been accused of bureaucratic and ideological rigidity in their application of structural-adjustment policies, which have often been seen as harming the poor. The PRSPs would seem to hold the promise of a more flexible and inclusive approach. Second, the reference to selection of macro-economic policies that benefit the poor is also suggestive of a departure from rigid adherence to market policies no matter what their effect on specific social groups inclusive of the poor.

Subsequent reviews of the PRSP initiative suggest that such promise has not been fulfilled as yet. A report on African PRSP documents by Thin et al., for Britain's Department for International Development (DfID), notes that while the papers acknowledge the multicausal nature of poverty there are still shortcomings in their analysis. They do not bring into play central concepts such as sustainability, inequality, or empowerment (see Chapter 7 for a dis-cussion of the latter concept). Nor do they properly utilize the sustainable-livelihoods approach despite its growing influence in development circles (see Chapter 3 for an examination of this approach). Many documents fail to men-tion livelihoods, and those that do use the concept in a "rudimentary" manner, referring to it only in the rural sector and ignoring it as a factor in examining the urban context. Indeed, Thin et al. argue that the papers tend to regard poverty as an essentially rural phenomenon despite mounting evidence of rising urban poverty levels.[44]

An Oxfam critique observes that in most of the countries undertaking PRSPs, the participatory aspect has been badly organized with minimal in-volvement of civil society. This is because timetables for completion of the documents have been rushed, one such example being Cambodia. A central factor in precipitating this haste is the perception of many states that the faster they complete a document, the quicker they will be given access to the con-cessional aid available under the scheme. It will be remembered that states are supposed to have their strategies in place in order to qualify for aid. Given that nations like Niger and Zambia were due to spend a quarter of their export earnings on debt in 2001, it can be seen why they might be inclined to skimp on preparation of their strategies in order to get access to badly needed fund-ing. Clearly, the Bank and the Fund have not taken adequate pains to correct for this tendency. In the case of Cambodia, this situation was further com-plicated by the fact that the Asian Development Bank was pursuing its own poverty strategy in the country at the same time that the Bank and the Fund were pushing the government to produce its PRSP. This suggests that the Washington institutions are failing to deliver on their promise to coordinate with other donors.

Oxfam further observed that the Washington institutions are failing to live up to their promise to make poverty reduction integral to their policies. The Oxfam critique quotes the IMF to the effect that its assistance given under the initiative should integrate macroeconomic policy with poverty reduction and should demonstrably be based on the relevant country's PRSP. However, it notes that "the process in many countries is working in the opposite direc-tion, with the economic policies within a PRSP being drawn from policy recommendations within Bank and Fund lending instruments."[45] Oxfam concludes that policy design is proceeding as usual in the Washington institutions. This situation is exacerbated by the fact that neither institution has undertaken a systematic analysis of the impact of their policies on poverty. Oxfam comments on this as follows:

> This is bad for policy design. It also means there can be no well-informed discussion in a country of realistic economic policy choices and trade-offs. If poverty reduction is the priority, then assessing the impact of proposed reforms on poor people must be a priority too.[46]

These observations are indicative that the Washington institutions have failed to deliver on the apparent promises of the PRSP initiative for changes to their operating procedures. It might be argued that the PRSP strategies are supposed to be designed by the recipient states, but both the Bank and the Fund are well aware that these states have little capacity and few resources to produce well-designed strategies. Rather than taking action themselves to help produce PRSPs that actually put poverty at the center of their policies, they seem to have lapsed back into their bureaucratic (not to mention ideological) routines, adopting what Oxfam describes as an attitude of "business as usual."[47]

CONCLUSIONS

In this chapter we have seen that the project form was initially viewed as the most effective means of mobilizing aid for development in the Third World. Thorough planning of investments to maximize efficient resource use was seen as the best path to development. However, analysts like Rondinelli and Schaffer quickly realized that in fact the blueprint approach was not effective in the face of the complexity and uncertainty of the development environment. Rondinelli in particular argued for a more adaptive, experimental approach that would be more suited to the complexities of the development context. The bureaucracies of the aid donors and recipients tended to take a different view, attempting to emphasize traditional bureaucratic virtues of control in the face of uncertainty. This emphasis on a top-down blueprint approach was reinforced amongst many donors by the enhanced levels of corruption encountered in much of the developing world. It would seem that a vicious circle had emerged in which the innate bureaucratic propensity to exert control over policy interventions had been found inadequate to deal with the complexity of the development context. Yet the response of donors was to retreat into a more rigid adherence to their traditional bureaucratic values and to try to deal with complexity by further emphasizing their control. The results have been that donors have still been unable to anticipate all of the problems however rigorously they have designed their projects, nor have they been able to eliminate corruption, however tightly they have tried to control implementation. Indeed, this reinforcement of top-down control is likely to prevent local bureaucracies developing the administrative and professional capacities essential to deal with development, that is, to respond flexibly and effectively to development situations as they emerge in the field. In sum, the top-down approach is antithetical to the qualities of flexibility and local participation and initiative required for a more effective development approach.

By the 1990s the shortcomings of the top-down project approach had become clear to most aid donors, and this has led to a change in emphasis in the emergence of various types of program approach, inclusive of SWAPs, CDFs and PRSPs. Our analysis has shown that the SWAP is indeed more flexible than the project form (at least in principle), but the aid donors are still concerned to exert control through conditionality. In this sense SWAPs are as much a top-down strategy of aid disbursement as projects. The same can be observed of the Washington institutions' PRSP initiative, where a failure to genuinely engage with civil society and to really change their policies to take account of poverty seems to have resulted in a continuation of traditional top-down operating methods. This means that many of the aforementioned problems of the top-down approach are replicated in various program approaches. The emphasis on conditionality leads to inflexibility and it constrains the development of local capacity to deal with the complexities of development. Furthermore, the actual recipients of aid have little or no opportunity to have a voice in suggesting what kinds of aid they may need. In future chapters we shall be examining how different approaches, such as participation, and different types of development organization, might lead to a more flexible, bottom-up working method that avoids the problems of the blueprint approach, while more effectively identifying and addressing the problems of those living at the grass roots in developing countries.

CHAPTER 3

The Environment and Sustainable Development

In the introductory chapter we saw that sustainability has become an important issue in development and project management. We briefly examined the significance of economic, administrative, and political sustainability in development projects. In this chapter we transfer our attention to the question of sustainability and the environment. Many readers will be aware of the environmental macro-crises emerging on a global scale, such as global warming, atmospheric deterioration, and depletion of rainforests and wetlands. All of these are crucial issues pertaining to both environmental sustainability as well as development, given that many of these crises originate in what numerous commentators see as unsustainable development patterns, particularly in the Northern states. Most of the industrialized states have based their economies on intensive use of carbon-based fuels as well as other environmentally harmful substances, and this directly contributes to the crises mentioned above. There are signs that these unsustainable consumption patterns are also being adopted by policy makers and elite groups in the South, further exacerbating degradation of the world environment. Important as these issues are, they do not constitute the central concerns of this chapter. In the first instance, they are dealt with extensively in many other publications (we might point to the yearly *State of the World* and *Vital Signs* publications produced by the Worldwatch Institute, which painstakingly document global environmental trends). Furthermore, such issues can only be dealt with at the level of global policy, whereas our main concern in this book is to examine issues concerning development management and administration at the field level. Consequently, the central focus of this chapter will be on how issues of environmental sustainability have been accommodated/incorporated at the project and program level. Reference will be made to macro-issues, especially in tracing the emergence of broad concepts of sustainable development, but our main concern is to examine how far environmental and developmental concerns have been reconciled at the field level.

As we shall see, questions of environmental preservation, or sustainability, were not initially seen as being complementary to development, especially when developmental change was conceived as consisting mainly of economic growth. This view was lent credence by the tendency for many traditional projects to damage the environment in various ways. Our analysis will commence by examining the contradictions between environmental conservation and development, briefly surveying some of the ways in which projects impacted on the environment. Subsequently, we shall briefly analyze the process through which a reconciliation of these contradictions was attempted in the form of the concept of sustainable development. This will reveal how a mainstream account of sustainable development has emerged that has shaped the policies and activities of many development and environmental agencies. Three central components of this mainstream account can be identified: market environmentalism (in which the role of the market as a force for environmental protection is explored), rational/managerial approaches to sustainable development (in which top-down blueprint approaches to development are adapted to deal with the demands of sustainability), and the sustainable-livelihoods approach (which proposes a bottom-up approach to attain the benefits of development without harming the environment). Each of these components of the mainstream view will be examined in turn to assess their implications for achieving a viable approach to a sustainable development. Throughout our analysis the central focus will be on the ways in which considerations of environmental sustainability have been grafted onto project design and implementation processes, both through top-down methods, such as Environmental Impact Assessment, and through bottom-up techniques such as the sustainable-livelihoods approach.

CONSERVATION AND/OR DEVELOPMENT

We have already noted that environmentalism and development are often seen as contradictory rather than complementary. This owes something to the origins of environmentalism. Adams traces environmentalism to a variety of sources, notably the science of ecology and conservationist thinking. He notes how concern for conservation of tropical environments and species arose in a colonial context and was, at least in part, colored by the racist views extant during that period. According to such views, indigenous people were usually deemed to be harming the environment by hunting animals or through the practice of shifting cultivation. Consequently, when national parks and protected areas were founded, one of the first actions was often to forcibly remove native populations in order to prevent them harming the area. In this way conservation was constituted in a manner that directly opposed the interests of local people.[1] Guha and Martinez-Alier cite the example of the Chenchu people who live in the hills and forests of the Krishna basin in Andhra Pradesh in India. Parts of the area where they live have been constituted as a tiger reserve under Project Tiger. This has restricted their access to forest products (which had already been curtailed when the state took over their forests early in the twentieth century). Obviously, the Chenchus resent the fact that their developmental interests seem to be have been sacrificed to those of Project Tiger.[2] Such cases are illustrative of the way in which conservationist interests have often come to be perceived as inimical to developmental interests.

Guha and Martinez-Alier trace how this process has played out in broader environmental debates. They point out that the British historian G. M. Trevelyan was one of the first prominent commentators to air the view that an increasing concern for nature seemed to linked to the growing urbanization and changes in the landscape that were part and parcel of industrialization. In other words, environmentalism can be seen as a product of economic and industrial growth. This leads to the view that environmentalism is a luxury that can only be afforded by those that have already attained a certain level of development and prosperity. Guha and Martinez-Alier quote a British journalist to the effect that "when everyone turns environmental, prosperity has truly arrived. Greenness is the ultimate luxury of the consumer society."[3] They go on to note that this is a view that is echoed by some of the most prominent contemporary commentators, such as Eric Hobsbawm, who claims:

It is no accident that the main support for ecological policies comes from the rich countries and from the comfortable rich and middle classes (except for businessmen who hope to make money by polluting activity). The poor, multiplying and underemployed, wanted more "development," not less.[4]

In this formulation we can see the clear juxtaposition of environment and development posited as opposing principles, in which environmentalism is conceived as a luxury that is only valued by those who are already developed. By contrast, it constitutes an obstacle to those that wish to attain development since environment is here conceived as entailing "less" development.

Certainly, there is evidence to suggest that this is the view that has been taken by many Third World states. Adams notes that many of the developing states reacted with some degree of suspicion to the proposal for the first of the major international conferences on the environment, the United Nations Conference on the Human Environment in Stockholm in 1972. It did not help that the conference was primarily the initiative of industrialized countries and that its agenda largely reflected their problems of industrial pollution. Third World states were also afraid that industrialized nations would seek to circumscribe their freedom to develop by such methods as raising antipollution barriers against their products. Moreover, the nonindustrialized countries tended toward the view that pollution was largely the result of the dirty technologies that the developed states had used to industrialize. Consequently, the Third World should not be expected to pay for any solution to a problem caused by the industrialized states. Indeed, there was a sense of palpable unfairness that the developed states might try to impose environmental limits on Third World industrialization strategies, having had the advantage of developing on the basis of polluting technologies themselves. This is a theme that emerges at various points in the debate on development and the environment.

As a result, efforts were made to incorporate certain environmental concerns of the Third World, such as desertification, soil erosion and water supply, into the Stockholm Conference. Assurances were also given that environmental concerns would not be mobilized by the industrial states in such a way as to harm Third World development interests. In fact the Stockholm Conference and its preparatory meetings saw the emergence of the argument that environmental preservation and development are complementary rather than contradictory. In this sense it marked the beginning of the formulation of the concept of sustainable development. However, as we shall see, the tension between environment and development has never completely dissipated and it reemerges periodically in the debates between environmentalists and developmentalists.

DEVELOPMENT WITHOUT ENVIRONMENTALISM

If pro-development forces have expressed reservations about the effects of environmentalism on development, green commentators might reasonably argue that there is much evidence to suggest that development is bad for the environment. Only in recent years have development agencies begun to pay attention to the effects their projects have on the environment. Prior to this development, projects were designed without taking any account of their potential effects on environmental conditions. This has resulted in a number of environmental problems, even disasters. Perhaps the central point to note is that adverse environmental effects have often proven deleterious to the developmental aims of the projects.

Most types of projects have some environmental implications, but it would probably be fair to say that amongst those with the most radical effects are dam-building projects. Dams have major impacts not only on the physical environment around the dam, but also on the population of the area to be flooded, who have to be relocated from their present homes and provided with new accommodations and means of making their living. Adams summarizes the ecological effects that often follow from dam projects as follows:

• Dams and reservoirs alter the pattern of river flows, typically lowering and extending flood peaks; they can affect sediment loads, alter patterns of erosion downstream, and cause channel movement and damage to infrastructure.

- Downstream physical changes in dammed rivers can cause changes in aquatic eco-systems (for example, to fish and hence people who fish) and in downstream flood-plain wetlands (for example, floodplain forests and farmlands). Socioeconomic impacts on people fishing, farming, and grazing can be significant.[5]

He provides numerous examples to back up these conclusions. Thus, the As-wân High Dam in Egypt resulted in reduced soil fertility in the Nile Valley due to lower sediment in floodwaters. Apparently, erosion in the Nile Delta due to lack of sediment caused by the High Dam has also led to declining catches for fishing villages.[6] Similarly, we may note that the Kainji Dam in Niger has constituted a total barrier to fish movement, as recorded catches at the foot of the dam have been high, while catches downstream were much reduced between 1967–69.[7] Reductions in fish catches below dams were also recorded in Nigeria, one example being on the Sokoto. Riverine woodlands can also be affected by changes in river flows caused by dams. The viability of forest ecosystems can be put into question by such changes, and any neg-ative ecological effects may only become evident decades after a dam has been built.[8]

One of the most notorious dam projects in recent years is the Narmada Dam Project in India. The Narmada Valley Development Plan proposes the construction of 30 large and over 3,000 medium and small dams on the Nar-mada River over about 50 years. The main element of the plan is the huge Sardar Sarovar Dam, which is planned to stretch 4,000 feet across the river and to rise to a proposed 455 feet.[9] The Sardar Sarovar Project alone is one of the largest water projects in India and one of the most controversial. Vari-ous claims have been made for the benefits to be accrued from the dam, for example, that it will irrigate almost 4.8 million acres (2 million hectares) of land and will supply drinking water to some 30 million people.[10] However, opponents of the dam claim that the 37,000 hectares to be submerged, to-gether with the 80,000 hectares to be used for irrigation canals, is actually more fertile than much of the land that is to be irrigated by the dam (http://www.narmada.org/sardar-sarovar/objectives.html). Caufield also notes that de-spite the claims that the dam will deliver drinking water, the project has no funds budgeted for village water supply.[11] Perhaps the greatest controversy concerns the some 200,000 people to be displaced by the dam, many of whom are tribal people (known as *adivasai* in India). Caufield records a number of instances where local people were tricked into moving from their home areas (which were scheduled for submersion), only to find that the new land they had been allocated was infertile and that the government would not provide health and other services that had been promised as inducements to move. The overwhelming response of such people was to move back to their homes despite the threat that they would be flooded.[12] An active popular resistance movement to the dam grew up in the area, gradually attaining national and international prominence for itself and its cause.

The role of the World Bank in this case is particularly noteworthy. The Bank provided financial support for the Sardar Sarovar Dam Project in 1985 despite knowing that no viable resettlement plan existed for those who were to be displaced. This directly violated the Bank's own policy, established in 1982, that "the Bank will not assist development projects that knowingly encroach on traditional territories being used or occupied by tribal people, unless adequate safeguards are provided."[13] In 1991 the Bank sent an independent review body to investigate the project in response to the intense popular opposition to the dam. A damning report emerged to the effect that nobody had given any consideration to the likely effects on populations living downstream; the dam would increase salinity, harming fishing grounds downriver; it would silt twice as fast as had been assumed and would deliver only half the irrigation water anticipated; and it was likely to have deleterious health effects, creating areas that would be breeding grounds for malarial mosquitoes. The Bank's immediate response was to try to quash the report and go ahead with the project anyway. However, the report was leaked, and the Bank was forced to withdraw from the project in some disorder.[14] Despite the Bank's exit, the Indian government is persisting with the project in the face of continued popular resistance.

It should be noted that dam projects are by no means the only type of development intervention that can harm the environment. Adams notes that irrigation projects are also particularly problematic. For an irrigation project to be effective, water must be efficiently delivered in accordance with participating farmers' needs. This is dependent on proper maintenance of canals, gates, and weirs. Effective management and implementation of this process is expensive and is seldom accomplished. Consequently, canals and other infrastructure tend to fall into disrepair, which leads to unreliable water supply to the farmer. Under these circumstances farmers tend to respond by appropriating as much water as they can when possible. This means that the wealthier are liable to get the lion's share of water and the poorer, together with those at the end of the canal, get least. Consequently some farmers overuse water, which can lead to waterlogged soils and resultant salinity or alkalinity, while others underuse it and are unable to achieve sufficient yields to make a profit. Furthermore, irrigation schemes bring associated health problems of malaria and bilharzia. It has been estimated that 60% of adults and 80% of children on the Gezira Project in the Sudan contracted bilharzia.[15]

We could cite many other examples of environmental damage (major and minor) arising from development projects in various sectors where the executing agencies have either been blind to environmental considerations or have ignored their own rules as the World Bank did in the case of the Sardar Sarovar Dam. The central point to draw from such examples is that the damage they cause does not stop with the environment. It feeds back into the prospects for developmental success. For example, the damage to land quality caused by inefficient irrigation projects feeds back into low yields that mitigate against project success. This could be seen as providing an initial corrective to the arguments we surveyed earlier that saw environmental and developmental goals as incompatible. Indeed, it could be taken as suggesting that environmental awareness is necessary for successful development. In the next section we shall trace how this perception took shape in development circles, leading to the genesis of the concept of sustainable development.

TOWARD SUSTAINABLE DEVELOPMENT

It has already been noted that the Stockholm Conference of 1972 marked the beginning of the process through which sustainable development has been defined. The conference agreed on 26 principles for action, which sought to reconcile environmental and developmental interests in the following way:

The fundamental point was that development need not be impaired by environmental protection (Principle 11). This was to be achieved by integrated development planning (13) and rational planning to resolve conflicts between development and environment (14). Furthermore, development was needed to improve the environment (8), and this would require assistance (9), particularly money to pay for environmental safeguards (12), and reasonable prices for exports (10).[16]

Adams notes that this drew on the technocratic roots of environmental thinking in ecology, which initially emerged as a science of environmental management. However, it can also be seen how this technocratic approach of management based on integrated and rational planning, also represents a very comfortable fit with the planning methods extant amongst the main development agencies at the time, which we examined in the last chapter.

Adams traces how this technocratic approach was reemphasized at almost every stage of the debate on sustainable development that ensued after Stockholm. Thus, the World Conservation Strategy, published in 1980 by the International Union for the Conservation of Nature and Natural Resources (IUCN), the United Nations Environment Program (UNEP), and the World Wildlife Fund (WWF), argued that conservation and development should be integrated at every stage of planning so that conflict between these objectives could be eliminated. This technocentric ethos is also intrinsically linked to a conception of sustainable development that is pro-capitalist in its acceptance of the necessity of economic growth. The latter element in this formula became evident with the publication of the Brundtland Report in 1988 and was reinforced by the Rio Conference in 1992.

The Brundtland Report was the outcome of a UN General Assembly resolution of 1983 calling for an independent commission to produce a report on the state of the world. Central to the commission's mandate was the investigation of critical environmental and development issues facing the world and formulation of realistic proposals for dealing with them. The resultant report was actually entitled "Our Common Future," but it is often referred to as the Brundtland Report after the chair of the commission, Gro Harlem Brundtland. One of the central achievements of the report was that it established what is still the best-known definition of sustainable development, which runs as follows:

[H]umanity has the ability to make development sustainable—to ensure that it meets the needs of the present without compromising the ability of future generations to meet their own needs.[17]

As many commentators have noted, this formulation lends itself to any number of possible interpretations. First, we may note that the stated objective of meeting the needs of the present could mean radically different things depending on one's interpretation of what the needs of the present actually are. Second, it is difficult, if not impossible, to calculate how far technological advances are likely to modify the ability of future generations to meet their needs, this being a factor that has direct implications for our present treatment of the environment. It might be argued that a technocratic optimist would suggest that we can rely on technological advance to solve many of the world's environmental and development problems, a view that would imply only a limited need to worry about our present treatment of the environment.

The spin that the Brundtland Report took on these issues was based on the view that much environmental degradation was caused by poverty, as when small farmers are forced to over-farm and exhaust land due to their socioeconomic marginality for example. The Brundtland Report followed the Brandt Report of 1980 in proposing that the answer to much Third World poverty lay in continued world economic growth, which meant "more rapid economic growth in both industrial and developing countries, freer market access for the products of developing countries, lower interest rates, greater technology transfer, and significantly larger capital flows, both concessional and commercial."[18] As Adams observes, the report did not question either growth or technology. It was assumed that economic growth, inclusive of aid and private investments, would relieve poverty in the Third World and that this would relieve pressure on the environment. This begged the question of what effects this growth would itself have on the environment. We have already seen that developmental interventions in the Third World often have radical environmental implications, and there is no reason to suppose that the enhanced aid and investment envisaged in the Brundtland Report would be any different. The report asserted that "the Commission's overall assessment is that the international economy must speed up world growth while respecting environmental constraints,"[19] but, as Adams notes, "it does not say how this balancing trick is to be achieved."[20]

One of the recommendations of the Brundtland Report was that a world conference on environment and development should be held. The UN scheduled its Conference on Environment and Development (UNCED) to take place in Rio in 1992. The Rio Conference, or Earth Summit, as it was variously known, involved representatives from 172 states and 3,000 representatives from NGOs. Any high hopes that environmental activists might have had for a breakthrough were soon dashed by the naked self-interest exhibited by many of the participating states, notably the United States, whose leader, George Bush, Sr., faced an election that year. Two of the main outputs of the conference were the Rio Declaration, consisting of 27 nonbinding principles on which to found future efforts at sustainable development, and Agenda 21, which was a much larger document that sought to set a broad agenda for a wide variety of activities toward sustainable development. Many commentators were agreed that the Rio Declaration was simply a bland compromise document, while Agenda 21 was so unwieldy that it was virtually impossible to implement it. Nevertheless, Adams identifies five ways in which the documents continued themes that had been prominent in the debate on sustainable development. First, progress was once again premised on the need for economic growth. This emphasized the conclusions of the Brundtland Report. Second, there was an emphasis on environmental management. Third, the technocentricity of previous documents was maintained. Economic growth will provide finance and technology will provide the means (i.e., the techniques, or hardware) to manage the world economy sustainably. Fourth, the multilateralism of the Brundtland Report was continued. Rio sought to build a consensus based on the shared interests of developed and underdeveloped countries in wanting to leave a benign legacy to future generations. These multilateral interests would be reflected in flows of aid and technology from the developed to the underdeveloped countries, which would be managed by international agencies. Finally, it followed a trend in development, noting that sustainable development should be participatory. However, the question concerning the terms on which participation was to take place was never addressed. Thus, the Rio documents evaded the question of whether or not those at the grass roots were to be given any actual say in deciding what shape sustainable development might take.[21]

It is worth noting that there were other significant outcomes of the Rio Conference. The Convention on Biological Diversity is aimed at protection of species and regulating conduct in sharing research, profits, and technology in the field of genetic research. The Framework Convention on Climate Change is concerned with lowering emissions of greenhouse gasses. Its operation was stalled for several years due to wrangling between various countries about their responsibilities under the convention. The Kyoto Conference of 1997 eventually saw a commitment by the industrialized states to lower emissions of six greenhouse gasses to 5% below 1990 levels by the years 2008–12. President George W. Bush decided to follow family tradition on environmental issues by reneging on that commitment on behalf of the United States. One might also mention the Forest Principles, which emerged from a plan for forest management and preservation. The original proposals caused major dissension between Northern and Southern state representatives at the conference, mainly because the South wanted the same rights to exploit their resources that the North had exercised. The South insisted that if the North wanted the forests of the South preserved they should pay for it, a principle about which the Northern states were less than enthusiastic. In the end a toothless set of nonbinding principles emerged.

While the conference was by no means a complete loss, it clearly failed to live up to expectations. Notably, it failed to secure any commitment by the Northern states to any substantial increase of aid for the environment or to any timetable for implementing reforms in national or international environmental policy. Its central effect was to establish the mainstream consensus on sustainable development defined above, which is the pro-capitalist model premised on economic growth, technological advance, and rational planning.

This consensus has identifiable impacts in terms of shaping approaches and methodologies for sustainable development. For example, its orientation toward capitalist growth finds expression in market environmentalism and such phenomena as pollution trading. Similarly, its emphasis on rational planning and managerialism is reflected in the emergence of environmental impact assessment (EIA) as a means of examining the ecological impact of development projects. Nor should it be forgotten that the participatory strand of this consensus at least opens up the possibility of a more populist approach to sustainable development, which is reflected to some degree in what has become known as the sustainable-livelihoods approach. In the rest of this chapter we shall examine several of these approaches and methodologies with a view to assessing their practicality for making an impact on the ground via development projects and programs.

ENVIRONMENT FOR SALE?

Low and Gleeson note that the core of market environmentalism consists in the view that the market is the best mechanism for regulating human exploitation of the environment and that intervention by the state is inefficient.[22] This argument is predicated on the tenets of classical economics to the effect that forces of supply and demand will act to reach an equilibrium where human needs will be met without the planet's resources being exhausted. As Beckerman puts it, "insofar as any natural resource does become scarce in a relevant sense its relative price will rise and this will set up a chain of market responses which will tend to discourage its use and the development of substitutes."[23] This process renders state intervention unnecessary, indeed inefficient.

A logical concomitant of this approach is that the environment should be treated as a commodity with a price so that it can be bartered on the market. This has led to market environmentalists proposing that in addition to such categories as human capital (skills and talents learned by people) and fixed capital (such as machinery and human-made infrastructure), one can identify natural capital, that is, the environment and its products (or products "created by bio-geophysical processes and not human action," as Adams puts it).[24] It is argued that in this way the products of nature can be represented and valued in terms of capital, which means they have a monetary price. Consequently, such resources can be commodified so that the market will have the same effect on them as other goods and the forces of supply and demand will operate to prevent overexploitation.

Indeed, market principles have made an impact on the environment in the shape of what has become known as pollution trading. This practice was given a particular impetus by the Kyoto Agreement, which emerged out of the aforementioned Kyoto Conference of 1997. It will be remembered that this committed signatories to a reduction of their emissions of six greenhouse gasses (GHGs) to 5% below 1990 levels by 2008–2012. However, the agreement also made the following provisions:

The Kyoto Protocol provides three **cooperative implementation mechanisms** that industrialized countries can use to supplement domestic actions for fulfilling their legally binding commitments to reduce GHG emissions:

Joint Implementation (JI) is a project-based approach that enables one industrialized country financing a GHG-reducing project in another industrialized country to receive "emissions reduction units" (ERUs) representing the emissions not generated by the second country **(Article 6 of the Agreement).**

Clean Development Mechanism (CDM) allows industrialized countries to accrue "certified emission reduction units" (CERs) in return for financing carbon reduction project activities in developing countries that help further their sustainable development **(Article 12).**

International Emissions Trading (IET) enables industrial country signers of the Kyoto Protocol to use GHG emissions trading to fulfill their legally binding commitments so that countries that reduce their emissions below the quotas can sell the excess to other countries in need of credits **(Article 17).**[25]

A number of countries, multinational corporations, NGOs, and other institutions have become involved in the pollution trade made possible through these mechanisms. NGOs have become involved in forestry projects since forests act as "sinks" for carbon dioxide (that is, they take in carbon dioxide and store it), thus helping to compensate for industrial emissions of that gas. Certain corporations are also supporting forestry and related projects with a view to earning credits against their own polluting activities. Various nations that are heavily forested are also seeking credits in respect of their forests with a view to benefiting their industries.

One of the earliest such projects was the CARE/Guatemala Agroforestry Project, started by CARE with USAID in the mid-1970s. In 1989, USAID involvement terminated with the end of their grant. At that stage Applied Energy Services Inc., a U.S. power corporation, became involved. AES was looking for a project to offset against its new power plant in Connecticut, which was expected to emit some 14.1 million metric tons of carbon over its 40-year life. They consulted the World Resources Institute (WRI), which recommended backing the CARE/Guatemala project. The project consisted of a number of components, including creation of community woodlots, application of agroforestry practices, terracing vulnerable slopes (to protect and improve agricultural production), and training of forest fire brigades. The WRI calculated that the project would sequester an estimated 16.3 million metric tons of carbon over 40 years, mainly through addition to the existing forest; demand displacement from the forest to the project's woodlots (that is, demand for timber could be met from the woodlots rather than the pre-existing forest); retention of some carbon in the soil; and the improved fire-fighting service. Consequently, AES helped finance the project, making it the first carbon offset project on such a large scale. The WRI qualifies its estimate by noting that this initial attempt at calculating the effectiveness of such a project was static, taking no account of how land use might change during the project. It has since developed an alternative method for assessing forestry projects' carbon-storing potential, known as the Land Use and Carbon Sequestration model (LUCS), which examines how the landscape will change over the life of a project. The WRI avers that even this only offers "first approximations, not revealed truth."[26]

The largest reported project has been initiated in eastern Bolivia by a consortium involving two large U.S. power corporations and British Petroleum. The consortium paid almost $10 million to buy a large forested area that was being worked by loggers. The land has been incorporated into the Noel Kempff National Park, thus giving it legal protection against logging and thereby protecting a number of the threatened species that live there, including river dolphins, jaguars, tapirs, and so on. The objective of the corporations is to claim credit for the carbon absorbed by the forest, which can be counted toward their targets for reducing GHG emissions.[27]

Totten notes that a number of countries are involving themselves in the "carbon trade" in the following terms:

In 1997 Costa Rica became the first country in the world to turn its forests into marketable carbon sinks by issuing "Certified Tradable Offsets" (CTOs), based on a forest carbon sequestration program with performance guarantees, carbon reserve pools, and third party certification.[28]

Costa Rica was followed in 1998 by the New South Wales (NSW) state government in Australia, which has formed a partnership with two electrical companies, Pacific Power and Delta Energy. Pacific Power invested in 4,500 tons of carbon rights secured on the basis of a sink of 1,000 hectares of eucalyptus hardwood plantations. Delta Energy bought 5,775 tons of carbon rights over 30 years based on a sink of 41 hectares of softwood plantations. NSW also developed a carbon-forestry investment product, yielding interest as well as carbon rights.[29]

It should be noted that there are some drawbacks to this national interest in carbon trading. At the climate talks in Bonn in 2002, four of the most heavily forested nations—Japan, Russia, Canada and Australia—managed to gain substantial concessions on the basis of considering their forests as sinks. According to environmental campaigners this has contributed to a less-than-fortunate outcome in that the cuts in GHG emissions agreed at Bonn will only be some 2% of 1990 levels by 2012. It will be remembered that the figure agreed at Kyoto was 5%. This is particularly unfortunate given that many scientists argue that GHG emission cuts of over 50% will be required at some point this century.[30]

These doubts about the environmental benefits of carbon trading are emphasized by recent scientific research that casts doubt on the effectiveness of forests as carbon sinks. The Hadley Centre for climate research in the U.K. published research arguing that the soil will start to emit more greenhouse gasses than the trees absorb as the climate heats up.[31] Furthermore, American researchers have argued that trees' carbon uptake declines after three years in the absence of other nutrients, notably nitrogen and water.[32] Such findings cast doubt on any process of establishing how far any forestry project can compensate for a given amount of GHG emissions.

This reflects the dubiety of the whole enterprise of commodification of the environment. The environment is extremely complex, and any economic formula for expressing it in monetary terms is likely to be reductionist. As Adams notes, "it is much harder to place a value on natural capital. . . . Most environmental goods are not subject to market relations, either because they are held in common (e.g., clean air), because they have only recently become scarce (e.g., clean groundwater, subject to slow and recent pollution penetration), because the structure of existing markets allows certain actors (usually established corporations and economic interests) to treat environmental costs as an externality, or because institutions for organising a market do not exist."[33] It can also be argued that natural capital is non-substitutable and so cannot be exchanged on the market. For example, if one proposed to convert 1,000 hectares of rainforest into ranch land, it would be impossible to exactly compensate for the ecological complexity of the rainforest in a substitute project. In short, economic environmentalism may be convenient for policy makers in that it enables them to place a value, or price, on elements of the environment and make policy on that basis, but such values can only be of the most dubious accuracy.

A RATIONAL APPROACH? ENVIRONMENTAL
IMPACT ASSESSMENT

We have already seen that the mainstream approach to sustainable development places a premium on rational planning and managerialism. Environmental impact assessment (EIA) represents a method of environmental protection based on rational planning. Essentially EIA is a means of identifying any environmental problems that are likely to emerge as a result of a proposed project with a view to minimizing or eliminating any resultant ecological degradation. EIA constitutes a planning process that can be grafted onto the project-planning process discussed in the last chapter. The positive aspect of this is that environmental planning can be grafted onto the existing development-planning process, but at the expense of further complicating an already complex procedure.

EIA's debt to rational planning is evidenced in the following account of its purposes:

An EIA is expected to have the following characteristics . . .

- It is a study of the effect of a proposed development project on the environment, the term "environment" including all aspects of natural and human environments.
- It considers both environmental and economic costs and benefits.
- It is a predictive mechanism; it estimates the changes in the quality of the current environment as a result of the proposed action.
- It compares all of the alternatives to the proposed project and evaluates them according to both environmental and economic costs and benefits.
- It is a decision-making tool that the decision-maker uses to arrive at the optimal selection of all possible alternative forms of the project, including the abandonment of the project.[34]

This indicates that EIA is subject to the same problems that characterize the project planning process, most notably the illusory assumption that all alternative options can be identified and weighed against each other in order to reach an optimal solution. We have already seen that such assumptions are unrealistic in development situations characterized by radical complexity. The addition of environmental considerations into the equation can only add to this complexity, further reducing any possibility of a fully successful outcome to the planning process.

As with the normal project planning process, EIA can be seen as consisting of a number of stages, which are illustrated in some detail in Figure 3.1. The first stage is that of screening the project in order to determine whether or not an EIA is actually needed. This is followed by the important and delicate process of scoping, which consists of determining the parameters of the EIA, that is, deciding what will actually be included in the assessment. After this, the actual process of assessment can take place. It is generally recommended that a baseline survey be undertaken in order to ascertain the state of the

Figure 3.1
A Generalized Procedure for EA

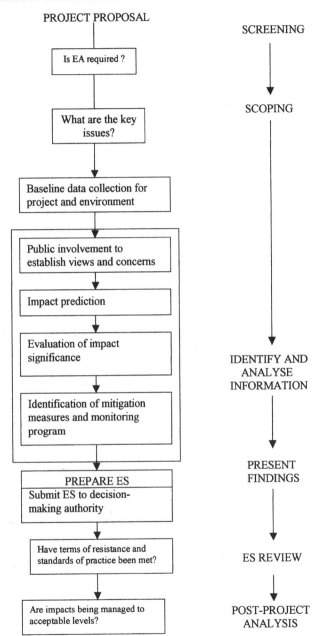

PROJECT PROPOSAL

SCREENING

Is EA required ?

SCOPING

What are the key issues?

Baseline data collection for project and environment

Public involvement to establish views and concerns

Impact prediction

Evaluation of impact significance

IDENTIFY AND ANALYSE INFORMATION

Identification of mitigation measures and monitoring program

PREPARE ES

PRESENT FINDINGS

Submit ES to decision-making authority

Have terms of resistance and standards of practice been met?

ES REVIEW

Are impacts being managed to acceptable levels?

POST-PROJECT ANALYSIS

Taken from D. Owen Harrop and J. Ashley Nixon, *Environmental Assessment in Practice* (London and New York: Routledge, 1999), 8.

environment in the project area at the start of the project. Certainly, we can see that without one it would be difficult to gauge how far the project was actually bringing about any change. The stages following the baseline survey consist in impact prediction and evaluation, processes that tend to be associated together inasmuch as identification of significant impacts inevitably entails consideration of the weight, or extent of the impact. These processes will culminate in the production of a report, referred to as an Environmental Statement (ES), "which describes the nature of the project (and possibly a range of alternatives), its environmental setting, the impacts associated with the development and proposals for dealing with those impacts considered to be potentially significantly adverse (impact mitigation)."[35] Finally, there will be an evaluation stage to review the ES and examine how far it meets professional standards. As in the project-planning process, these stages are iterative and tend to flow into one another. We have noted the association between impact prediction and evaluation, but the process of scoping also tends to touch on these issues, because any consideration of what should be included in an EIA must also address such questions as "What impacts are likely to happen?" and "How severe are they likely to be?" It is also generally recommended that stakeholders in the project should be consulted and kept informed at all stages.

A variety of techniques are used in performing such processes as screening, scoping, and impact evaluation. Checklists are often used in the screening process. For example, a basic checklist might list all the environmental factors that could be affected by a project so that planners can run down the list to see which items their proposed project is likely to affect. If they find items on the list that may be affected this alerts them to the possible need for an EIA. More complex checklists can be used in impact evaluation, notably scaling checklists, which rank impacts according to severity, or magnitude. Matrices are also used for this purpose. One of the most widely used applications in EIAs is the Leopold Matrix. Gupta and Asher describe this as follows:

The Leopold Matrix is a large arrangement with 88 environmental factors along the vertical axis and 100 development characteristics along the horizontal one, giving rise to 8800 cells. . . . Each cell is divided by a diagonal line, and magnitude and importance of the impact are written (one in each half of the cell) on a scale of 1 to 10, 10 being the maximum.[36]

They note that the Leopold Matrix has a number of advantages, for example, that it enables the planner to get a visual impression of the overall impact of the project on the environment, while also showing which part of the project is causing the greatest impact. It also shows both beneficial and harmful impacts, given that either a plus or minus sign can be put in front of the figures in the cells.[37] However, it has also been described as "large and unwieldy," one estimate suggesting that only about 20–50 project-environment interac-

Figure 3.2
Conceptual Framework of the Impact Network

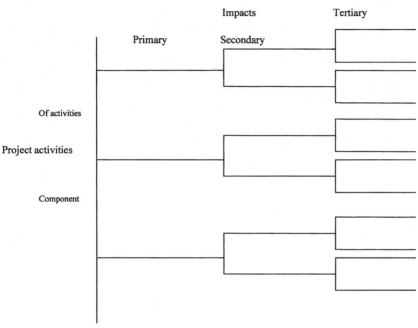

Taken from Asit K. Biswas and Qu Geping, *Environmental Impact Assessment for Developing Countries* (London: Tycooly Publishing, 1987), 204.

tions were likely to be significant in most project proposals.[38] Criticisms that have been made of both checklists and matrices note that both approaches compartmentalize the environment into separate elements, each of which are separately affected by discrete elements of the project. This means that they focus on primary impacts, overlooking any secondary impacts that a project may have. Furthermore, where a value is assigned to an impact, this is dependent on the subjective judgment of the assessor, introducing the danger of bias.[39]

The failure to consider secondary impacts can be corrected using network methods (see Figure 3.2), which entail listing project activities in order to identify their possible impacts on the environment. On this basis, secondary and then tertiary impacts can be identified. This is useful in consideration of impact-mitigation measures because it draws attention to the need to counteract a series of environmental impacts rather than just the primary, or initial impacts. The downside is that networks are complex to compile and quickly become visually complicated. They also fail to address weighting, or magnitude of impact.[40] Similar criticisms of complexity can also be made of overlay techniques, alternatively known as environmental features mapping. In this method, overlay maps of the project area are drawn, each of which illustrates the potential effect of the project on a particular environmental factor. Magnitude of impact can be indicated through different levels of shading, so that a severe effect might be represented through a dark gray, whereas a slight impact would be shown by use of a lighter gray. Again, this quickly becomes visually complicated as more overlays are added. This can be alleviated by use of computerized Geographical Information Systems (GIS), which enables the planner to examine environmental impacts as a whole, singly, or in any combination required. Thus, information can be aggregated or disaggregated as required, although use of GIS assumes access to computer technology, which may not be available to Southern planners.

Our analysis of EIS thus far is indicative of the extent to which it further complicates the project-planning process. This is not to condemn the entirely laudable ambition to incorporate environmental considerations into the development-planning process. We have already seen the frequently lamentable results of failure to factor in the environmental effects of proposed development projects. In light of such examples any attempt to take account of the environmental consequences of our actions has to be seen as welcome. However, such enthusiasm has to be tempered by the knowledge that incorporation of environmental variables into the planning process increases the already high level of complexity and uncertainty associated with the development context. This renders the task of adequately planning development projects even more problematic. None of this is made easier by the fact that developing countries tend to be characterized by inadequate baseline environmental data, inadequate resources for gathering such data, poor funding, and poor capacity, both at governmental level and at the level of the individual planner. While all these problems may make it difficult, even impossible, to adequately plan for all the consequences of our development interventions, it should still be clear that at the very least EIA can be effective in alerting us to some (though not all) of the potentially harmful environmental consequences of our actions.

ENVIRONMENTALISM FROM THE BOTTOM UP?

In previous sections we have examined arguments to the effect that environmentalism is often inimical to the interests of the poor, who need the benefits of development more than they need a clean environment. We also noted the example provided by Guha and Martinez-Alier of the Chenchu people, who were denied access to some of their traditional forests due to a conservation project to protect tigers. All of this tended to suggest that the poor were more likely to suffer than benefit from environmental projects and programs. However, Guha and Martinez-Alier also provide evidence to suggest the opposite. For example, they note that Thai peasants under the leadership of a Buddhist monk, Phra Prajak Khuttajitto, have taken direct action to protect their local environment. The Thai government was introducing eucalyptus-tree plantations in the Packham district with the intention of exporting wood chip and paper pulp. In the process it was clearing existing deciduous forests. This process was harmful to local peasant interests because the high water consumption of the eucalyptus trees had an adverse effect on their rice crops. Consequently, in 1988 and 1989 they burned down eucalyptus nurseries, planting local trees instead. It is worth noting that not only did they destroy the trees that harmed their rice crops, they also took steps to try and restore the environment to its previous balance by planting local species. In this instance grassroots environmental action coincided with development action. This leads Guha and Martinez-Alier to the conclusion that "poor countries and poor individuals are not interested in the mere protection of wild species or natural habitats, but do respond to environmental destruction which directly affects their way of life and prospects for survival."[41] It is this sort of understanding of the coincidence between development and environmental needs of the poor that gives rise to the sustainable-livelihoods approach to environmentally sustainable grassroots development.

The sustainable-livelihoods concept was popularized by Agenda 21, but it also owes a great deal to the work of Robert Chambers, one of the central advocates of participatory development. In 1988 Chambers argued as follows:

[T]here is mounting evidence that when poor people have secure rights and adequate stocks of assets to deal with contingencies, they tend to take a long view, holding on tenaciously to land, protecting and saving trees and seeking to provide for their children. In this respect, their time perspective is longer than that of commercial interests concerned with early profits from capital, or of conventional development projects concerned with internal rates of return. Secure tenure and rights to resources and adequate livelihoods are prerequisites for good husbandry and sustainable management.[42]

This takes the insight of Guha and Martinez-Alier a stage further. Where the latter realized that the poor would react to oppose environmental depredations that harmed their abilities to make a living, Chambers recognized that if the poor were given secure rights over their share of the land and its resources, together with an adequate livelihood, they would actively protect their environment. Herein lay the basis of the sustainable-livelihoods approach.

Chambers argued that there are five necessary elements to a sustainable-livelihoods intervention.[43] First, he advocated an adaptable learning approach of the sort commended by Rondinelli, which was examined in the last chapter. Adaptability is necessary to respond to the needs of the poor, which vary according to location and will also change over time. Second, people's priorities must be at the fore of any intervention. This is necessary because people must feel that their true needs are being addressed by a project if they are to genuinely take ownership of it. Furthermore, people at the grass roots often have the most reliable knowledge of what will work best in their varying environments. Chambers cites the example of soil conservation in West Africa, where official programs focussed on construction of earth bunds with little success, while local farmers preferred stone bunds, which proved to be much more resilient.[44] Third, as already indicated, the poor must acquire secure rights and gains if they are to be given the incentive to live in an environmentally sustainable manner. Chambers supports this contention with evidence from Haiti and Kenya, which confirms "that when peasant farmers are secure in their ownership of land and their rights to do what they like with trees, they are likely to plant them in considerable numbers," whereas "in parts of the Sahel and of India, where government regulations restrict rights to cut, peasant farmers are reluctant to plant."[45] Fourth, Chambers stresses that a self-help approach is central in promoting sustainability. While subsidies and food-for-work approaches can play a useful role in dealing with the very poor, it is more likely that people will be genuinely committed to a program that they have voluntarily worked on, and concomitantly it is more likely to be sustainable. Fifth, an effective sustainable-livelihoods intervention is dependent on a high-caliber, committed staff that works on the project for a substantial period. Adaptability and the capacity to learn are essential, while continuity amongst the staff is essential for learning to take place and adaptation of the project to be properly implemented.

It can already be seen that such an approach would make unfamiliar demands on the blueprint-obsessed, rule-bound development bureaucracies examined in the previous chapter. Even so, a number of agencies have introduced the sustainable-livelihoods approach into several of their activities. Amongst them are the UNDP and Britain's Department for International Development (DfID). The UNDP elaborates its approach as follows:

[S]ustainable livelihoods (SL) offers both a conceptual and programming framework for poverty reduction in a sustainable manner. Conceptually, livelihoods connote the means, activities, entitlements and assets by which people make a living. Assets, in this particular context, are defined as not only natural/biological (i.e., land, water, common-property resources, flora, fauna), but also social and political (i.e., community, family, social networks, participation, empowerment), human (i.e., knowledge creation by skills), and physical (i.e., roads, markets, clinics, schools, bridges).

The sustainability of livelihoods becomes a function of how men and women utilize asset portfolios on both a short and long-term basis.[46]

Having translated sustainable livelihoods into the language of economics, envisaging the poor as rational utility maximizers manipulating portfolios of assets, the UNDP goes on to define sustainability as consisting in the following four characteristics. First, it involves the "ability to cope with and recover from shocks and stresses." Second, it entails economic effectiveness, defined as "the use of minimal inputs to generate a given amount of outputs." Its third element is ecological integrity, that is, ensuring that the way people secure their livelihoods is environmentally sustainable. Finally, it involves social equity, "which suggests that promotion of livelihood opportunities for one group should not foreclose options for other groups, either now or in the future."[47]

The UNDP has developed a five-stage methodology "for the design, implementation, and evaluation of SL programs at the country level."[48] These are as follows:

- A participatory assessment of the risks, assets, entitlements and indigenous knowledge base found in a particular community. These are usually manifested in the coping and adaptive strategies pursued by men and women. Coping strategies are often a short-term response to a specific shock such as drought. On the other hand, adaptive strategies entail a long-term change in behaviour patterns as a result of a shock or stress. Both have implications on the composition of the assets (i.e., depletion, regeneration) from which they are derived;

- Analysis of the macro, micro and sectoral policies, and governance arrangements which impinge on people's livelihood strategies;

- Assessment and determination of the potential contributions of modern science and technology that complement indigenous knowledge systems in order to improve livelihoods;

- Identification of social and economic investment mechanisms (i.e., micro finance, expenditures on health and education) that help or hinder existing livelihood strategies; and

- Making sure that the first four stages are integrated and interactive in real time.[49]

It is interesting to note the ways in which this methodology differs from the approach proposed by Chambers. We may observe that Chambers's emphasis on the need for adaptability, learning from people at the grass roots, and putting their perceived needs first are all somewhat underemphasized in the UNDP methodology. Certainly, the initial assessment of assets and risks is supposed to be participatory, but it is notable that the next three stages are all couched in terminology redolent of analysis and planning from above. Indeed, when we examine the following passage on how the decision is made to start a UNDP SL program in a particular country, it tends to raise doubts as to how participatory the initial stage of the methodology is:

For UNDP, the programming cycle is the initial entry point for promoting SL. UNDP indicates its interest and comparative advantage in the SL approach through its Advisory Notes. Policy makers are then engaged at an early stage to consider a sustainable livelihoods framework. . . . If there is broad agreement on pursuing a SL programme, specific priority areas will have to be identified, along with potential partners for the design and implementation process.[50]

It is eminently clear that the initial framework and parameters for an intervention are set by the UNDP in cooperation with national politicians. Local communities are not involved at this crucial stage where the terms of the program and its "specific priority areas" are identified. This is suggestive that the UNDP has shifted the emphasis of the sustainable-livelihoods approach away from the discomfiting challenges of Chambers's participatory approach and toward a more top-down style of planning that fits better with its existing bureaucratic working methods.

Given this tendency, it is hardly surprising that the UNDP has identified the following problems with its approach to SL. First, it has noted that involvement of the broad range of stakeholders in a project has often been neglected, or overlooked, which suggests that participation, a fundamental element of SL, has not been properly implemented. Similarly, the UNDP points out that gender issues have often been neglected, despite the fact that women are often amongst those most in need of assistance to attain sustainable livelihoods. It also points to a dilemma in empowerment, noting that while the local community are supposed to be empowered, "local government (i.e., District) will have greater ownership of the SL process given that it is to be part and parcel of their District Planning Process."[51] The UNDP also refers to the difficulties of converting local bureaucracies to participation given that "they are based on vertical authority structures, risk-averse and punish experimentation." Reference is also made to the fact that it is difficult to get different government organizations to work with each other for much the same reasons.[52] It would seem that the UNDP maintenance of its own top-down operational approach has fed into an atmosphere where participation is often relegated to a low position on the agenda.

Even so, the sustainable-livelihoods approach has borne fruit in a number of projects and programs. The UNDP program in Malawi revealed that maize output on small farms was inadequate to satisfy food requirements for the cultivators and their families as well as meet market demand. This led to a realization that a strategy based on agrarian production for the market has to be balanced with food security for the farmers. As a result, agricultural incentives were devised to promote the combined production of maize and other drought-resistant crops such as sorghum and millets. Furthermore, the assessment phase revealed that traditional laws played an important role in protecting fruit trees and processing local plants. This was taken into account in formulating reforestation policies and programs for Malawi.[53] Turton has also shown that elements of the sustainable-livelihoods approach have been used to good effect in some watershed development programs in India. In the case of a project in Orissa, SL was used to examine the situation of the poor and was instrumental in revealing that their poverty was not merely a function of "poor productivity of natural resources," but that "its nature and structure are embedded in a complex web of historical, political, and social relations, which enable a small, powerful minority to deprive the disempowered majority of their entitlements."[54] Consequently, the project has been structured into two phases. In the first two-year phase, the focus will be on identifying opportunities to enhance the position of the poor that are unlikely to provoke opposition from the powerful. The intention is that the poor will break out of the debt cycle and acquire skills and confidence that will enable them to negotiate with the power brokers for more contentious gains during the second phase of the project. It can be seen that in such instances the sustainable-livelihoods approach actually does have promise for empowering those at the grass roots as well as delivering environmental gains in the shape of reforestation and watershed development projects.

ANOTHER DECADE, ANOTHER CONFERENCE

At the time of writing this chapter the 2002 World Summit on Sustainable Development (the Johannesburg Conference) is approaching. Prior to the conference some of the central development agencies, including the World Bank, the UNDP, the European Commission, and DfID, joined together to produce a concept paper outlining policy challenges and opportunities in the field of sustainable development. It is notable that their recommendations to the conference stressed the need to reduce poverty as part and parcel of achieving the goal of a sustainable environment. Indeed, it could be argued that the main tenor of the document was suggestive of the emergence of a somewhat more nuanced account of the interface between the environment and development. In examining how to reduce poverty and improve the environment, some of the donor agencies' traditional obsessions were revisited, notably the need for good governance and reduction of corruption by aid recipients. However, attention was also given to the need to directly help the poor to protect and expand their asset base. The report also noted that growth is not a sufficient condition for poverty reduction and that "quality of growth is what matters both in terms of promoting pro-poor growth and in terms of reducing impacts on the environment."[55] They clearly rejected any contention that the market alone can be relied on to save the environment. The paper also asserted that "(i)ndustrialized countries need to reform international trade policies on trade, investment, global public goods and aid in order to better support developing country efforts to address poverty-environment concerns."[56] The need for more aid and debt relief was also affirmed. All of this seemed promising and was suggestive of a move in the mainstream position on sustainable development away from its aforementioned faith in capitalism and toward a focus on a sustainable-livelihoods approach.

Unfortunately, the Johannesburg Conference conspicuously failed to deliver on much of this promise. Its main achievement was the agreement to halve the number of people without proper sanitation by 2015, an initiative that should reduce disease and save many lives. There was also some positive movement on fisheries and chemicals. However, there was no delivery on the aforementioned promises of trade reform and more aid. Nor were there any substantive commitments to developing renewable energy sources or to protecting endangered species of plants and animals. Jan Pronk, the special envoy to the conference of UN General Secretary Kofi Annan, summed up the situation by saying, "(w)hat's been missing here is a sense of urgency."[57] Perhaps one of the more salient comments was made by Justin Friesen, a Canadian 11-year-old (and a member of a children's delegation at the conference), who noted that "(t)oo many adults are too interested in money and wealth to take notice of serious problems that affect our future."[58] In short, the Johannesburg Conference followed the too familiar pattern evidenced at the Rio Conference, of raising expectations only to have them dashed by the self-interest of the developed countries. It remains to be seen whether this can be broken in time to prevent the "serious problems" so presciently anticipated by Justin Friesen.

Can Development Organizations Be Reinvented? Organizational Reform and Decentralization in the Developing World

INTRODUCTION

All students of development can reach a universal agreement on one very impressive achievement of the World Bank—its ability to reinvent itself with each wave of criticism. The same adaptability is true of most development organizations, including bilateral ones and NGOs. The pure irony of the situation is that these change agents never apply the same threats of reforming for accountability, transparency, and participation to themselves as they impose upon the developing governments (in exchange for millions of development-project dollars). To understand this dynamic, we find postmodern concepts, especially Foucault's idea of *résistance* and Gramsci's basic analysis of political economy, to be essential. We turn to our postmodern political economy shortly, but first we must explain one of the latest thrusts of the development establishment—the ideas of reforming and decentralizing the development process and organizations.

ORGANIZATIONAL REFORM IN DEVELOPING COUNTRIES

Over the last decade, the World Bank, along with numerous other change agents, has spent millions of dollars reforming developing governments. On the surface, this seems to be a logical crossroads of the trajectory of the development discourse, or international conversation, about development. Since we have found that the millions in aid for so many years have yielded insufficient results in reducing poverty, we continue to search for answers as to how to make the shrinking aid base more effective. As we discussed at the end of the first chapter, part of the response to criticism that aid is overly centralized and supports corrupt governments has been to co-opt (or become partners with) NGOs. The second response by donors has been to place a major impetus on programs to reform the corrupt host governments themselves, generally under the rubric of "good governance." Good-governance development aid seems to include everything from anticorruption measures to creating whole new judicial branches, but almost every aid donor seems to be in on this latest game. The origins of this answer are not germane to our analysis here, but they are part of the international set of ideas called the "new public management" (NPM) that arose in the 1980s to reinvent government in the U.S. and Britain as government's roles and budgets shrank. Governance projects deserve much closer scrutiny.

There is a huge and growing literature on the NPM, but for our purposes we can simply review the basic principles here. The basic meta-idea is to make government run as closely to a private company as possible. This idea is in line with the international rise of neoliberal thought that I have discussed elsewhere.[1] According to neoliberal thinking, government agencies should introduce as much competition as possible into their efforts. The areas of reform include a new emphasis on results-based management, contracting and procurement, personnel management, and creating new decision-making structures through autonomy and decentralization. The NPM was supposed to have solved the two basic problems diagnosed with regard to the public sector: government, as a monopoly enterprise, is supposedly inherently inefficient, but it has also been unresponsive and unaccountable to public needs. Therefore, we can talk about three basic legs, or principles, in the NPM stool: providing accurate evaluation and measurement of public sector activities, thus creating a means of accountability; creating more flexibility in hiring, firing, and promotion activities, so that the measured accountability can be used to create a more productive incentive structure; and a horizontal management structure, so that information sharing, decision-making, and responsibility flow naturally, along with the ability to react quickly, creatively, and decisively in a tailored fashion to changing situations.

USAID is a prime example of an organization that has wholeheartedly been reengineered by the NPM principles. Their new guidelines explicitly call for results-based management and evaluation of all projects. The thinking behind results-based management of the public sector is straightforward. In private industry, the overriding criterion of success is clear—posting a profit. In the public sector, there is no such measure of success. The result is that *there is simply no good measure in most cases of how well government agencies are run.* Second, as we explained in Chapter 1, development organizations all rely on resource flows, in most cases from developed world governments. Given the lack of any sense of urgency for aid in the post–Cold War climate, the U.S. Congress and other developed world governments have not only cut back on aid, but also demanded that aid demonstrate that it is being well spent. As a result, both the World Bank and USAID have heavily stepped up their evaluation efforts to demonstrate steady progress in the success rates of their projects. We discuss the evaluation game in a later chapter. For now, let us simply state that the NPM has led to a whole host of attempts to benchmark, or provide a baseline for development projects, and a new set of indicators by which to measure their success. Unfortunately, though it is early, most studies of results-based management, mainly centered on British and American efforts to reinvent government, have shown mixed, if any, real improvements in operating performance. Thus, the results-based management seems more talk than substance.

USAID has also vastly changed the way it runs its contracting and personnel operations, as has the World Bank. The NPM pushes for market-oriented solutions, and thus there has been a push throughout the public sector internationally to contract out as much work as possible. The supposed benefits are that competition in the contracting sector for the work will lead to better results at a cheaper price. Second, as government budgets for all functions, including aid, are being cut, this gives government agencies a way to cut the personnel and overhead costs. Part of the NPM allows for more flexible labor relations within the public sector. This means that civil servants, previously untouchable in many countries, now may be dismissed or fired. It also means that salaries for remaining personnel are to be upgraded to levels closer to the private sector. The idea behind this is that the public sector has traditionally been seen as an employer of last resort, with less desirable and lower-paying jobs than the private sector, and thus the human resources have been equally substandard. With the NPM reforms, the civil services of countries should become leaner, of higher quality, and more responsible and responsive.

In practice, the NPM has simply been a way to legitimate downsizing in the public sector.[2] In most countries, it is still very difficult to fire a civil servant. Civil servants are still underpaid, though the reforms have led the way for a small coterie of "super-bureaucrats," whose salaries are much higher than most of their colleagues. In terms of contracting out work, because of the budget process, much contracting may appear off-line, which therefore allows agencies to accomplish the same work for the same money while appearing to cost less. What actually happens is that, because of the nature of the contracting process, which we expose further in the evaluation chapter, a small group of contractors have been able to capture most of the work, and attract many of the best employees from the civil service. The end result is a demoralized and reduced work force in the civil service and, perhaps more important, the inability to develop any long-term knowledge or skills base, since the contractors are now able to capture these benefits.

The last, but not least, leg in the stool of the NPM, is the idea of creating a more horizontal and decentralized decision-making apparatus. We will discuss decentralization at length in the next section, but let us summarize these aspects of civil service reform as intending to create more flexibility and accountability within the public sector. The NPM idea is to make government agencies think of the public as clients, that is, as customers, who must be serviced not only as efficiently as possible, but in as tailored a manner as possible. Thus, every government and development agency now seems to include a survey with most publications, to get feedback from readers. Outside contractors also make money by conducting occasional surveys of the public to help government to evaluate its clients' perceptions. Internally, the NPM has led to the fragmentation and creation of greater autonomy among government agencies and, within those agencies, more purported independence within individual units or departments. Second, the NPM reforms supposedly allow individual employees and managers greater autonomy to work within their particular area of responsibility, so long as results continue to improve.

As we might guess, while these are good ideas in some ways, simply declaring them does little for changing organizations that date back hundreds of years and an ingrained culture of doing things in a different way. In fact, despite the slew of organizational behavior studies pushing for the horizontal organization, it is only in some of the very small, high-tech companies ("dotcoms") that we find anything close to this kind of organization. Thus, while the NPM has its heart in the right place in terms of creating awareness of the need for responsiveness and the need for greater individual responsibility, in a period of massive government cutbacks, these attempts at reengineering have largely failed.

Of course, this has not stopped the World Bank and other aid agencies from pushing the NPM reforms upon developing governments. Indeed, despite the Bank's own assessments that many of the early civil service reforms, such as those in Nigeria, failed to show any significant improvements in institutional functioning,[3] aid agencies have continued to pour money into bureaucratic reform projects. I do not wish to imply that there has been no positive effect of the reforms, such as incentives for performance, but by and large, the effect of the NPM internationally has been to cover up downsizing on the one hand, and to blindly apply an untested set of principles to unique and idiosyncratic situations on the other, with predictable (failing) results.

DECENTRALIZATION

Since we are advocating a participatory approach in this book, you will probably think we should be very high on any approach involving decentralization of governmental functions. This would mean that local recipients of development projects would have more direct access to actual decision-makers, since they would now be more local, and that development projects could be better tailored to meet local conditions. Unfortunately, here again, the practice of the development community has been to co-opt the idea of decentralization in order to actually avoid meaningful reforms. Nonetheless, decentralization has become one of the key new elements of the new development practices and the magnet for a large and growing percentage of scarce resources.

What do we mean by decentralization? Like NPM, decentralization is a reform train that has been gaining resources and steam over the last decade. The basic idea is that development organizations in general, and the state in particular, are overly centralized, top-heavy, and therefore unaccountable and unresponsive to the problems at the grassroots. To the extent that government decision-making can be decentralized, these problems should be solved, and the participation that could lead to sustainability established. Decentralization would, furthermore, allow for tailoring efforts to local problems, and mobilization of local populations and resources.

Decentralization is usually considered in three aspects: political, administrative, and financial. Political decentralization means the central government cedes some of its powers to smaller, more local government or nongovernmental authorities. It is often divided into the terms *delegation, deconcentration, devolution,* and *decentralization,* depending on the type of change in administrative structure.[4] I would identify the first two as types of administrative decentralization. Only the last two are political, since they involve plans to actually moving national decision-making to the local level—devolution over a long period of time and decentralization within a foreseeable period. An example of political decentralization occurs when the national government may provide education grants for the regions in the country, but allow them to choose exactly how they will spend those grants according to local needs. Administrative decentralization might mean, by contrast, that a national education policy is followed, but that the central government creates local representatives to implement policy according to local circumstances. Fiscal decentralization, meanwhile, refers specifically to the tax and expenditure powers of the central government being ceded to local authorities. Thus, a central government may allow local authorities to administer a new local sales or value-added tax.

In practice, of course, each of these types of powers is interrelated. In fact, the conclusion of most analysts is that decentralization programs have overwhelmingly failed to deliver local autonomy. An interesting case is the Provincial Development Plan Projects (PDP) carried out in Indonesia and funded by USAID in the 1970s. USAID evaluation reports of the project point out that little real delegation or authority was achieved by local Indonesian governments, after millions in development aid. Why? There were two essential reasons for the failure. One was that the Indonesian government, like all developing-country governments, comes from a long legacy of extremely centralized decision-making. Furthermore, Indonesia, like many other developing countries, suffers from an artificiality in terms of the creation of the national entity. Indonesia was created by colonial design from a vast archipelago of islands with no history of national authority and divided by different cultures, languages, and ethnicities. Thus, during the independence period, most nationalists saw a very strongly centralized government as being essential to preserving territorial unity. Moreover, once the local Dutch administrators left, there was very little capacity or experience of governance on the local level. Thus, like most international development projects, the PDP was extremely naïve in thinking that creating a new set of rules for Indonesian governance would be supported by the central government in such a short period of time. In fact, the Indonesian central government seems to have made a good-faith effort to create local authorities, but it never was willing to give those local units genuine administrative or fiscal authority to create their own local political authority. Instead, the local representatives were still tightly controlled by the central administration and poorly prepared to deal with local conditions.[5]

This case, along with well-documented other ones from Argentina, Bangladesh, and the Philippines, tells us a few things about the reality of decentralization.[6] First, the political reality of most developing governments is that they have very strong predispositions toward centralized government. This aspect of their political culture will take decades to change, if it will change at all. Second, even when local authorities are created, they tend to be poorly trained and have limited abilities to create their own tax base. Third, and perhaps most important, there is no reason to believe *prima facie* that local government will be any more representative, less corrupt, or more competent, than central governments. In fact, most local, particularly rural, areas of the developing world have a thoroughly undemocratic culture, in the sense that local landowners or chiefs make decisions. Fourth, in many cases, there may be desirable national and international goals, such as the education of women, that may be resisted to a greater degree by local authorities. Moreover, most developing countries are marked by strong regional and local disparities; thus, a central government with some ability to redistribute income and wealth is needed. It does not make any sense, for example, for the regions of a country to try to compete for jobs through continually reducing taxes and cutting public services, with no view to the national interest for equity.

As the reader will no doubt have appreciated by now, the real solutions to the problems of local governance and participation are far more complex than the superficial nature of current development practices would lead us to believe.[7] We have shown that local participation, mobilization, and tailoring of projects is an important goal in and of itself. We have also shown that the key tenet of postmodern development practice is that the local people themselves should be the principal actors in deciding which types of development projects should be implemented. However, we have also shown that a central government is essential for pursuing national interests, such as regional equity and women's education, and that local governments tend to be poorly equipped to take over much of the authority in the short run. Moreover, most fiscal analyses conclude that the ability to create efficient local tax bases is highly limited, including primarily a local property tax. A local value-added tax, for example, is not only difficult to administer but may simply drive customers to the next state. Given the problems with reforming the central government that we reviewed in the previous section, we can only imagine the practical difficulties of creating well-functioning local governments in a period of shrinking resources.

Thus, our hope must be to move beyond a simplistic spectrum of national to local when it comes to decentralization issues. John Cohen and Stephen Peterson's book *Administrative Decentralization* provides us with a key concept that can help us to move beyond this impasse: *institutional pluralism*. They point out, first of all, that the level of centralization of government involved in a project depends inherently on the nature of the task at hand. A large infrastructure project, such as a new hydroelectric dam, would have national-level effects in terms of power and environment and would require enormous amounts of capital and expertise, a task that probably only a national government could handle. At the other extreme, creating local cooperatives, such as micro-finance clubs along the lines of the Grameen Bank, might be best left to local communities to organize themselves, with some financial support from local, national, and international authorities. Somewhere in the middle might be agricultural extension, work to increase the productivity of local farmers, which would require input from agricultural researchers, seed companies, local outreach workers, local financial organizations, and the farmers themselves.

Besides scale, institutional pluralism implies another important aspect for consideration. That is, for too long developing governments have been the sole dominant actor, in collusion and occasional conflict with their international financiers. Thus, the proliferation of NGOs is seen by many in the development field as a saving corrective to the inevitable arrogance of the central government. However, as we have discussed elsewhere in the book, NGOs tend to have their own political economy of resources that constrains their actions. What is needed, and is implied by a growing literature on the rise of "civil society," is an active, aware population that has a multitude of organizational avenues to influence decisions, including NGOs, government representatives/voting, political parties, local cooperatives, local governments, unions, and student organizations. In our view, the more the groups, the better the chance that government will be representative, accountable, and responsive. In the short run a new proliferation of groups may lead to difficulties in achieving action, but in the long run the achievement of some consensus, even a negotiated one, will create the tacit and cultural backing for development that will finally lead to sustainable results. NGOs, particularly local ones, could provide a very important mobilization and agglomeration function to create constituencies for the poor, if they are well organized. The Movement for the Landless (MST) in Brazil is an example of a local NGO that has successfully created a national-level organization pushing for social justice.

Still, local participation ultimately depends first and foremost upon re-sources. Decentralization cheerleaders rightly expect that a true devolution and ceding of authority would lead to much greater possibilities for mobilizing greater local resources. If we are talking about already impoverished groups, the levels of their resources will be very limited, even if highly and efficiently mobilized, which is rarely the case. Thus, increasing local resources depends upon national reforms. In most developing countries, the tax base is very limited—the rich generally have loopholes or evasion techniques so that they are able to avoid many of the taxes. Second, developing countries have very poor tax administration and enforcement. Their taxes tend to be focused on easily administered taxes, such as taxes on exports and imports, or a basic sales tax, which is regressive in hurting poor people more. This means that devel-oping countries borrow a lot more from the developed world than they need to, *simply because they cannot marshal their own resources.*

In sum, most decentralization projects have failed because they operate on the premise that a swift change in organizational charts will lead to local input. The reality is that a pluralistic approach is needed to develop multiple modes of participation, that creating this type of culture will take a long time, and that the ability to reform public resource gathering and expenditures is the key to making any level of government work. Most important, decentralization should be organized to strengthen existing communities, rather than simply be an exercise in administrative reorganization. We turn now to explaining why development organizations have not moved to this level of analysis, before providing some suggestions as to how to achieve its recommendations.

A POSTMODERN POLITICAL ECONOMY ANALYSIS OF ORGANIZATIONAL REFORM

As we pointed out in Chapter 1, the aid game is one in which host govern-ments collude with international and bilateral development agencies and NGOs largely funded by developed country governments. These organizations, which are at the forefront of institutional reform and pushing the banners of trans-parency, accountability, and decentralization, have some explaining to do. Why? First, they are among the least transparent and decentralized organi-zations one can find anywhere. The World Bank and the IMF keep much of their information and agreements secret from the public. Most NGOs, like the international development organizations, including the United Nations, do not show clearly where they spend their money. Most NGOs also do not reveal from where they obtain their funding. As members of the public, we would like to know what implicit compromises are being made to the donors of these funds. We also find that most development organizations do not appear as horizontal-matrix organizations with clear responsiveness to local impoverished peoples. Instead, they tend to have small coteries of decisionmakers in central offices (removed from the field) making the key policy and budget decisions according to their own estimation of local people's needs and the organizations' priorities. Thus, any tailoring for local conditions, or input from the actual impoverished peoples who make up the project has to work within the organizational constraints. It seems hard to believe, therefore, that these types of organizations could create genuine participatory, bottom-up development, and not surprising that they instead are trying to impose participatory solutions on local populations.[8]

A related push is the new international campaign against corruption. Like other organizational reform efforts, this one is marked by a very superficial analysis and therefore a waste of resources. The basic thinking is that aid agencies can go in and mandate certain new rules of the game, and that developing countries will automatically follow the developed world's more controlled corruption. This seems to be a particularly naïve assumption given the long historical roots of corruption in many of the developing countries' cultures, including the private sector.[9] Again, we are talking here largely about international-development organizations that enjoy the same public space (or lack of private market competition) for which they criticize and try to reform developing country governments. Thus, in our mind, while corruption is a genuine problem, maybe the conversation should also include the corruption of the poverty brokers at international-development organizations who live lives of luxury even with comparison to the local developed-world standards.[10]

Why, then, would these organizations espouse motivations contrary to their own values and operations? In fact, the writings of Foucault as well as the Marxist writings of Antonio Gramsci, loosely applied, can explain this conundrum. Foucault introduced the idea of *résistance*. For our purposes we can take this to mean that even if development organizations are dominated by a certain hierarchy of values, that hierarchy itself inevitably creates winners and losers. We all know that of the millions spent in aid, very little seems to effectively reach the actual recipients, and almost none deals directly with the recipients' own desires. Thus, we could interpret the ideas of decentralization, grassroots participation, and small, nimble, flexible, and responsive NGOs as a form of resistance to the impositions of development practice from the large organizations representing developed world interests, or the hierarchy of development priorities within a world capitalist system. However, the very unevenness of hierarchy creates a natural resistance to it, which is an idea echoed in Marx's basic writings in terms of natural antagonisms that have occurred throughout history. Gramsci, a Marxist, took this aspect a step further by positing that those who control knowledge and ideas in a society can reinforce the natural hierarchies and inherent differences of a capitalistic system. Thus, a Gramscian might say that the very idea of free markets leading to greater efficiency, while we live in a reality in which many First World markets, such as agriculture, are subsidized and closed, is a way that the First World legitimizes the interests of the world capitalist class. I believe that the same aspect can be applied to the present discourse of participation, decentralization, and institutional reform, which is implemented in rather ineffective ways. My diagnosis is that one of the main reasons that the World Bank started participating with NGOs and talking about organizing impoverished groups was simply to co-opt, head off, and take over the growing *résistance* and opposition to the policies and practices of the development community. This includes the recent vogue of hiring previous critics of the World Bank and including anthropologists and sociologists along with the dominant formal economists in new hiring, all of whom no doubt thoroughly enjoy the perks of the good life. The good side of this diagnosis is that to some degree, the World Bank and other development organizations actually have to follow through on their rhetoric to demonstrate an ongoing modicum of credibility. This opens the way for development activists to push toward reforms that might more truly serve the interests of the poor (if they could first come to include them).

A WAY TO MORE MEANINGFUL ORGANIZATION REFORM, STARTING WITH INTERNATIONAL DEVELOPMENT ORGANIZATIONS

What, then, would be a better way to improve development organizations? I have pointed out that the problem with the NPM is as much in its naïve application as its principles. As Judith Tendler points out in her case study of the well-run Ceará state government in Brazil, the heart of success in government depends as much on tacit understandings, attitudes of sacrifice and devotion to the public interest, and long-standing cultural complexities as it does on setting up a new set of rules.[11] Thus, the push for institutional reform, like much of the current academic fad of new institutionalism, really misses the boat in terms of the complex, tacit, and deeply ingrained nature of the problems in developing-country organizations.

Perhaps the most important actor from this point of view is having a viable and active media that can expose corruption to the public at large. Unfortunately, what we actually see is the creation of monopolies and oligopolies of media companies throughout the world. While academic vogue sees the Internet as a corrective for this problem in terms of opening up new sources of information, in developing countries the Internet still is far removed from the daily lives of the most marginalized groups.

Last but not least, all motivations aside, a key failure among development agencies is the almost complete lack of information sharing. Instead what we see in impoverished countries is a series of competing projects among competing donor agencies that continually reinvent the wheel and may even work at cross-purposes. The weakness of host governments underscores their general inability to direct foreign-development organizations toward projects of true national priority or even to cooperate with each other on larger or more integrated concerns.

The keys to organizational reform of governmental and development organizations are transparency and accountability through the development of new mechanisms of governance. These mechanisms can come from the top and from the bottom and should reflect local cultural and contextual complexities. From the top, all World Bank, host government, and NGO agreements and budgets should be made transparent and open to all. All development organizations and host governments should also account for how they spend all tax revenues, borrowings, and donations in easily understood public fora. All development organizations should develop an "information protocol" in which project evaluations and designs could be shared through a virtual database available to all who are interested. Moreover, host governments should be funded and trained to develop a coordinating agency for all foreign-development organizations, which would also serve as a cooperative forum for developing national and regional integrated strategies. Host governments also need to engage in meaningful tax reform and begin the long process of creating viable local governments. As local governments become more capable, they should be given increasingly significant transfers of national tax payments and explicit redistributive funds for marginalized areas.

From the bottom, a strategy of institutional pluralism should be followed. NGOs, especially local ones, should be funded transparently by government grants to serve the purpose of mobilizing local and marginalized populations. Local groups should be actively encouraged to form their own cooperative groups and promised funding to pursue their own goals for their communities or groups, provided that they work transparently and democratically. These groups should be actively organized for marginalized groups, such as rural impoverished women. Truly independent watchdog organizations, in government, in NGOs, and in local communities, should be given guaranteed budgets, access to organizational information, and recourse to the media with the responsibility of pushing for accountability of resources. Independent media should be actively formed and encouraged both on the local and national levels. More important, the hegemony of information by which foreign and central government development organizations dominate the discourse must be reduced. We need presses, newspapers, and Internet sites funded so that the voices of the poor, the espoused target of development of assistance, can speak directly to the problems of development. We can anticipate the reaction to this set of proposals to be the old elitist one that local groups given grants from the central government will simply waste resources and that their ignorance will lead to dead ends. While acknowledging the importance of national-level projects and developed technical expertise, we believe the ultimate arbiters of efficiency should be the recipients themselves. As long as they are open about their intentions and the spending is for the good of the group, who can better decide what is efficient and optimal? How will we know unless we make them true partners in the conversation? We believe ultimately that there is tremendous goodwill among individuals in the development business and that a more honest self-assessment about these issues could move the discourse (the conversation and the actions that follow it) to a more productive and healthy level.

CHAPTER 5

Participation: Development from Below?

We have spent much of our time examining the problems arising from traditional approaches to development, notably the top-down blueprint approach to project/program design. In this chapter we shall focus on an alternative approach that has come to prominence at least in part as a response to top-down methodologies and their shortcomings. This is the participatory approach, which is supposed to reverse the normal hierarchies of development so that power and decision-making flow from the bottom up, rather than the top downwards.

As we shall see in our analysis, participation as a practice is not something that can be adequately taught in an academic text such as this. Most of the proponents of the participatory approach are agreed that it is something that can only be learned by doing it. A central reason for this is that participation is not simply a methodology, or way of doing things, in which set rules and techniques can be learned and then put into application in the field. In this sense it is different from traditional project methodologies in which project design and management techniques can be learned and applied generally to different situations. Many practitioners of participation would argue that a formalistic and repetitive application of participatory techniques is self-defeating and will actually damage the prospects of real participation by those at the grass roots. This means that participation is only partly about the techniques used in the field by development workers to try and engender participation. Indeed, there is no set procedure or technique that can be guaranteed to bring about participation. While participatory techniques can be useful, the attitudes and behavior of the organizations and workers involved in participatory strategies are much more important in determining whether or not their interventions will succeed in mobilizing people to participate. Obviously, the question of how genuinely they wish to engender participation is central, but the nature of the attitudes and behaviors required for good participatory practice will be examined further below.

The problematic nature of participation means that this chapter cannot provide a straightforward account of how to do participation (as we have noted, participation can only be properly learned through practice). What it can do is give an account of what is generally meant by participation, provide a sense of how participation works through analysis of specific examples, examine its advantages and problems, and comment on the conditions necessary to enable good participatory practice. Consequently, we shall start by examining some alternative definitions of participation, briefly surveying its emergence and history as a development approach. We shall then turn our attention to some of the central methodologies and techniques of participation, bearing in mind that the participatory approach is only partly about methodology. This will lead into a consideration of problems of participation, a central one being that many observers focus mechanistically on methods and techniques, thus failing to create the conditions for genuine participation. Finally, we shall examine the organizational, behavioral, and other factors that help create the conditions for effective participation. Case-study material will be taken into account throughout our analysis.

WHAT IS PARTICIPATION?

A variety of definitions of participation have been offered. Oakley et al. gathered together the following:

(a) Participation is considered a voluntary contribution by the people in one or another of the public programmes supposed to contribute to national development, but the people are not expected to take part in shaping the programme or criticizing its contents (Economic Commission for Latin America, 1973).

(b) With regard to rural development . . . participation includes people's involvement in decision-making processes, in implementing programmes, their sharing in the benefits of development programmes and their involvement in efforts to evaluate such programmes (Cohen and Uphoff, 1977).

(c) Participation is concerned with . . . the organized efforts to increase control over resources and regulative institutions in given social situations on the part of groups and movements of those hitherto excluded from such control (Pearse and Stiefel, 1979).

(d) Community participation [is] an active process by which beneficiary or client groups influence the direction and execution of a development project with a view to enhancing their well-being in terms of income, personal growth, self-reliance or other values they cherish (Paul, 1987).[1]

All of these definitions share the view that development will be enhanced if people are actively involved in the projects that affect them. However, it would be fair to say that statement (a) on the one hand and statements (b), (c) and

(d) on the other hand represent radically different approaches as to how far such participation should be taken. The first statement suggests that people are mobilized to volunteer some work on a project without actually having any substantive voice in determining what it will do and how it will do it. However, statement (c) makes it clear that people at the grass roots are to be given a measure of control over resources and within institutions, while statements (b) and (d) indicate that project participants will have a say in the design, management, and evaluation of the project. Statements (b), (c), and (d) entail empowerment, whereas (a) does not.

These different approaches may be related to Oakley et al.'s observation that one can identify two broad schools of thought concerning the efficacy of participation. He characterizes these as follows:

- One school saw "participation" as the key to the inclusion of human resources in development efforts; previously development planners had overlooked the contributions that people could make and the skills that they could bring to development projects. If, therefore, one could incorporate the human element in such projects and persuade people to participate in them, then there would be a stronger chance that these projects would be successful.

- The other school saw this participation in a very different light. It saw participation as more linked to tackling the structural causes of people's poverty rather than as yet another input into a development project. People are poor because they are excluded and have little influence upon the forces which affect their livelihoods. Participation is the process whereby such people seek to have some influence and to gain access to the resources which would help them sustain and improve their living standards.[2]

It can be seen that the first school takes an instrumentalist view, seeing participation as a way of mobilizing people to make projects work better. This viewpoint is often associated with the suggestion that participation should be seen as a way of making participants feel a sense of ownership for the project. It is argued that if people have expended work and other resources on a project they are more likely to feel that it is their project. Concomitantly, they are more likely to work effectively on the project and to sustain it when the donor agency has departed. In this way, participation can be seen as a tactic, or a methodology, for enhancing sustainability.

The second school has a more radical tendency. In this view, the purpose of people's participation is not an improved project, but rather their own empowerment. Through participation in a project, people are seen as developing the capacity to take initiatives and to gain control of resources and institutions so that they can improve their lives. This is generally what is meant when development analysts refer to empowerment. The difference between the two schools is linked to the question of whether participation is considered as a means that is used to achieve project objectives or as an end in its own right. For the first school, participation is a method of attaining project outcomes, whereas the second school sees participation as an end in itself (i.e., a project objective) inasmuch as it is the key to empowering people.

Of course the division between these schools is not always as clear-cut as has been suggested thus far. We have emphasized the differences between them in order to clearly explicate their different implications. In actual project situations one often finds an overlap between the two schools of thought, with a project seeking to attain certain pre-designed goals while also specifying empowerment as an objective. However, it would probably be fair to say that most projects incline more in one direction than the other, with the emphasis usually being on the instrumentalist approach. Most bureaucracies want the reassurance of having clear, measurable objectives that they can point to as achievements, rather than having to attain an unquantifiable value such as empowerment.

The interplay (and tension) between these two schools may be illustrated with reference to the history of participation. Thomas-Slayter argues that participation initially manifested itself in three broad approaches: first, people's organizations and cooperatives; second, community development or *animation rurale*; and third, guided participation in large-scale projects. The first category includes people's own organizations, such as cooperatives, as well as welfare organizations, which might include NGOs. Community development and *animation rurale* are techniques whereby an external force, often the state, enters a community to organize it to undertake a project with some limited outside help. Such strategies often find their roots in the colonial period, as with the French strategy of *animation rurale*. Guided participation sometimes implies that project "beneficiaries," or recipients, may have a measure of decision-making control in a project, but this is ultimately controlled by the bureaucrats running the project. It may be noticed that all of these approaches (with the possible exception of organizations set up by the people themselves) retain top-down hierarchical decision-making structures in the final instance. They use participation essentially as a means to achieve project objectives. The people are mobilized to do externally directed work on externally decided project objectives. They are not empowered in the sense of being given any decisive measure of control in the project. In this respect these approaches are clearly more related to the first instrumentalist school of participatory thinking.

Thomas-Slayter observes that recent decades have witnessed the growth of criticism of these traditional participatory approaches, notably to the effect that they easily become coercive and manipulative.[3] To the extent that bureaucrats retain ultimate control over a project, it is easy for them to co-opt it and to manipulate people into doing what the bureaucrats want rather than what they themselves want. Such so-called participatory projects evoke dissatisfaction and frustration as people become aware that their work has not achieved what they hoped for. These negative attitudes toward projects are not conducive to project beneficiaries developing any sense of ownership toward the project. Consequently, they are unlikely to feel any incentive to sustain the project after the sponsoring agencies have left. In short, these top-down versions of participation were not even very effective in attaining instrumental project goals such as sustainability.

Dissatisfaction with these initial versions of participation led to the emergence of more radical approaches focused on empowerment. Chambers premises his critique on an analysis of the shortcomings of top-down project design. He points out that those at the top (whom he often refers to as "uppers") are ill equipped to diagnose and solve the problems of those at the grass roots (the "lowers," as he terms them). Their knowledge is derived from textbooks and laboratories that often do not apply to the situation at the grass roots. They tend to visit and research the locations of their projects for short periods that are insufficient to gain a knowledge of the area as it actually is. Instead, they tend to rely on expert accounts of the project area, whether from old reports, or from members of the local elite, such as academics or bureaucrats. In all too many cases, such accounts turn out to be inaccurate. Often, aid personnel do not even manage to meet the poorest people because those who are really poor tend to live off the beaten track in inaccessible places. Chambers makes a number of recommendations as to how these shortcomings can be corrected, notably by staying longer at the project site, going off the beaten track, and listening to the poor and learning from them about their perceived problems and their lives. In this way, expert knowledge is superseded by local knowledge (people's knowledge) and local people gain a greater say in the projects that affect them. Chambers argues that this bottom-up approach will lead to more relevant and effective projects. It is notable that his approach also incorporates a strong element of empowerment.[4] We can see that Chambers's work represents a major influence on the second school of thought on participation. Cohen and Uphoff make similar points, arguing that participation should entail the following elements. First, people at the grass roots should have a voice in deciding what a project will do. Second, they should be fully involved in implementation. Third, they should share in the benefits of any project or program. Finally, they should be involved in evaluating the project.[5] This makes it explicit that people should be empowered through participation at every stage of a project. It is also a major departure from the top-down blueprint approach. If the beneficiaries are to have a voice in the design of the project there can be no blueprint. All this is indicative that participation can be much more responsive to conditions as they develop on the ground, a major problem with the traditional project approach.

While the instrumentalist approach to participation has not been completely displaced, it is clear that the ideas of such commentators as Chambers and Cohen and Uphoff have exerted considerable influence on the discourse of participation, which itself has become increasingly influential amongst development agencies. It is now normal for such agencies to claim that they implement participatory programs. Increasingly, they also refer to participation as entailing an element of empowerment. Oakley et al. note that the World Conference on Agrarian Reform and Rural Development (WCARRD) "emphasised the importance of a transfer of power as implicit in participation" in 1979.[6] More recently, the World Bank has embraced participation, defining it as "a process through which stakeholders influence and share control over development initiatives, decisions and resources which affect them."[7] As we shall see, this does not indicate that aid bureaucracies have all been completely won over to the empowerment-oriented school of participation. However, our analysis so far does show that participation has become more influential over recent years and that it is generally seen as entailing some measure of empowerment for project recipients. In the next section we shall examine how participation has been operationalized, analyzing some of the central techniques for engendering participation. We will also pay attention to factors affecting the efficacy of these techniques in bringing about grassroots participation, whether as an instrument for achieving project goals or as a process of empowerment.

PARTICIPATION AS PRAXIS

How then does participatory development work and in what sense can it be seen as bringing about empowerment? It often (if not usually) has to be started by an external agency. Oakley et al. point out that while groups have emerged spontaneously in some areas, notably India and Latin America, "more commonly an external agency takes the first step in initiating the process."[8] Usually the first step will involve sending one, or possibly two, change agents to work in a community. Burkey cautions us against attempts to work with a whole community, noting that even small rural villages will be characterized by social differentiation between different interest groups, particularly those who are better off and those who are worse off. Relations between these groups may well be characterized by exploitation. Burkey notes that the Community Development Movement that started in India in 1952 assumed the existence of a rural social solidarity, only to find that the richer members of the rural communities were using their influence to appropriate the lion's share of any benefits from the movement's programs. He draws the conclusion that account must be taken of the differential interests of variant sectors of the community in identifying a group with whom to work. Only through developing such an understanding of the community can the change agent discover which groups are most in need of aid. Furthermore, it is often best to work (at least initially) with a group characterized by broadly common interests, as this militates against tendencies toward disagreements as to what the group's central aims should be.[9]

Attaining an understanding of the community and then identifying a suitable group with whom to work is bound to take time, and it is implicit in participatory development that the change agents will take some time to achieve these initial tasks before venturing into any actual development activities with the community. Oakley et al. cite the example of a female change agent working in Brazil who spent a year observing some fisherwomen before one of them took the initiative and made contact with her. Several further contacts with various fisherwomen led to the formation of groups that conducted some successful welfare activities.[10] This is perhaps a rather extreme example inasmuch as the agent waited until the local community approached her. Most agencies would not want to spend a year waiting for something to happen and would want the change agent to take an initiative in working with the group or community. However, this does not obviate the need for agents to take some time to learn about the community. As we shall see, this is something that tends to be forgotten as agencies rush to an often ill-considered implementation.

If change agents are usually required to take the initiative in making contact with local people, this raises the question as to how they might do this and start the participatory process. One can distinguish a number of broad approaches to engendering participation, which are often viewed as participatory methodologies (although many of them are little more than grab bags of various techniques for stimulating participation). Thomas-Slayter identifies six, these being Participatory Rural Appraisal (PRA), Methods for Active Participation (MAP), Training for Transformation (TFT), Productivity Systems Assessment and Planning (PSAP), Participation and Learning Methods (PALM), and Participatory Action Research (PAR).[11] As we have just noted, most of these approaches are characterized by reliance on a variety of methods to commence a participatory process, usually focusing on use of different types of meetings, group activity, and information-gathering techniques such as mapping. Thus, MAP, TFT, and PSAP all involve various kinds of meetings such as seminars and small group activities for purposes that include information gathering, analysis of the data thus gathered, and consideration of strategies and options for action. PAR is rather different and might be characterized as consisting in an educational process through which a target group is motivated to formulate strategies and initiate activities to improve their collective situation. PALM is a methodology that originates in India, which places emphasis on participatory techniques for information gathering so that people can use it to start their own development processes. The techniques that are used bear a strong resemblance to the most widely spread methodology of participation, PRA.

PRA is used throughout the developing world and is clearly the most influential of the methodologies mentioned above. It owes a great deal to the work of Robert Chambers who characterizes it as "a growing family of approaches and methods to enable local people to share, enhance and analyze their knowledge of life and conditions, and to plan, act, monitor and evaluate." This makes it clear that he envisages PRA as a process, entailing grassroots participation at every stage of a development intervention from planning to evaluation. Chambers goes on to note that "(p)ractical applications have proliferated, especially in natural resources management, agriculture, health and nutrition, poverty and livelihood programmes, and urban contexts."[12] Figure 5.1 (also compiled by Chambers) provides an extensive list of such applications that have been used in various contexts under the rubric of PRA. Amongst the most commonly used applications are mapping and wealth ranking. Louise Fortmann gives descriptions of how these applications have been used in Zimbabwe, which give a sense of how they play out at the grass roots and the effects they can have. She describes resource mapping as follows:

Mapping is just what it sounds like. You ask people to draw a map. You can have them map anything you need to know about—the village, the wealthy, water, markets and so on; I asked people to map where they obtained tree products. For this they need a long stick and a lot of twigs: the stick is for drawing the map on the ground, and the little twigs represent trees. Rocks and other props are also useful. For example, one group of men filled a cup of water for a dam. A group of women fashioned a wonderful windmill out of cornstalks. . . . Drawing on the ground with a stick (or many sticks as people get into it) avoids any school and learning connotations that pen, pencil and paper carry, although there is a certain vulnerability involved. For example, the agricultural extension agent drove his motorcycle right through the village research team's practice map.

After people had done their maps, I asked them what it looked like in 1970, in 1980 and what they would like it to look like. Not surprisingly, everyone said there used to be more trees and they wished that there were more once again. . . .

The maps provided a useful visual indication of resource clusters. They were also the most accurate check on elite myths, in particular the myth of the community woodlot. The Chairman of the Grazing Scheme proudly took visitors around the community woodlots: an area of substantial eucalyptus and an area of regenerating indigenous woodland. This, the story went, was where the villagers came for their wood. But with the exception of the elite grazing committee, when villagers drew their maps of where they obtained tree products, the village woodlots were conspicuous by their absence. Survey data confirmed that only the rich used these woodlots. Their absence from the maps tells an even more powerful story—most villagers do not even think of the woodlots as an available resource. No survey can tell you that quite so clearly.[13]

This passage illustrates many of the virtues associated with participation in general and PRA in particular. It is indicative of the informality that is necessary to encourage the involvement of poor people who tend to be intimidated by the formality and authoritarian attitudes that characterize top-down development situations. We may also note that information is communicated in a visual way that the illiterate are able to understand and which enables them to contribute their knowledge. It is also worth noting how this use of mapping provided an opportunity for some local people to demonstrate their skills (as with the woman who made the model windmill), thus helping to

Figure 5.1
Some Typical PRA Methods and Approaches

- *'Handing over the stick' and they do it*: basic to PRA is facilitating, handing over the stick, chalk or pen, enabling local people to be the analysts, mappers, diagrammers, observers, researchers, historians, planners and actors, presenters of their analysis, and then in turn facilitators: women, men, poor, non-poor, children, parents, schoolteachers, farmers, local specialists.
- *Do-it-yourself*: roles of expertise are reversed, with local people as experts and teachers, and outsiders as novices. Local people supervise and teach skills: to transplant, to weed, plough, level a field, mud a hut, draw and carry water, fetch firewood, wash clothes, cook a meal, stitch, thatch.
- *Local analysis of secondary sources*: most commonly the analysis of aerial photographs (often best at 1:5000) to identify soil type, land conditions, land tenure (Dewees, 1989a; Mearns, 1989; Sandford, 1989). Satellite imagery has also been used.
- *Mapping and modelling*: people's mapping, drawing and colouring with chalks, sticks, seeds, powders, pens, etc. on the ground, floor, or (often later) paper to make social, health, or demographic maps, resource maps of village lands and forests, maps of fields, farms and home gardens, thematic or topic maps (for water, soils, trees, the incidence of pests, etc.) (P. Shah, 1995), service or opportunity maps, maps of the location of anti-personnel mines (pers. comm. Michelle Barron for Mozambique), three-dimensional models of watersheds, etc. (Hahn, 1991; Mascarenhas and Kumar, 1991). These methods have been amongst the most widely used and can lead into household listing and well-being ranking, transects, and linkage diagrams.
- *Time lines and trend and change analysis*: chronologies of events, listing major local events with approximate dates; people's accounts of the past, of how customs, practices and things close to them have changed; ethno-biography—a local history of a crop, an animal, a tree, a pest, a weed ... diagrams, maps (see Sadomba, 1996 for retrospective community mapping) and matrices (Freudenberger, 1995) showing ecological histories, changes in land use and cropping patterns, population, migration, fuel uses, education, health, credit ... and the causes of changes and trends, often with estimates of relative magnitudes.
- *Seasonal calendars*: by major season or more usually by month to show: distribution of days of rain, amount of rain or soil moisture; crop cycles; women's, men's and children's work, including agricultural and non-agricultural labour; diet and food consumption; illnesses; prices; animal fodder; fuel; migration; sources of income; expenditure; debt etc.
- *Daily time-use analysis*: indicating relative amounts of time, degrees of drudgery, etc., of activities, and sometimes seasonal variations in these.
- *Institutional or Venn diagramming*: identifying individuals and institutions important in and for a community or group, or within an organization, and their relationships (for examples, see Guijt and Pretty, 1992).
- *Linkage diagrams*: of flows, connections and causality. These versatile diagrams have been used for the analysis of sequences, marketing, nutrient flows on farms, migration, social contact, and impacts of interventions and trends, and for income and expenditure trees (Archer and Cottingham 1996b: 135).

continued

Figure 5.1
Continued

- *Well-being (or wealth) grouping (or ranking)*: card sorting into groups or rankings of households according to local criteria, including those considered poorest, worst off and most deprived, often expressing key local indicators of well-being and ill-being. A good lead into livelihoods of the poor and how they cope (Grandin, 1988; Swift and Umar, 1991; Mearns et al, 1992; RRA Notes 15: passim; Turk, 1995; Booth et al, 1995).
- *Analysis of difference*: especially by gender, social group, wealth/poverty, occupation and age. Identifying differences between groups, including their problems and preferences (Welbourn, 1991). This includes contrast comparisons: asking one group why another is different or does something different, and vice versa (pers. comm. Meena Bilgi).
- *Matrix scoring and ranking*: using matrices and counters (usually seeds or stones) to compare through scoring, for example different trees, or soils, or methods of soil and water conservation, or varieties of a crop or animal, fields on a farm, fish, weeds, conditions at different times, and to express preferences (see, e.g., Drinkwater, 1993; Manoharan et al., 1993; Posadas, 1995; Maxwell and Duff, 1995).
- *Team contracts and interactions*: contracts drawn up by teams with agreed norms of behaviour; modes of interaction within teams, including changing pairs, evening discussions, mutual criticism and help; how to behave in the field, etc. (The team may consist of outsiders only, of local people and outsiders together, or of local people only).
- *Shared presentations and analysis*: where maps, models, diagrams, and findings are presented by local people, and/or by outsiders, especially at community meetings, and checked, corrected and discussed. But who talks? Who talks how much? Who interrupts whom? Whose ideas dominate?
- *Participatory planning, budgeting, implementation and monitoring*, in which local people prepare their own plans, budgets and schedules, take action, and monitor and evaluate progress.
- *Drama and participatory video-making*: on key issues, to enable people to discover how they see things, and what matters to them, and to influence those in power.
- *Short standard schedules or protocols* as alternatives to questionnaires to record data (e.g. census or similar information from social mapping) in a standard and commensurable manner.
- *Immediate report writing*, either in the field before returning to office or headquarters, or by one or more people who are designated in advance to do this immediately on completion of fieldwork.

Source: Robert Chambers, *Whose Reality Counts? Putting the First Last* (London: Intermediate Technology Publications, 1997), 117–119.

build their confidence to participate. In addition, this exercise in mapping was effective at eliciting information that showed something of the ecological history of the area and suggested the potential for a project. It was found that there had been more trees in the past and that many people wished for more trees in the present, which suggests the desirability of a forestry project. Of particular interest is the fact that a careful analysis of the local people's maps (or in this instance of something missing from the maps, the so-called community woodlots) revealed crucial data about the monopolization of resources by the village elite. This is clearly something that would have been missed in a top-down approach to developing the village in which the local people would almost certainly not have been consulted. It can be seen that this particular exercise in resource mapping went some way to fulfilling most of the aims of participatory development in that it encouraged people to take part, it obtained useful information, and it helped illuminate the social structure of the village. Of particular note is the fact that it gathered data that could be used to design an intervention that would be much better adapted to conditions in the village than a traditional blueprint approach.

Similar points can be made about Fortmann's description of a wealth-ranking exercise that she performed in the same village. She describes it as follows:

Participatory methods for wealth ranking involving card sorting are pretty standard. I sat down with my research team [consisting of people drawn from the local village] and said, "Tell me what rich people have, tell me what poor people have." I wanted a five point scale. They pushed me to six. Their scale included the usual cast of variables—cattle, house type, and employment. But also included among their variables was one I had never thought of—secondary education, where (in the village or in town), and how continuous. They laid out categories of people who were dependent on other people for livelihoods. There was a huge argument over the importance of owning means of production (ploughs, cattle, fields) against owning consumer durables (fancy house, radio).

Then I asked each village researcher to rank all our respondents, leaving blank anyone they could not or did not want to rank. What I found particularly interesting in these rankings was that they ranked a number of widows much lower than I would have ranked them. Why? They ranked widows on what they themselves personally controlled/owned as opposed to what their children were able to give them. Since their children might withdraw their favours, or be run over by a bus, their largesse did not count. There was a very strong sense of vulnerability in these rankings.

These rankings were eventually used in statistical analysis. They correlated highly with the traditional measures (cattle ownership, tin roof) of wealth. But they reflected the nuances of local reality far better, and the research team got practice for future use in thinking through categories of people and how they were affected differently by various things happening in the village.[14]

This passage is particularly illustrative of the way in which participatory techniques can reveal perspectives that would probably not occur to development professionals, but which nevertheless have vital implications for development activity. Thus, Fortmann's village researchers persuaded her that wealth is not merely a function of what a person has, but also of that person's entitlement to what she has and how easily it can be taken away. Consequently Fortmann obtained a more nuanced view of social reality, while her village researchers were also exposed to the techniques of development analysis.

However, it is also interesting to note her almost throwaway comment at the beginning of the passage to the effect that "methods for wealth ranking involving card sorting are pretty standard." The point is that her standard ranking system proved to be inadequate to represent the complexity of reality in the village and had to be adjusted by her village research team. This is symptomatic of a problem mentioned in the introduction to this chapter, which has become general with the spread of PRA in particular. Participatory techniques are often applied in a mechanical and formalistic manner that undermines their purpose of motivating people to become involved. Clearly, Fortmann was flexible enough to correct for this problem, but as we have seen, such flexibility tends to be the exception rather than the rule with the bureaucracies that usually deal with development. In the next section we shall focus on some of the main problems that have affected participation in practice.

PROBLEMS OF PARTICIPATION

It is worth noting at the outset that Chambers has always insisted that PRA consists of more than a set of techniques. Indeed, a perusal of Figure 5.1 reveals that the first two items in his list of techniques and approaches have more to do with attitude and behavior than method. The first is "handing over the stick," which denotes handing over the initiative to local people, while the second is "do-it-yourself," which also refers to the need to let locals take the lead in undertaking activities. Chambers reinforces this point in the following terms:

In good PRA, participatory behavior and attitudes matter more than methods. Facilitators have to learn not to dominate. This learning is not easy. Many trainers find it difficult (I do). To confront behavior and attitudes is harder than to teach methods.[15]

Chambers lays considerable emphasis on the importance of good training, particularly on the role it must play in changing attitudes and in counteracting the biases of top-down development. He stresses that it should involve a field component (in which trainees learn by doing) rather than simply taking the form of an academic classroom-based exercise in which traditionally bureaucratic authority structures based on expertise are reinforced, thus undermining the overtly participatory message. The focus on the primacy of attitude and behavior is also reflected in Chambers's suspicion of manuals, which is illustrated in the following passage:

[T]he formalism of manuals with set procedures can fossilize and stultify. With any innovation there is an urge to standardize and codify, often in the name of quality. Manuals are called for and composed. Paragraphs proliferate as intelligent authors seek to cater for every condition and contingency. As texts lengthen, so too does training. The more there is on paper, the more reading and lecturing become the norm, and the more inhibited and inflexible participants become in the field. Big manuals and bad training go together.[16]

Rather than lapse into a routinized form of PRA in which the same techniques for popular mobilization are mechanically used time and time again, Chambers advocates adherence to what he terms the "one-sentence manual for PRA—'Use your own best judgement at all times.'"[17]

However, many observers have noted that formalism has grown with the spread of PRA and its institutionalization as a working methodology that has been adopted by an increasing number of development agencies. Indeed, this should not be unduly surprising in view of our previous analysis of traditional aid bureaucracies (see Chapter 2), with their emphases on rule following, hierarchy, procedure, and playing safe. Leurs observes that "(p)erhaps the biggest challenge facing PRA at this level [the organizational level] is the hierarchical organizational culture which is still so pervasive in non-governmental (including aid-funded projects) as well as government organisations."[18] A common pattern seems to be for development agencies of all kinds to adopt PRA in name so that they can claim to be participatory, only to try and institutionalize it as a part of their existing top-down procedures. Leurs comments that "much PRA has been reduced to the increasingly mechanical application of standardized sequences and combinations of methods."[19]

A study of the way that PRA has been used in Kenya comments that "for some agencies PRA has, it seems, simply become a bureaucratic requirement—a box that needs to be ticked for a project to proceed."[20] It also observes that:

"Doing participation" has, in some circles, become practically equivalent to doing PRA. A number of people highlighted the dangers of conflating the two. "Donors want PRA, *not* participation," one practitioner complained: they want a clearly delimited product that would serve to meet the procedural obligation for consultation, not a process that could throw up challenges and possibilities beyond the bounds of the projects they had in mind. As an international NGO worker reflected, "it seems like PRA is a thing you do to communities, rather than something about participation."[21]

This approach to PRA has the following costs:

One . . . is that PRA is simply slotted into existing practice, providing little challenge to institutionalized patterns of behaviour. Another is that without a closer understanding of what PRA involves in practice—that is, without doing PRA—it is easy enough for people to latch onto elements of the approach. In so doing, they come to regard "doing PRA" as equivalent to, for example, applying a set package of tools or as an event, "a PRA," rather than as part of a process that has other aspects and entailments.[22]

All of this is illustrative of how a tokenistic use of PRA undercuts participation. The common tendency to adopt a few tools, use them on a one-off basis in each community, and mechanistically repeat them from one community to the next, is far from conducive to a genuine process of participatory mobilization. Clearly, exposure to a one-time PRA is less likely to mobilize people than the processual approach that Chambers specifies. This is especially the case if the agency or personnel doing the PRA are simply going through the motions, with little if any intention of initiating a genuine participatory process in the first place.

A number of commentators have focused on the effects that such approaches have on local communities. Wordofa makes the following points about the dissemination of PRA in Ethiopia:

• There is the danger that it will create fatigue: villagers cannot afford to be on call for outsiders wanting to do PRA, since they have to devote most of their energies to making ends meet. Villagers in many areas may already be seeing PRA as a time-consuming and tedious task that does not do much for them.

• If every training workshop, fact-finding mission and researcher continues to drag communities out for PRA-related meetings, expectations will continually be raised and frustrated, and villagers may in the end devalue the approach. This has already been presented as a problem in several places.[23]

Of course people are all the more likely to be fatigued and disenchanted if PRA is used simply on a symbolic basis with no real intention of fulfilling any local expectations of participation. Cornwall et al. note that development practitioners in Kenya feared that local people were becoming tired of PRAs that seemed to have little if any positive output for them and that "(i)t was only a matter of time . . . before villagers would refuse point blank to take part in yet another PRA."[24] Pratt also found this to be a recurring concern amongst aid personnel in Nepal. They observed that PRAs raised expectations amongst the participants and that disappointment of such expectations was likely to lead to popular disenchantment with participatory development techniques.[25]

In making these points it should not be forgotten that many agencies are carrying out good work of the sort illustrated by Fortmann, but bad PRAs are common enough that many people feel that they are a genuine reflection of what participation can achieve. For example, many Kenyan practitioners expressed the view that "there is nothing about PRA that is automatically sensitive to issues of difference within communities."[26] In particular, it was felt that PRA was gender blind and that it elided wealth differences in communities, consequently reinforcing inequalities between men and women, and between wealthy and poor. Yet, we have already seen from the Fortmann examples that a sensitive use of techniques associated with PRA can be very effective in identifying just such lines of difference. Clearly, the contrast between the Kenyan case and Fortmann's Zimbabwean examples revolves around bad practice as against good practice. It is clear that in Kenya, many practitioners are rushing the process and failing to start their interventions with a preparatory phase in which they familiarize themselves with the community or village with which they intend to work.[27] We have already seen that all too many of them approach PRA in a tokenistic way, failing to actually engage with the people in an attempt to mobilize them. By contrast Fortmann avoided at least some of these pitfalls. Rather than using the wealth-ranking techniques in a purely routine manner, insisting that they be applied exactly as specified in the manual, she used them as a starting point with which to communicate with the local researchers. This enabled her to draw on local knowledge, which enhanced her understanding of the social intricacies of the community, and led to a group decision to modify the wealth-ranking tool so that it was better adapted to the needs of the community. She departed from a routinized approach in order to actively engage with the community. In this sense she came much closer to observing Chambers's dictates of handing over the stick and following one's own best judgment than to a bureaucratic approach.

The question arises as to how to ensure some level of quality control in participatory work. This raises a complex of interrelated problems concerning how to reconcile the somewhat contradictory demands of development agencies for rules and regularity (which might be seen as implying top-down hierarchy) with the demands of participation for spontaneity, handing over the stick, and use of judgment. We have already seen that a bureaucratic approach often leads to formalistic PRAs that are unlikely to lead to a genuinely participatory process. However, Wordofa expresses the fear that the less scrupulous may translate Chambers's one-sentence manual, "use your own best judgment at all times" into a license to "do it the way you want; there is no formula."[28] Such an approach could also lead to abuses of the participatory process and is suggestive of the need for some sort of structure to prevent, or minimize their occurrence. How can enough structure be provided to prevent such abuses without it stifling the qualities of spontaneity essential to good participatory praxis? A number of suggestions have been made as to how the problems of participation might be solved and in the next section we shall examine several of them with a view to establishing how far they successfully reconcile the competing claims of structure and spontaneity.

QUALITY CONTROL AND PARTICIPATION

It will be recalled that Chambers places considerable emphasis on training as the crucial factor in ensuring good participatory praxis. His view is that training must be based on learning by doing rather than by academic exercises. He approvingly cites the example of a large-scale training program set up in India by an organization called MANAGE, in which there were only two lectures, an inaugural and a closing lecture. All the other activities were interactive and practical. Chambers explains that "(w)here training is not through lecturing, but through learning by doing and experiencing, a culture or style is set, which can carry over into fieldwork, into organizations, and even into the family." This is "a culture of self-critical awareness and of participation." It is built through activities and games, such as shoulder tapping, in which the participants tap each other on the shoulder if they begin to act in a dominating manner or display any other bad habits endemic in top-down bureaucracies.[29] Leurs also views training as important and approvingly refers to an approach that "focuses on the role of the facilitator and his or her relationships with different community members." These are reviewed and the facilitator is encouraged to analyze his/her experience and to generate training materials on this basis. This approach also provokes the facilitator to be self-critical and aware of his/her own actions.[30] It can be seen that effective training of this sort could have a beneficial influence on field workers. The emphasis on self-criticism and analysis would help to correct for tendencies toward routinization of participatory activities.

However, training does not in itself change organizational culture, and if the organization puts pressure on the facilitator to produce specific results in a certain time, this may tend to counteract any positive influence that good training may have had. It is for this reason that many commentators, including those close to Chambers (e.g., many of his colleagues at the Institute of Development Studies at Sussex University), have advocated the need for a new type of development organization, the learning organization (a model that is derived from business studies). Chambers quotes Peter Senge to the effect that the organizations that will function best in the future will be the ones "that discover how to tap people's commitment and capacity to learn at *all* levels in an organisation."[31]

An IDS workshop gave consideration to the changes in procedures, systems, and structures that would be necessary to turn top-down development bureaucracies into learning organizations. Under the rubric of procedural change, they recommended that aid donors and governments should move away from an obsession with the need for a tightly defined, quantifiable product, or output, and toward a greater concentration on process and capacity building. Rather than looking for physical outputs, such as a school or a health center, they should focus on the process of assisting people to enhance their capacities to undertake and participate in development. Such a change would entail a departure from the blueprint approach in which every activity of a project is planned to take place at a certain time. Instead, aid bureaucracies would have to be much more flexible in just what aid interventions did, when they did it, and how long it would take. In particular, they would have to be supportive of facilitators during the essential preparatory phase when the worker is familiarizing him/herself with the community or target group s/he hopes to work with. Equally essential is official willingness to hand over the stick to people at the grass roots so that they can undertake their own development activities, rather than insisting on adherence to a blueprint.

Another of the workshop's recommendations was that incentive schemes should be introduced to reward participatory behavior by personnel, both in the office and in the field. The following behavior patterns were deemed particularly deserving of reward:

- *tolerance and mutual respect*—the willingness to accept and value that the perceptions of others may not agree with one's own;
- *openness and adaptability*—the willingness to talk about mistakes and to embrace change; and
- *wisdom*—acknowledging that experience, and in particular, the development of initiative in the field, i.e., methodological innovation and experimentation, should be encouraged as it creates opportunities for learning.[32]

These entail radical changes from the hierarchical, risk-averse behaviors typical of top-down bureaucracies. Particularly notable is the avocation of Chambers's principle of "failing forwards." In top-down bureaucracies officials are likely to try to conceal their mistakes for fear of being punished for them. Such fear also stifles their capacity for innovation, because it is often through innovation that mistakes are made. By contrast, Chambers argues that mistakes should be acknowledged and studied as opportunities to learn for future implementation. This entails that learning organizations would not penalize officials for mistakes and should reward innovative behavior.

Other procedural prerequisites for a learning organization include introduction of feedback mechanisms so that information is shared; and organizational willingness to allow stakeholders a role in evaluating their development activities. With regard to the former point, the IDS Workshop noted the tendency for different sections of bureaucracy to behave secretively and conceal information from each other, whereas an ability to learn is founded on availability of information. Consequently, different departments and offices in development bureaucracies should make information easily accessible to each other. This willingness to share information should also be reflected in the acceptance that aid recipients have the right to examine and evaluate what is being done for them. The IDS Workshop explains that "(e)valuation is not about judging others, it is about creating a space in which to systematize and learn from experience, to reflect on a program's activities to see how these might be improved."[33]

A number of structural and systematic changes are identified as being necessary to support these procedural adaptations. First, the use of "flexible, ad hoc, innovative learning units" is commended. These can help to break down the aforementioned boundaries between different sections or offices in an organization. They can also help to counteract traditional bureaucratic propensities to inflexibility. As the IDS Workshop notes, "the separate units [bureaucratic offices] cannot easily combine forces and respond flexibly to the unplanned events and outcomes that are, by definition, the stuff of participatory programs." They continue:

Hence the need for a task culture made up of a network of loosely connected "commando" units with a high learning potential. Each unit is composed of a team with a strong sense of purpose and clearly defined tasks. Units move across the organization as if they were on a grid, helping information move more rapidly and ad hoc decisions to be made when necessary.[34]

This would help the organization to become more flexible and responsive to situations and opportunities as they arise in the field.

The second structural/systemic change recommended is flexible budgeting. As the IDS Workshop puts it, "rigid, pre-set budgets, in which specific amounts are tied to particular activities (to be done within a set time-scale, usually far too short), do not allow for the unplanned requirements of participatory projects." The essence of participatory work is that many development activities cannot be preplanned and budgeted because they emerge out of the discussions between facilitators and beneficiaries. This leads to the following suggestion:

For staff to respond adequately to the unexpected requirements of participatory schemes, the following minimum changes in accounting procedures are needed:

- increasing the number of people entrusted with the handling of accounts (minor staff should be trusted as much as possible to draw from accounts without having to wait for the appropriate signatures if the need is urgent);
- the ability to switch money from one budget heading to another; and
- the ability to roll unspent balances forward.[35]

Some devolution of responsibility for finance and the ability to switch money between budget headings are essential to provide the necessary flexibility to fund activities that have not been pre-planned. The ability to roll unspent balances forward would solve one of the major problems of bureaucratic waste of aid, that is, the tendency to relax standards in appraisal of projects toward the end of the financial year. The necessity to spend every last penny allocated, for fear that money will otherwise be withdrawn, has led to many agencies approving projects that they knew to be substandard toward the end of the financial year. Removal of this threat through the ability to roll unspent funds forward would not only provide the greater financial flexibility required by participatory activities, but also eliminate a major source of waste. The IDS Workshop points out that some donors are adopting some of these reforms, setting up contingency funds and permitting movement of funding between budget headings.

The final point made by the IDS Workshop concerns accountability. They observe that the essence of top-down projects is that accountability runs upward with project personnel being responsible to the official above them in the hierarchy, so that those in the field are accountable to their superiors at head office, who are accountable to the donors. The people with least control are often the supposed beneficiaries of the aid at the grass roots. In a participatory intervention, accountability should also work downward. This is not to say that upward accountability becomes irrelevant, since donors and central offices have a right to know how funds are being spent. However, those at the base, the recipients, have just as much right to know how the aid that is being used in their name is actually being spent. Indeed, participation necessitates downward accountability given that it entails recipients making decisions about what will be done. While it points out that downward accountability is necessary, the IDS Workshop fails to specify any systemic or structural changes that would help to bring this about, stipulating only that a "profound change in the behavior and attitudes of those in positions of power, those who control accounts, may be necessary." They suggest that taking senior personnel into the field to show them the need for flexibility may be effective in convincing them to make such changes. However, they also draw inspiration from the example of the Japanese management model exemplified by Toyota, which they describe as follows:

The premise of the Japanese model is that to respond quickly, effectively and efficiently to changes in demand . . . communication across hierarchies in the company must be allowed to flow with minimum interruption. Some have called this a "flat management" structure. Not only can workers assembling cars communicate ideas directly to the executive and R&D staff, they are also rewarded for taking initiative and formulating ideas on the spot. They do not work as isolated individuals on the production line, but as part of a team.[36]

It may well be that this example of a commercial success based on participatory principles represents one of the more powerful incentives to move toward a bottom-up approach in today's market-obsessed development milieu.

One can point to evidence that some aid agencies are moving toward the participatory approach even though they may not meet the criteria for a learning organization. GTZ, the German Technical Cooperation Agency, initiated a project entitled "Critical Factors and Preconditions for Success in Participatory Approaches" to examine the effects of its participatory projects. Amongst its objectives was to determine how "participatory methods fit in with the existing management instruments, regulations and procedures of GTZ, and which modifications emerge as necessary (planning methodology, monitoring and evaluation methods, staff—and policy—evaluation instruments, etc.)."[37] Thompson also notes that certain development projects have attempted to introduce learning mechanisms into their operation. The Badulla Integrated Rural Development Program in Sri Lanka, the National Irrigation Administration of the Philippines, and Kenya's Soil and Water Conservation Branch have all made efforts to develop institutional learning mechanisms. Thompson describes them as follows:

All three agencies . . . used pilot programmes as learning laboratories for testing, modifying and refining their new participatory approaches. These lessons were analysed and discussed in great detail by key decisionmakers from the agency and, in some instances, other external resource persons in a variety of workshops, review meetings and working groups. The emphasis in all of these sessions was on critical reflection, open sharing, constructive dialogue and learning. Various forms of process documentation were also initiated, including regular village reports, catchment reports, process reports and socio-technical profiles. All of these forms of documentation were distributed and discussed by a wide array of key stakeholders on a regular basis.[38]

This use of pilot projects is reminiscent of the experimental approach commended by Rondinelli (see Chapter 2), which is also directed toward facilitating a learning approach to development interventions. In the above examples this approach is conjoined with elements of the "learning organization" model, notably self-critique, wide-ranging and free discussion both within and outside the organization, information sharing, and moves toward downward accountability. All this is suggestive that at least some development organizations are moving away from the top-down blueprint model toward a more experimental approach that involves at least an element of participation.

Thus far, we have seen that theorists of participation have specified good training and institutional change as essential to the achievement of good participatory practice. While it can be seen that these represent enabling conditions, it also seems clear that none of these can ensure good practice. They may be necessary, but they are not sufficient conditions for good participation. If we were to try to identify the elements that are core to good praxis we would probably find ourselves focusing on the synergies that emerge from the positive behaviors emphasized by Chambers and the attitude of self-critique (which has also been emphasized as essential to participation), which underlies and motivates such behavior. Something akin to this perception is evident in the views of many Kenyan practitioners who agreed that "creation of more opportunities for interchange and debate" is essential to improve participatory practice. Cornwall et al. elaborate on these views as follows:

For some practitioners, the starting point for these discussions should be the core concepts underlying interpretations of "participation." Conceptual clarity would, they suggested, help practitioners to differentiate between different forms of practice, and also to see the potential of using different participatory methodologies to pursue the broader goals of participation. Others argued for the establishment of nonthreatening spaces in which practitioners could interact around the dilemmas of practice. These ranged from "problem clinics at which less experienced practitioners could gain support and advice from their more experienced peers, to open sessions to which practitioners bring recent experiences and explore together ways to resolve problems they face. Others still suggested starting from a discussion of outcomes, from which debate might be generated around indicators of impact, particularly for non-tangible outcomes like "empowerment." This could also take the shape of an open discussion of standards of practice—whether framed in terms of minimum standards, a code of ethics, or what a commitment to best practice actually involves.[39]

It can be seen how a widespread and open debate on such issues could deliver quite specific benefits in terms of mutual support, dissemination of various techniques, and greater general understanding among practitioners that participation involves more than the routinized use of a few tools such as mapping and wealth ranking. Perhaps the most crucial benefit lies in the self-critical awareness that such ongoing debate is likely to foster, since this in itself constitutes the most effective safeguard against a formalistic praxis.

This gives rise to the question of how such debate might be ensured as a normal part of the participatory process. Such a question may seem superfluous given the emphasis that has been laid on the necessity for self-critical awareness by such prominent participatory theorists as Chambers, not to mention his many followers. Arguably, the problem lies with the methodology that Chambers is most associated with, PRA, also the most widely used methodology. The problem is that this self-critical component is not particularly central to the process of undertaking a PRA. It is too easy for practitioners to see PRA as a grab bag of tools and techniques that the facilitator performs with a community. Certainly, there is the admonition to hand over the stick and to let the villagers do it themselves, but there is no specific moment in a PRA that necessitates any self-critical debate amongst any of the parties involved, inclusive of the donors and the aid beneficiaries. A good practitioner is likely to understand the need for such debate and critique and to introduce it as Fortmann did (see above). However, it is all too easy for a facilitator to focus on the tools and to forget about the principles that are supposed to underlie their utility.

This suggests the need for a methodology in which the elements of debate and critique are central to the process in the sense of being built into it. In fact such a methodology exists in the shape of Participatory Action Research (PAR). We have already seen PAR characterized as "an educational process through which a target group is motivated to formulate strategies and initiate activities to improve their collective situation." Burkey defines it as follows:

Participatory action research takes place in time as part of the analysis-action-reflection process where the people are both the subject and the object of the research; where the investigator not only shares this reality, but in fact participates in it as an agent of change. Participatory action research is thus an active research with a clearly defined purpose of creating knowledge to be shared by both the people and the investigator, knowledge that leads to action and, through reflection, to new knowledge and new action.[40]

It is clear that analysis and reflection are an integral part of the process of undertaking PAR, which consists of a cycle wherein analysis leads to action, followed by reflection, leading to further action. The centrality of these elements of debate and critique is demonstrated by the fact that PAR is mainly based on the dialogic approach, which Burkey describes as consisting of "an interchange and discussion of ideas based on a process of open and frank questioning and analysis in both directions between the investigators and the people, both individually and in small groups."[41] PAR is not something that is done to a target group. The people are fully involved in the processes of analysis and reflection. They are not reduced to the position of objects of research because they also operate as subjects actively researching their own situations and strategies for improving their lives. The objective of PAR is that people should become capable of producing their own analyses and plans of action. As Comstock and Fox assert:

The validity of the results of participatory research can be gauged first, by the extent to which the new knowledge can be used to inform collective action and second, by the degree to which a community moves towards the practice of a self-sustaining process of democratic learning and liberating action.[42]

All of this indicates that reflection, analysis, and self-critical awareness are central to the performance of a PAR intervention in a way that is not the case in PRA. It is intrinsic to PAR that the facilitator must embark on some form of analytical dialogue with the target group. The fact that such reflection involves aid recipients is also significant in that it means that any knowledge, analysis, or critique produced is not simply confined to the aid practitioners. It brings into play people's knowledge and contributes to people's knowledge. This mobilization of the recipients as contributors to critique and analysis makes it all the more likely that facilitators will be prompted to reflect and analyze what they are doing in order to operate effectively. Thus, the dialogic approach can be conducive to synergies between the specialist knowledge brought by the facilitator and the people's knowledge brought into play through the dialogue. Such synergies encourage the facilitator to remain critical and to develop his/her knowledge (consequently improving practice), while also encouraging the people to develop and use their knowledge for their practical benefit. Such popular mobilization is also one of the core aims of participation and represents an indicator of at least a measure of success.

In this section we have examined how far some of the central problems of participatory praxis might be remedied. We have seen that problems of formalism, routinization and bad practice can be addressed by means of good training and reform of development organizations so that they are more flexible and receptive to innovation. However, it has also been argued that there is a need for participatory methodology to incorporate an analytical moment that prompts practitioners to think critically about what they are doing and whether or not they are actually helping to empower people. Ideally this should bring into play people's perspectives so that it is also playing an active role in empowerment. The methodology that seems to come closest to meeting these criteria is PAR.

Of course, it can be argued that it would still be possible to do a PAR approach badly. Facilitators can be as domineering, or as disinterested in PAR as they can be in PRA, or any other approach. What differentiates PAR from PRA is that a critical moment is central to the process of implementing PAR in a way that is not the case with PRA. Consequently, it is not quite so easy for practitioners to lapse into bad practice with PAR. It must also be acknowledged that in the final instance good practice is the result of an ethical decision. Aid practitioners at all levels could theoretically be provided with all the necessary facilities (analytical and practical) to undertake good aid interventions, but in the final instance it is still up to them to decide whether or not they are going to use those facilities to the best of their abilities. One of the authors has argued elsewhere that the imperative to engage in development is based on an ethical obligation to assist others.[43] However, the essence of ethics is that such obligations can be refused as well as accepted. The best that we can do as development analysts is to try to specify as far as possible the conditions that will be conducive to good practice and that will make it more feasible for practitioners to take ethical decisions. Hopefully, this analysis has made some small contribution to such an aim.

CONCLUSIONS

In this chapter we have seen that participation has been widely adopted by a large number of agencies and that most of them accept that it entails an element of empowerment for aid recipients. It is clear that the approach can and does have a number of beneficial effects in terms of mobilizing people to analyze their situations and undertake development activities. However, there are problems with the spread of participation, notably tendencies toward formalism and routinization, which tend to undercut the participatory possibilities of the strategy. While good practice can never be absolutely assured, we have argued that good training, moves toward a learning organization, and adoption of the PAR methodology (with its important critical element) all help to create enabling conditions for good practice. What is clear is that participation represents a decisive departure from top-down development, with its problems of rigid blueprints that tend to be ill adapted to conditions on the ground. Good participation holds out the prospect of a development approach that is adaptable and flexible enough to deal with the complexities of development at the grass roots.

CHAPTER 6

The Growth of Gender Perspectives in Development

INTRODUCTION

Social-constructivist theory and everyday reality confirm to us that we live in a world of ideas as much as physical experiences. The rise in importance of certain issues in development, like those concerning women and the environment, can be traced to changes in conscience in the 1970s. Just three decades ago, women experts in development began making forceful and successful pushes for the recognition of the particular problems that women face in development. Many development agencies, such as the World Bank, are just now developing and implementing clear strategies on gender.[1] Despite these new efforts, the movement toward gender equity in development remains marred with confusion, dissonance, and symbolic but non-substantive actions. I hope to use the lens of postmodernism in this chapter to show that the questions raised by feminist theory are much deeper than those concerning women. Postmodernism, in my opinion, implies a fundamentally distinct orientation for equity, one based upon a more participatory structure of relationships, rather than an imposition of standards considered necessary for equity.[2]

At first glance, we might think that women's issues in development are not any more important than the issues surrounding any other minority group in development, whether that group is defined by ethnicity, class, geographical area, caste, or some other socially constructed (created) category. However, women's issues are particularly important because of the unique characteristics of this group. First, women make up more than half the population of the planet. Second, women universally have been relegated to inferior status to men. Feminist theory argues about exactly why, but estimations include biological facts of child rearing, weaker physical capacity, historical legacy, and capitalist relations. Third, regardless of the origins of the inferior status of females, even in developed societies that openly espouse gender equality, they continue to suffer discrimination in all areas of life. In fact, females overwhelmingly do the job of child raising and household maintenance as well as now occupying professional positions at less pay than their male counterparts. Many feminist theorists have pointed out that much of the work done by women around the world, such as child raising, occurs in a parallel, nonremunerated capacity, ignored by the formal economy of paid work. Fourth, like all social institutions, development organizations are dominated by men and patriarchal systems that perpetuate their dominance. Fifth, but certainly not least, women tend to be among the most marginalized and impoverished groups in the developing world. Women tend to be excluded from equal access to education. Women suffer the most in terms of both economic and physical abuse, including domestic violence and female genital mutilation (FGM). In general, gender inequalities increase as the poverty of the group does.

PRIMARY PERSPECTIVES ON WOMEN AND DEVELOPMENT: WID VS. GAD

There are two primary perspectives on gender and development, and they have developed sequentially.[3] The first and predominant mode of thinking is called "Women in Development" (WID). WID was the original set of demands created by women development activists in the 1970s to create focused avenues for dealing with the special problems that women face in development.[4] By institutional measures, WID has been spectacularly successful and continues to grow in the development agendas of development organizations. Most mainstream development organizations now have a special WID unit, specialized WID policies, project and evaluation guidelines that seek to include gender impact as a an important criterion, and WID awareness training. While the consensus is that there has been substantive progress, studies of development organizations show that WID units tend to be marginalized, with WID employees kept from promotions to higher activities. WID generally tends to be seen as an additional activity rather than being mainstreamed into the consciousness and daily practice of development aid. The proliferation of women's NGOs internationally over the last 10 years constitutes an important pressure to correct these oversights. Still, on a national and local level, even basic attention to women's issues is far from being achieved.

The Gender and Development (GAD) approach emerged as a critique to the WID policies in the 1980s. In fact, WID had been criticized from the beginning by activists who took a Marxist perspective that WID was an inadequate response to basic oppression caused by world capitalist relations and that development agencies were agents of this oppression. GAD casts a wider theoretical net with important differences in policy implications than the well-known Marxist line of thought. GAD sees women's issues as not simply a matter of paying special attention to a particularly marginalized group, but as a reflection of a general condition they call "patriarchy." By patriarchy, GAD theorists refer specifically to the fact that the *power relations of gender exist in all aspects of society.* In this sense, they appropriate the lessons of postmodernism that power has important aspects of social construction, and not just or ultimately economic or class oppression, as Marxists would claim. By social construction, we mean that society creates certain archetypes, such as "the homeless," "immigrants," or "the poor," which actually represent widely diverse and varied subgroups and individuals. When social constructions are married to value hierarchies, conceptions are created or reinforced about what is good and what is bad, which informs and constrains policy. In postmodern parlance, analysts call this act "difference," and it can refer to any assignment of identity, value, or expectation, not just what is good and bad. As a simple example, in different ways, we idolize sports heroes in our cultures. Thus, someone who is born with particular gifts and is able to nurture them has a chance to become a "hero" in our societies, while someone without those physical gifts, or, more important, without the same types of opportunities, is not. In a developing society, a young woman will be inundated with exclusively male heroes, whether they be Bolívar in South America, Nehru in India, or Nasser in Egypt. At the same time, we also live by the Western myths that individuals, in good part, create their own destiny, through "hard work," "intelligence" (sometimes measured in standardized tests), and "entrepreneurship." However, for women, these create a significant cognitive dissonance in the sense that women are still expected to provide the caretaker role for household needs, and their ability, symbolic and practical, of professional success is similarly compromised. The dissonance is even greater if we think about the conflicting messages concerning sexuality for women. On the one hand, role models from Barbies to advertisements push physical attributes as a means of power, while on the other, social norms dictate a conservative chastity in practice. We can only imagine the levels of dissonance in developing countries where the messages of Western media and a new generation clash with more traditional cultural forms. The result could be an a new form of hybridity between the Western culture and the traditional culture(s), but the shock of difference and the rapidity of the change make such new and comforting syntheses difficult, even within the Western world (between old and new values).

In GAD terms, we consider females as being different and treat them as a separate group, with separate social status and norms. Therefore, there are some all-female schools, there are separate female sports, and, more generally, there are different roles and expectations assigned to females than to males. These are all elements of the hierarchy of subordinate values assigned to females under the socially constructed systems of patriarchy. The cultural constructions reinforce and match social institutions and practices.

GAD has a very potent and all-encompassing critique of the way that the social construction of gender pervades all aspects of our lives and reinforces the inferiority of females in tacit as well as overt ways. GAD analysts would look at development ideas, organizations' practices, and cultural norms, as well as simply demand changes in resource flows. In fact, some GAD analysts point out that *the creation of separate WID units actually reinforces the "difference" by separating out females as a separate group, and reinforcing the construction of women in developing countries as feeble and helpless.* A defender might make the case that WID was a pragmatic approach intended to work within existing separations to improve women's lots so that they could someday claim equality. However, when we look at the paternalistic images of women in development manuals and reports and examine the policy approaches and projects designed for women, we find that GAD proponents have a strong case that development agencies themselves are sexist.

A step that takes GAD analysis further is to point out that postmodernism suffers from its own critique. That is, *why wouldn't postmodernism itself be judged to be an imposition on others?* A new movement called Women, Environment, and Development (WED) points out precisely that there is a basic lack of "authenticity," in some ways, to the women's movement within development. That is, the *women in developing countries have very little voice in the development discourse*, and therefore, development projects do not reflect the ground reality of their subjects. Thus, WED pointed out that while GAD may be a helpful step forward, it still does not capture the depth and complexity of the issues facing women in developing countries.

If we take the salubrious logic of WED further, we note that even among NGOs with bases in the South, the predominant membership and voice tends to be that of well-to-do women who can afford to engage in such activities. Thus, GAD and WED together point out that there are important differences between women in the North and women in the South, as well as along other lines of social construction, including class, race, ethnicity, actual geographical location, generation, and experience. This has fed into the more general ideas that women in developing countries need to be empowered, rather than simply led. We agree with both the GAD analysis and with the idea that the proper role for the development agency is empowerment of women to solve their own problems; however, as we discuss later, actually implementing these ideas is another story. Development agencies' primary role should be providing resources and encouraging, training, and otherwise aiding women to organize themselves. Empowerment implies a fundamental change in power and will therefore face great resistance from within existing development organizations and local cultures. In this sense, the agency of the institution and the agency of empowered women are in two different trajectories.[5] Thus, we should consider the development-project process as a negotiated one in all instances. From this point of view, WID was a first step and its limitations understandable for the context of the times, but the improvements of the GAD and WED perspectives have yet to be implemented in a meaningful way.

CURRENT STRATEGIES OF MAJOR AID AGENCIES

The 1995 Fourth Conference on Women in Beijing brought women's issues to the forefront of the development agenda, and as has been the case in other fora, a diverse audience participated. That is, at least in conferences and some journals, there seems to be a conscious effort to include women from Southern NGOs. However, this effort at representation does not seem to be reflected in development-project policies. For example, while every major aid agency now has full-fledged separate units to deal strictly with women's issues, these units generally seem to be more focused on increasing gender sensitivity in projects rather than a legitimate effort to create projects that deal with gender inequalities head-on.

Indeed, like so many issues in development, no one is openly against gender inequality, but there is little agreement on what should be done and even scantier evidence of strong action to create new projects and programs. Because an open embrace of gender-oriented development is so new, there is even less information about the design, implementation, and evaluation of projects designed with gender sensitivity in mind. Moreover, development organizations seem to be at a loss in terms of how to organize gender initiatives, since they cut across all types of sectors, regions, and projects.

Gender development initiatives by project agencies fall into several basic issue-areas. The first are initiatives on reproductive health. Oftentimes, reproductive-health projects are folded in with general efforts to reduce population growth and improve health. These projects constitute the initiative area with the longest track record in women's projects. The second category is women's education projects. These have become perhaps the most fashionable of all women's projects, as there is a broad consensus that women's education has a wide variety of beneficial impacts, including the reduction of birth rates, reduction of poverty, the improvement of economic productivity, and the creation of greater independence for women. The third basic category is poverty and emergency relief-oriented programs designed particularly for women. There have been a number of recent analyses pointing out the important and differential role of women in these situations who serve as the anchor for family ties and the main organizers for coping mechanisms in hardship. We might consider the new concerns toward the impact of structural adjustment on women in this category. Structural adjustment concerns regarding women's relationship to the short-term and economic effects of economic policy decisions, and it involves similar kinds of projects to help women cope with what are expected to be temporarily difficult conditions. The fourth basic category would include institutional programs designed to increase the proportion of women in important positions in the working world. These "affirmative-action" programs translate not only into hiring preferences in the First World, but occasionally proactive training and mentoring programs by development agencies and women's networks. Last but not least, there are a number of new initiatives that seek to increase the political power of women through developing political organizations, networks, and resource funds directed at both traditional and nontraditional political actors. While long-standing in the First World, there has been a mushrooming of women's NGOs in the last decade throughout the developing world, in the hope of creating stronger political pressure for change as well as self-help organizations.

In general, development agencies seem lost in terms of what to do about gender. While most agencies formally embrace gender initiatives and show that gender-conscious projects have a higher rate of success,[6] there seems little purposive action.[7] The insights of GAD and WED do not seem to have been translated into actual policies, probably because they entail changes in power relationships. A recent evaluation of aid agencies shows efforts to include gender considerations in projects have met with generally marginal success.[8] While all agencies have at least gone through the motions of policy action, in general, gender is not effectively mainstreamed into agency activities. The shortfalls include everything from data to guidance to evaluations of gender results. Of course, part of the problem here is the one we address in the evaluation chapter, namely that aid organizations are their own monitoring and evaluation agencies. There are few clear data on how much and how agencies are addressing gender.

There are a number of other factors that affect how well development agencies respond to gender. Perhaps the foremost is a steady external pressure on the agency by outside groups. The second is the level of dedication, interest, sympathy, and positioning of internal staff members toward gender issues. The third is the level of organization of women beneficiaries of projects. The fourth, but also quite important, is the degree to which agencies hold divisions and project managers accountable for clearly defined and measurable goals of increasing gender sensitivity.[9] This would suggest that some gender sensitivity training may be a useful prerequisite or accompaniment to an aid agency's normal portfolio. Of all the agencies, as in most other areas of development, the Nordic development agencies seem to be at the forefront of not only suggesting but also acting upon GAD's insights.[10] While development NGOs seem more thorough in going through the motions of gender sensitivity, indications are that they have neither been more successful in practice.[11]

Since there are a number of new problems that require new approaches in gender projects, new types of projects will be created. For example, there is increasing concern about working conditions for the growing population of women workers in low-wage, labor-intensive export processing zones. There are also strong concerns for the emerging international trade in prostitution, domestic labor, and related exploitation of children. Certainly of utmost importance is the growing crisis of AIDS throughout the developing world, which clearly requires a gender-oriented policy. On the other hand, none of these new concerns seems to require agencies to push beyond the WID framework, which is probably the way they want it.

DEVELOPING A NEW STRATEGY FOR INCORPORATING GENDER IN PROJECTS

Perhaps one of the key problems is the lack of well-developed policy frameworks on gender. On one hand, some agencies, like the World Bank, tend to subsume gender as one of many variables measuring poverty. In this approach, gender has tended to be buried in practice as a secondary concern for development projects and large quantitative analyses using "female household" or a similar proxy variable to measure differences and results. On the other hand, most new development projects aimed at women are geared toward specific issues, such as literacy or developing craft-type skills such as weaving. The point of the GAD framework is that gender involves a nexus of problems that must be considered simultaneously. Poor, rural women in developing countries need safety from domestic violence, nutritional aid, reproductive and child-care assistance, literacy, and political empowerment. However, if we genuinely believe in empowerment, the beneficiaries themselves should create the priorities and have a major influence on resource allocation. If, for example, beneficiaries' priorities place the economic above the reproductive, then their wishes must be respected for empowerment to exist.

A few clear lessons have come out from our limited project knowledge so far. One thing that is clear is that development initiatives must be very strongly proactive on gender issues to make a difference. Simply hiring a female on a project, or including some gender-related objectives in the project documentation as secondary to the main thrust of the project, virtually ensures that gender will be ignored. Women face too many obstacles in development settings, at home, in institutions, and in development organizations themselves to be relegated to secondary status in development projects.

Second, all too often, WID units are considered places of exile for both issues and promotions. Gender equality should therefore be incorporated explicitly into all aspects of a development project and integrated into each of the agency's development activities if it is a true objective. Mainstreaming gender means an explicit commitment to reworking training, hiring, promotion, project selection, implementation, and evaluation guidelines to consider gender. Simply adding a gender component to project management seems to result all too often in gender being viewed as another bureaucratic obstacle in project implementation, rather than a genuine incorporation of gender as a key lens of the overall perspective.[12] However, even adopting a comprehensive approach that includes gender will not change well-entrenched organizational cultures.[13] Including male specialists on gender could have a beneficial effect in mainstreaming gender and reducing stereotypes that result in political isolation.

However, the problem is much deeper than just agency renewal. Development agencies continue to ignore the local conditions faced by women. The thrust of most gender initiatives, whether we are talking about the World Bank, UNDP, AID, or even SIDA seems to emanate from a top-down apparatus and in a series of sweeping policy statements, though these often include multiple incantations of "empowerment." Similarly, as noted above, evaluation of success in gender equity is done in a top-down fashion, according to predetermined criteria—generally, increasing overall numbers and/or ratios of females hired. In general, country-level offices of development agencies seem less responsive to gender initiatives, both from headquarters[14] and from women affected by the project. Certainly, anyone who has traveled to the developing world has noted that women will have a harder time in negotiations with host-country governments. While there is a dominant male discourse and posturing even in the developed world, the machismo found in most development-country norms seems more heightened. Unjustifiably so, but women may be taken less seriously or have a harder time in developing a rapport with host-country managers, which makes project management more difficult. Therefore, as Jane Jaquette pointed out to me, a strong and absolute commitment by top management is essential to overcoming these built-in sources of resistance.

Development projects in all cases require local tailoring, but even more so in projects where gender is an issue. Women in developing countries, especially in rural areas, face strong pressures for conformity from their husbands; thus, projects must be sensitive to this dynamic in order to reduce the level of conflict at home that could lead to nonparticipation by women. In line with this, gender-sensitive projects, like all projects, should be designed around the particular development objectives of the women in question. For example, the group may be more interested in a small-income producing project that allows them the flexibility to reasonably continue their normal home duties, as opposed to an educational project with less clear immediate benefits and longer out-of-home time requirements. In practice, we find no development agency that formally includes the voices of impoverished women in its decision-making process on projects. Even ad hoc consulting groups on women and development are dominated by women with elite backgrounds.[15]

Local NGOs may or may not be able to play a bridging role for the aid agency. Many developing country NGOs are based in capital cities and run by women with the education and means to do such work. Most of the more activist women in developing countries also come from elite backgrounds. If the members of the NGO contain their own biases, they could circumvent the project's goals, or worse yet, recreate power differentials based on other factors, such as education, income, or class.

Even in Communist countries in the developing world, such as Cuba, China, and Vietnam, where new norms of gender equity are openly espoused, scholars have pointed out serious shortcomings. While the conditions may be slightly better than in other countries in the region, women in Communist countries still are limited in terms of participation in decision-making. Usually, the Communist Party in the country sets up a separate woman's rights organization, however, most analysts agree that these organizations are dominated by an old-fashioned male patriarchy in the form of a commanding-party apparatus.[16] While there certainly were early gains among Communist regimes, these gains in equity are clearly more than reversed as Cuba and North Korea stagnate economically and former Communist countries China and Vietnam open up their markets.

Let us now turn to a few examples that expose these points further. A recent International Fund for Agriculture and Development (IFAD) document reviewed several development projects geared toward improving household food security in Guatemala.[17] The projects were in good part oriented toward "improving the status and security of women" in rural areas involved in micro-agricultural production. The review of the projects found that the project interventions to move agricultural producers toward more profitable crops had limited success, because smaller households were apparently much more cautious about entering enterprises with higher risks. The review called for greater attention, therefore, to insurance and marketing aspects of the projects. A USAID international review of programs to aid girls' education consistently points out that community empowerment and participation are key to project outcomes,[18] yet fails to identify measurements or criteria by which to judge the extent to which those aspects of the projects were successful. The bulk of the report focuses on easily quantifiable measures of participation, therefore underplaying these vital, if latent, factors. This brings up the broader question of whether education projects are education for its own sake, or for empowerment. If the latter is the goal, then there is no clear conceptualization, plan, or measurement for how girls' education feeds into other systems, particularly, economic gains. In other words, a truly effective education project would not only include the latent factors of empowerment within the community, but also measure the postgraduation results, as well as the participation and testing rates. An FAO report on gender and participation in agricultural development planning projects internationally reaches some of the same conclusions we have here.[19] It states:

The mainstream agricultural planning literature ... has rarely taken the gender-focused literature into account. . . . In the "real world" as well, gender analysis has rarely, if ever, entered the planner's tool kit. Neither, in fact, has PRA, except in a very preliminary manner that tends to confine participation to the official village leadership. . . . Village or community level planning is still rare. . . . How responsive is current agricultural planning to gender and socio-economic differences? We really don't know.

We would like to see development projects in which the goal is not to produce small handicrafts for tourists, but to create genuinely open paths for women's empowerment, beginning with the decision-making and allocation process in development agencies themselves.

CONCLUSION

Postmodern thinking brings up interesting questions about gender and development. One basic question is a perennial one for postmodernists: how to recognize "difference" without creating power differentials. As we have seen from our review above, women's issues have been superficially embraced by aid agencies, and while progress has been made, undoubtedly agencies maintain male-dominated organizations that continue to marginalize women's pressing needs.

A second intriguing parallel question is how we can respect others' cultural beliefs and rights to create their own preferences, a core theme of our book, while also recognizing the importance of some basic standards of human welfare.[20] In other words, on one hand, unlike development agencies, we are reluctant to pass judgment on developing societies as "inferior" because of gender differences. We should see the folly of the common attempts in development projects to recreate developed-world women's conditions and self-definition, with the possibility of recreating all the tensions, angst, and problems. Developed-world women face different circumstances than do their counterparts in the developing world. Developed-world women face a situation of attempting to expand and claim enforcement of already-created (at least formally) norms and rights, whereas in many cases in the developing world, ideas of gender equality are still contested and articulated (highly differentiated). The gender situation of the developed world represents a "cultural milieu," or nexus of historically embedded social identities and experiences, that does not really apply to the developing world. At the same time, we find unacceptable the level of violence, in physical, emotional, and psychological terms, in the treatment of women in the developing world. The clear harm that is caused not only by the extreme cases of genital mutilation, but also by the inequality of opportunities, is impossible to ignore.

One important postmodernist principle here is not to enshrine any key difference. Identities are flexible,[21] and while gender is a basic creator of identity through differentiation, it is not the only one. Obviously, there is some confusion about the definition of gender in practical terms in some cases. More important, there are important differences among women as well. Women face different and varying levels of mistreatment that vary by their location (e.g., Middle East vs. Latin America; rural vs. urban); economic activity (professional vs. informal); income level and class; religion; and levels of education, to name just a few. We might dare to say that all men are not the same, either, and some could prove valuable allies. Unfortunately, but expectedly, women's organizations tend to be dominated by those with greater access to power and resources; thus, we have an additional problem of a lack of representation by a huge subset of the women suffering the most in developing countries. In sum, while gender issues transcend poverty, and a comprehensive approach is needed, patriarchy is too general a term to lead to purposive action in the highly varied situations that different groups of women face.[22]

There is no neat solution to this problematique. Rather, we repeat several of the themes of the book. First, women's development efforts must include access to resources and decision-making as well as window-dressing units and reports. Second, women's organizations themselves must embrace internal differences and promote participation. Third, the ultimate source of victory lies in changing culture—norms and beliefs that, as Gramsci and Foucault pointed out, underlie the tacit and informal support of power differentials. As Kate Young says:

"Women become empowered through collective reflection and decision-making. The parameters of empowerment are: building a positive self-image and self-confidence; developing the ability to think critically; building up group cohesion and fostering decision-making and collective action." What is meant is enabling women collectively to take control of their own lives to set their own agendas, to organize to help each other and make demands on the state for support and on society itself for change. . . . It also implies some degree of conflict: empowerment is not just about women acquiring something, but those holding power relinquishing it . . . so men must undergo a process of reflection and transformation which makes it possible for them to recognize the ways in which their power is a double-edged sword, that it structures their relations with other men in competition and conflict, and makes cooperation and building on advances highly problematic.[23]

Yet we must avoid creating a rubber stamp in terms of a First World model of gender relations.[24] One of the main messages in this book is that for any change to be sustainable, it must be done without coercion and through dialogue and persuasion, rather than imposition. Moreover, we must not allow our goals to get in the way of the need for solutions to be weaved through the intricacies of local actors and conditions. In the end, then, we are proposing a new set of projects—one that aims toward an open-ended process, which might include several overlapping steps. The key actors in this negotiated process would have to be the aid agencies and the host governments as usual, but also the participants of the projects themselves. On a wider scale, we should recognize from the GAD and WED analyses that the construction of inferiority of gender has deep historical roots and reinforcing social planks. Thus, in a longer-term policy sense, changing the hearts and minds of developing societies is necessary to challenging patriarchy. The first step would be exposure, including increasing awareness of the problems faced by women and the opportunities for society-wide improvement through the reduction of inequality. This step could be characterized as *accurate exposure*, in presenting not only the suffering of developing-country women, but also the hypocrisy of aid agencies that make claims on gender equity but do not deliver and host governments and societies who proclaim equity but practice the same old game. The second would be to promote dialogue and experimentation for finding solutions to these inequalities. This step should be taken diplomatically, in the sense that the social means of conversation about topics are bound to differ from one place to another. The third would include information dissemination and analysis to relate to, and learn from, the situations and solutions offered by those dealing with the same kinds of issues. The fourth would be the assertion of power by pro-women groups in societies to institutionalize these norms, including meaningful access to legal and other social recourse and aid. Again, giving resources and encouragements should be differentiated from commanding from afar.

To various extents, agencies have made apparent efforts in the directions of many of these principles, yet the reality is far different. Here are some suggestions for more concrete policy changes that could be considered on an internal level:

- Refocus internal agency efforts toward changing the organizational culture, norms, and incentive structure, so that gender awareness is part of the entire organization and not just an isolated unit or a numbers game (in terms of hiring).

- As stated in our other projects, make each phase of development projects, a *co-managed enterprise between the participants and the donors.* This means the project conception, criteria for evaluation, and allocation decisions should be made in good part by the local women beneficiaries of the project, not project handlers. This is a truer sense of empowerment.

- Women, and not just those of elite background, should be part of the decision-making apparatus of development projects. Women not affiliated with the agencies, and not just those working for NGOs, should be able to propose their own projects to agencies for funding.

- Women from developing countries should be given a greater voice in the development discourse. Though efforts are being made in this direction, the conversation between the Western and the developing world still seems haphazard and disjointed. Based on incentives and opportunities, women from developing countries are more likely to say what sponsors want to hear than to represent more authentic concerns. Thus, there is still a great deal of indirect co-optation for legitimation by donors and Western women alike.

- Women in developing countries should be given encouragement in personal, economic, political, and social empowerment, but should be allowed to select the means and rate that they find appropriate. Working through political parties may be fine for some countries, but not others. Attending political meetings may endanger other aspects, such as economic ones, or women's struggle for empowerment. It might make sense to support female-only schools if that allows greater access to education. Similarly, projects must consider the huge variation in conditions faced by various women, even within the same locality. Local and personal conditions, in short, require much greater attention and tailoring than is presently being given.[25]

- In line with the last point, sustainability involves community support. Women must be empowered within the parameters of their own societies, not in a way suitable for other societies. Challenges should therefore be appropriate to the situation and task at hand. If basic human needs are involved, such as physical abuse or FGM, a strong external challenge may be justified, but even there will only be successful to the point where it can *persuade* the community to change norms. Challenges for less urgent tasks of empowerment should not lead to the isolation or ostracizing of women leading such moves. The result of this is too great a dependency on outside donors and ideas (mimicry), and the creation of a sense of social isolation, imposition, or "otherness" about the very causes that are designed to benefit the majority of women in the area, a heightening of the dissonances we discussed earlier. Designing a challenge within more accepted social norms and practices of appeal—for instance, references to women's rights in the Qu'ran—will have a much greater chance of success because they fit within the culture, perspective, and means available to most women. Empowerment may be a very long-term process, requiring new institutions and norms, which can only be partially aided in the project format. This requires a delicate dance of negotiation between the donor, host government, local authorities, and the participants themselves—much more subtle, complex, and requisite of diplomatic skills than the "whirling dervish" approach of most development agencies now.

- The bottom line of this thinking is that the development agency must transform into an enabler and leave the proposing, executing, and evaluation roles largely to local participants. From this point of view, there is no dissonance between the governance-reform issues of Chapter 4 and a bottom-up orientation. Instead, we suggest conceptualizing a new role for institutions.

We believe that the challenge of gender-related projects reflects the postmodern challenge to development—that is, that the act of increasing genuine participation and decision-making in the project is an end in and of itself, and that development projects should be evaluated along these lines. If some of the decisions made by developing-country women are not embraced by developed-country women, the latter should keep in mind that the core idea behind empowerment is some control over one's own decisions. Last but not least, to breakdown patriarchy, women need to work with men. If women's inferior status is a social construction, so is men's superior status.[26] Greater enlightenment among men is the key, then, to breaking down these artificialities that are behind categorical power discrimination. By recognizing the artificiality behind such propositions, we can, in postmodern fashion, liberate ourselves from such illusions and the legitimation games that help to cover them up. In the end, we feel that empowerment and allowing for self-learning are the end goals of a truly liberating feminist/postmodernist approach to development project management.

CHAPTER 7

How to Help a Failing Patient: The Difficult State of Evaluation in Development Projects

INTRODUCTION

If you are reading this book you will agree that one of the most remarkable things about being human is our difficulty to learn. Development projects are no exception. Let us put our cards on the table: *evaluation as currently practiced in development project administration is a virtue often preached but rarely practiced.* Indeed, most comparative studies cite the figure of a minimum of 25–30% project failure in most aid agencies.[1] It seems to be a no-brainer that any development project will yield scores of potential lessons for other projects to be undertaken in the future. Moreover, evaluation is essential to accountability of resources. In a world of poverty, we want to make sure that every penny that goes into development is well spent, which means we need to measure results. Thus evaluation should be clearly incorporated into the project cycle, such that:

$$\text{evaluation results} \quad \Rightarrow \quad \text{new project analysis}$$

$$\Uparrow \qquad\qquad\qquad\qquad \Downarrow$$

$$\text{new project implementation}$$

This would yield a virtuous circle in which we continually learn to conduct better and better development projects.

Unfortunately, one of the most dismal aspects of studying developing projects is finding out about two essential and ubiquitous shortcomings: the failure to coordinate actions and the failure to learn through evaluation. *Both evalu-*

ation and project selection go together, since an appropriate pre-project analysis should incorporate information and lessons from previous projects. In practice, we do not see any evidence of serious project evaluation in current development-project administration, for reasons we will discuss. Certainly there is no shortage of evaluation initiatives, but the good intentions have not really led yet to a virtuous circle of learning.

In this chapter, we will discuss the traditional and emerging methods of evaluation of development projects and then compare the advantages and disadvantages of each. While our previous chapters discussed how participation can positively shape each stage of the development project, in this section we will focus on participation in the post-project evaluation stage. Then we will discuss why focusing merely on different evaluation methods is misplaced, because the politics of development impede both information sharing and evaluation. Finally, we shall make some suggestions about ways in which evaluation could be improved in development projects, keeping in mind the political obstacles.

TRADITIONAL METHODS OF PROJECT SELECTION: THE PITFALLS OF FINANCIAL EVALUATION OF DEVELOPMENT PROJECTS

This section will focus on the traditional financial criteria used to evaluate prospective development projects based on their rates of return in terms of financial and social costs and benefits. Primary focus is placed on cost-benefit analysis and the limitations inherent in the necessary assumptions for this type of analysis. Cost-benefit analysis (CBA) is the predominant way that projects are selected and appraised by development agencies. Because cost-benefit analysis is difficult for non-evaluation specialists to understand, we spend most of each section on explaining a basic principle of CBA. Those who are familiar with the basic techniques will want to skip to the latter part of each subsection for the commentary on potential problems. A number of references, including basic manuals, are provided in the Bibliography.

Cost-Benefit Analysis

The basic idea behind this type of analysis is to quantify the costs and benefits of the project alternatives under consideration, over time, and to favor the project or (version of the project) that will yield the highest *social* return. Cost-benefit analysis in this context has been subject to a continuing criticism that pervades the debate over the importance of welfare economics in general.[2]

The costs and benefits of development projects are often converted to foreign exchange,[3] which is the most scarce and necessary resource for economic development, particularly in terms of purchasing power for imported capital and technical inputs. This reflects the reality that most donor-agency costs are denominated in their home currency and allows for comparison of projects in different countries.

One of the major complications in any cost-benefit analysis is that projects are often not mutually exclusive. In other words, the adoption of one project often affects the viability and rate of return of others.[4] Another pitfall is the possibility of double-counting benefits. For example, an increase in agricultural output might be mistakenly added to the overall estimation of the social benefits of facilitated transportation routes, which would already include the benefits of increased agricultural output.[5] In practice, it may be quite difficult to disentangle both benefits and costs in order to avoid double counting. In the following sections, the tools of cost-benefit analysis, and some of the problems in using them, are discussed.[6]

Discount Rate

The discount rate is the measure by which costs and benefits are weighed over time. The idea is that everyone prefers to have goods now, rather than later. That is why interest rates for the lending of money always have positive interest rates. A higher interest rate means that money invested now must yield higher net benefits later to be equivalent in value to us at the present. In other words, in the private market, the higher interest rate would mean higher current borrowing costs, and so the need for a greater stream of benefits over time. Discount rates for project outcomes should be calculated in real terms by deducting the projected rate of inflation. The choice of the discount rate, then, determines the rate of interest that will be used to compute the net present value, or the value of the stream of benefits to be accrued in today's terms. The discount rate is the way that we can work time into our analysis of projects' costs and benefits. Thus, even projects with very different time lengths can be compared against each other.

The discount rate is used not only to figure out the net present value of projects, but also for the internal rate of return and the benefit-cost ratio. The internal rate of return is the discount rate by which the net present value becomes zero. In other words, it shows how high the interest rate must be before the project no longer provides net benefits. The higher the internal rate of return, the better the project. As Rosen points out,[7] however, the internal rate of return (IRR) can lead to confusing results since it consists of relative rather than absolute comparisons. Therefore, a project with a lower IRR *may* still be preferable if it produces larger absolute benefits. While the costs would also be higher, if a significantly larger population benefited, the absolute spread of benefits *should* be considered along with the rate of return. The benefit-cost ratio is simply the net present value of total benefits divided by that of costs. Rosen demonstrates in this case that a simple manipulation of an additional item being considered as either a cost or as a decrease in benefits can change the whole benefit-cost ratio, and therefore the basis for comparison of projects.[8]

Obviously, the choice of discount rate is crucial in the analysis. A higher discount rate will favor projects with benefit streams occurring earlier than ones with somewhat higher benefits that are accrued later. Unfortunately, in most developing country countries, a lack of institutions including property rights that can be used as collateral, as well as very high transaction and information costs, prevent the smooth functioning of the credit market. Therefore, while the clear choice for a discount rate should be the projected interest rates over time, the volatility of developing country credit markets makes such projections precarious indeed. Partly for this reason, many cost-benefit analysts try to create social indicators as evaluative criteria in addition to the financial ones.

Shadow Indicators

Similar market imperfections abound in all aspects of most developing-country economies. For example, the commonly known dualistic character of those economies, in which the presence of a formal, unionized sector sits alongside widespread underemployment, leads to unrealistically high formal wages. The high transaction costs due to lack of infrastructure and institutions, such as national commodity exchanges and adequate transportation between cities and rural areas, occur not only in the credit market, but also in product markets. A last example is the distortions created by government intervention in the economy, such as the presence of state-owned enterprises that suck up credit and affect private sector viability, for example, by providing inconsistent electricity to industries, as has been the case in Nigeria for some time, or in overvalued exchange rates, which lead to credit and price distortions in the value of imports and exports. Little and Mirrlees summarize these distortions, which require shadow prices and rates, as the following conditions in developing economies: very rapid inflation; currency overvaluation; underemployment; imperfect capital markets; the externalities of large projects, which will be discussed below; inelasticity of demand for exports, which makes industry protection more attractive than may be financially apparent; and protectionist measures, such as tariffs, which distort prices and can negatively affect exports.[9]

Cost-benefit analysis attempts to deal with these distortions by assigning more realistic rates or prices, which are called "shadow" rates or prices. Shadow rates or prices not only attempt to assign distortion-free market prices, but also include considerations of social benefits, such as increased employment.[10] Shadow prices are therefore assigned to both inputs and outputs of development projects. For example, as noted above, shadow wage rates will most often be set below the prevailing (formal) wage rates in order to reflect the social benefits (or "true opportunity costs") of increasing the amount of (currently underemployed) labor input in a project. Shadow prices are also sometimes calculated net (after) of prevailing taxes on goods and services, since tax revenues (minus administrative costs) are transferred to the government. However, the key questions in regard to taxes should be how they are used and what their effects are on the economy. If government capacity is low and tax revenues are not used efficiently, a project administrator should consider including taxes as a net or marginal loss. On the other hand, some taxes may reduce rather than create economic distortions,[11] as in the case of leveling the proper level of taxation on natural monopolies or reducing externalities, such as pollution. Shadow interest rates, meanwhile, are often higher than prevailing interest rates, since capital in the form of credit is often the scarcest input in a project, and developing country governments logically want to direct the use of that scarce resource. Shadow exchange rates are used to measure the true foreign-exchange value of a project when the exchange rate has been manipulated by the government, generally through intervention to overvalue the rate and thereby favor capital equipment imports, or through excise taxes or duties that distort trade.[12]

As is probably clear from the above discussion, the problem with shadow prices and rates is correctly assessing both distortion-free and socially considerate figures. While world prices for commodities are used to correct for price distortions in tradeables, such prices do not accurately reflect the price and rate differentials of the domestic economy. In particular, world prices should not be used to consider the prices of non-tradeables in the domestic economy, which could figure prominently in development projects, such as unskilled labor. Moreover, particularly in the larger developing country economies, differences between world and domestic prices are to be expected, considering the many scarcities in developing economies, such as the lack of technical skills. The rates of return on those factors in shortage would, absent internal and external economic distortions, be higher than they are in the developed country. Little and Mirrlees's suggestion that previous and current project experience and industrial and agricultural surveys be used to find the shadow rates and prices is helpful, but will not conclusively resolve the uncertainty involved.[13] The key point is that projects will not have infinitely substitutable factor inputs, so that factor prices do not equalize in a developing country setting. Social-welfare considerations, including a prioritization and definition of social goals, furthermore, will be assessed differently by every person and differently over time. Therefore, not only inconsistencies but also pure opinions will abound in applying social-welfare considerations to development projects.

Finally, as may have been surmised, the application of shadow prices and rates, even in the unlikely case that it is consistent across different types of projects with different inputs and outputs, does not reflect the *true* costs and benefits that will be accrued in the actual implementation of the development project. Therefore, project managers often lose sight of the financial, especially cash, flows that are needed by focusing too much on the economic rates of return. Certainly one of the keys to project failure is the lack of consideration for *long-term financing*, sustainability, and capacity building.[14] Even slight user fees and host-government matching, from this point of view, creates a real stake in the project outcome and an interest in the viability and efficiency of the project delivery.

Externalities

One of the non-market aspects of projects that must be considered is externalities. These include both positive and negative benefits of a project that would not be captured by market transactions. Projects that would be highly beneficial for the economy as a whole may not be undertaken by private concerns because of high risks in recouping costs or the collective nature of the benefits.[15] For example, while it may take many years to recoup the costs of building a highway in tolls, the road may lead to the economic development of an underdeveloped section of a country and to the ability to much more inexpensively move agricultural goods produced in the interior of a country to the larger cities, thus reducing the costs of food to industrial workers and increasing agricultural exports. These economic linkages can also be crucial in reducing overhead costs and in facilitating the achievement of economies of scale. Negative externalities could include, for example, the production of pollution or increasing incentives for urban migration by agricultural workers. While such externalities might be considered, for example, by reducing the shadow-wage rate by the costs of further migration,[16] very detailed information and analysis would be required, such as the marginal effect of new urban employment on migration flows. There is a quickly burgeoning literature on environmental economics on both the project and national level.[17]

Another type of externality that must be considered is the effect that a very large project will have on the domestic-market structure. For example, a large project that produces intermediate capital goods may, in effect, come to occupy a monopolistic position in the market.[18] While this might be a necessary state of affairs, at least initially, the fact that domestic innovation and entrepreneurs could be stifled is a key point to remember. Any developing country government should therefore consider other options, such as financially encouraging joint ventures with foreign firms to provide the service or good, or contracting the service to domestic corporate bidders while providing the start-up capital.

While externalities must be considered, they are extremely difficult to quantify, even in developed countries. For example, in considering health risks associated with a project is impossible to find a universally agreeable currency value for human lives. Development-project planners may be able to make some rough estimations of external benefits and costs, such as the expected increases of health problems due to pollution, but much of externality analysis will remain imprecise.

In regard to economic linkages, Little and Mirrlees point out that the project as a whole must still be profitable (have a positive rate of return), or all of the expected linkages in terms of related industries will be similarly unprofitable.[19] The ignorance of this basic logic in the past seems to have led at times to over-subsidized infant industries, with the result that most, in effect, had continuously negative rates of return—in other words, they never grew up.[20]

Income Distribution

Income-distribution considerations also play a role in development-project selection, since in many developing countries, income distribution is highly unequal. Projects that will worsen income distribution, therefore, may not receive the same consideration as ones in which lower income or wealth groups benefit. On the other hand, a balance must be achieved between income-distribution considerations and the expected declining savings rates of lower income classes.[21] As mentioned before, the lack of capital is one of the principle blockages to economic development, and any savings will have an economic multiplier effect as investment, which creates new resources and frees other resources for further economic investment and growth.[22] The amounts of collateral or savings might have to reach a critical mass size, that is, be large enough for entrepreneurs to borrow enough to create new businesses and jobs. In either case, the administrative as well as the opportunity costs of redistributing income in the project selection process must be considered.[23] Income-distribution considerations can be made a part of the cost-benefit analysis through the assignment of marginal weights to the benefits according to the accruing income class. Benefits to lower income groups therefore are valued more highly. Another method would be to assign weights to the expected increases in consumption by income class.[24]

As might be expected, the main problem is the choice of distributional weights. These weights will, once again, be difficult to apply consistently and will rest on the value judgments of the decision-maker. Political considerations, as might be surmised, will probably play the most important role in this case. Income distribution between generations is likely to be the least controversial in that future generations are likely to have many fewer advocates than do proponents of current consumption.[25]

Related Project Measurement Methods and Risk

Other methods of selecting projects on a financial basis are often applied in conjunction with the cost-benefit analysis methods that have been described above, oftentimes to consider the risk and uncertainty of project benefits. Input-rationing analysis considers the ratio of the use of a scarce resource, such as foreign exchange (to buy inputs), per expected benefit amount.[26] Cost effectiveness measures the costs of various combinations of project inputs, given a certain operational process of using the inputs.[27]

Uncertainty and risk analysis are often completed alongside cost-benefit analysis. One method of risk analysis is sensitivity analysis, in which each of the main environmental variables, such as the cost of inputs, is changed and the effect on project benefits is seen. The percentage change in the variables that renders the net present value of the project zero are sought after, in order to see the likelihood of project failure if one of the variables changes.[28] Regardless of the outcome of the sensitivity analysis, some allowance should be made in the project budget for uncertainty.[29] The amount to be set aside could be determined by another related method, which is to assign probabilities to the changes in the variables and, from them, to find the expected value benefits. These probabilities should be derived from past experience, including statistical distributions of outcomes and actuarial data from insurance of related risks.[30]

The "impact approach," which has been used by U.S. and Swedish development agencies in project assessment, links the immediate expected impacts of projects to more general goals of social and economic changes. It attempts to do so by including sets of verifiable indicators of the expected impacts in the project assessments.[31]

Once again, these related analytical techniques are fraught with danger, in that the changing of any one or more of the necessary assumptions can affect the outcome of the process and, therefore, the selection of the development project. In a strongly politicized context, then, there will be multiple opportunities to manipulate measures to favor certain projects. Moreover, the measurement of the risk of different types of projects will have to be on different time and space scales, as acceptable risk will vary from economic sector to sector, geographic region to region, and so on, and will depend on the overall scope.[32]

Conclusion: Traditional Methods of Development-Project Evaluation

While cost-benefit analysis of development projects could be a valuable (though limited) tool, it has not been rigorously utilized by the development agencies.[33] Even within developing countries, the centralization of budget decisions that is required for application of cost-benefit analysis has been resisted by developing-country politicians and bureaucracies.[34] This points to a basic lack of capacity, which also means an opening for manipulation through technical wizardry. Finally, the continuing pressure to lend within the multilateral institutions has led to considerably less scrutiny of development projects than is warranted.[35] Thus, we must conclude that the poor application of cost-benefit analysis has led to great abuses and manipulations in development-project practice according to the politics of development agencies. Before we get to that, we should first discuss the new techniques of participatory assessment that have come to challenge traditional project-evaluation techniques. The key point here is that in all this discussion of project selection techniques, there is little to no formal place for input by the beneficiaries!

Surely, if we want to assign social weights to project outcomes in order to consider these factors alongside project financial factors, only the beneficiaries themselves would know how much they value each expected aspect/outcome of the project.

AN EMERGING PARADIGM: PARTICIPATORY METHODS OF EVALUATION

Introduction

In the context of worsening relative inequality, which we discussed in Chapter 1, and the feeling that development agencies were out of touch with the reality of the most impoverished groups in the developing country, a wide-ranging critique developed. Though the methods of participatory rural appraisal (PRA) have been explicated in Chapter 5 by Parfitt, I will make some additional comments here in line with our present argument. For our purposes, we will focus here on suggestions from that critique about how participatory techniques could work hand in hand with more traditional development-project evaluation techniques.

The movement toward participatory methods of evaluating projects began in the 1970s but really has gained steam in the last decade. The basic motivation behind participatory evaluation is that at the center of this book: the need to allow development recipients[36] a voice in shaping the development project. Critics of development agencies from this point of view, including those in developing-country NGOs, felt that the evaluation of development projects along traditional lines missed a large part of the picture of what was actually happening at development project sites and that this blindness led to numerous mistakes in the field, poor evaluations, and a general miscasting of the direction of development-project efforts. The pioneers of this movement, such as Robert Chambers, think that the criteria for the success of a development project should come directly from the recipients themselves.[37] The fact is that recipients alone have intimate knowledge of their own goals, constraints, and relationships; in a sense, the goal of participatory evaluation is to empower recipients to have a voice in all stages of development projects and to be the ultimate judges of the relative success of the project. By making participants an intimate part of the process, we enhance the direct impact and sustainability of our development efforts. Participatory evaluation should be incorporated in both the selection and post-hoc learning of a project.

Basic Methods of Participatory Evaluation

The key idea behind participatory evaluation is to understand the beneficiaries' perspectives and to use them for shaping development projects. This means that the evaluator has to spend considerable time understanding the context of the area in which the project will take place. He/she must find out the motivations and desires of the target population, help them to develop a list of priorities, help them to find indicators of success, and conduct surveys and interviews to allow them to evaluate the results. This evaluation would then be used to improve the development project (design and/or implementation) according to recipient wishes and ideas. More important, participatory techniques create an atmosphere of strong energy and ownership by the recipients, so that the project has a much higher likelihood of success and sustainability. Last but certainly not least, the experience of participation has a value itself and may lead to important long-term beneficial externalities and spillover effects, such as empowering a marginalized group to make greater demands or instilling confidence and/or organization within it.

Participatory techniques thus allow for much greater and ongoing tailoring of project evaluation. For example, a participatory evaluation may bring out subtle differences among subgroups of the recipient group, who experience different effects of the projects. It may be that women are affected differently than men or that older women of a certain socioeconomic group have a particular experience that is different from the rest of the group. The broad, quick, post-hoc survey techniques of traditional evaluations would probably miss these important aspects of the project.

Participatory evaluation in its best forms does attempt to be systematic and consistent. A key concept is "triangulation," which refers to using a wide variety of sources and techniques to provide overlapping evidence for ideas about how the development project is working. On the ground level, participatory evaluators should use maps, "walk-throughs," interviews, diagrams, and indices, according to the literature, to understand the local context of the project. Some sources recommend having participants rank priorities and outcomes, measure outcomes in common terms, identify changes, and clarify expectations. In short, the recipients' statements themselves should occupy much of the evaluator's report.

Where Participatory Evaluation Falls Short

While participatory evaluation techniques seem to be spreading like wildfire, when poorly done they create evaluation problems as serious as the traditional techniques we dissected earlier. Participatory techniques can be subjective to the point of inconsistency. This inconsistency may arise from a number of sources, including an inadequate representation from all groups. As is well known, the most vocal of a group may not represent all points of view, and subgroups in many developing countries' cultures may be reluctant to share open opinions unless they have a very strong relationship with the evaluator. Second, participatory evaluation leads to major questions ironically related to the advantages of the scale. On one hand, participatory evaluation allows for intimate, complex portrayals of local situations; on the other, participatory evaluation reports may not say much that would be helpful in conducting future projects in other areas. Moreover, the potential for unsystematic evaluation information could not only impede the overall learning curve for the development agency, but also may have only limited effects in programming priorities, where much more adjustment is called for. As an example of the latter, imagine a donor agency facing refunding requests from multiple projects, all of which have had participatory evaluations, with the expected mixed results. Without some clear kinds of guidelines, it will be very difficult to evaluate which project(s) should get funding priority.

Unfortunately, most of the agencies who have adopted participatory techniques have done so in a very cursory manner, paying lip service without really changing their practices.[38] The result is that participatory techniques have had an indirect influence on development agencies' language and ideas, but only an occasional demonstrable impact on actual development-project administration. This is not to underestimate the importance of participatory techniques in changing the focus of development administration, particularly among NGOs. But participatory techniques still leave us with the key question of how to create a systematic method of participatory evaluation that a) truly incorporates the recipients into the decision-making process and b) measurably allocates scarce resources in the most efficient way. We will discuss the political obstacles to the further spread of participatory evaluation techniques in our political economy section below.

CHOOSING THE RIGHT EVALUATION METHODS

So, how are we to decide between the systematic but oblique evaluation methods traditionally used and the emerging ones of the participatory paradigm? Of course, the answers must be well anticipated—it depends on the context, and use both as much as possible. First, let's talk about the context of development projects. Development aid, in general, is disbursed in two general avenues: programmatic and project aid. While this book has focused on project aid, programmatic aid—aid that is geared toward creating a more favorable macro-environment for development—is arguably becoming the more important of the two. Most of the new initiatives in the development-agency literature center on renewing institutions and reforming macroeconomic policies, in line with the neoliberal platform of the First World that we discussed in Chapter 1. Thus, the scale and scope of programmatic aid is dramatically different than that of project aid. Second, even with project aid, scale and scope vary tremendously. Thus, the traditional focus of most development aid, large infrastructure projects, differs dramatically from the focus of most new, small-scale project aid by NGOs. This might lead us to the general principle that large-scale projects are better suited to traditional cost-benefit methods and participatory techniques to small-scale projects.

We would argue, by contrast, that *a combination* of both techniques, albeit to different degrees according to the context, is needed *in cases of both pro-grammatic, large-scale projects and grassroots, small-scale projects*. In both cases, we are facing problems that can be aided by both sets of evaluation techniques. First, we always face highly limited and politically constrained budgets. This means that we will always be in the difficult position of choosing among competing projects. Second, we need to be able to measure results, both in order to incorporate learning into an overall evaluation of development efforts and to see which projects should be continued as is and which substantially modified or dropped. As an example, think about several education projects occurring simultaneously in the same area of a country. The projects may (should) be set up with different mixes of training, materials, and direct ser-vicing of recipients. The different techniques that come out of each experience are invaluable guides for what may be more and less successful in the next round of projects. Third, there must be a way to link the project information with an overall sectoral, country, and programmatic strategy. The project data should give us feedback that helps us to realistically adjust our programmatic priorities and strategies. In sum, there must be some *systematic* method of pri-oritizing, measuring, and evaluating projects. Traditional project cost-benefit analysis, when properly done with an open mind, can provide an important tool in this effort.

However, we have also seen all too often that cost-benefit analysis comes up short in terms of capturing the roots of project success and failure. In other words, cost-benefit analysis is very helpful in describing *how much* in terms of project results and costs, but it says very little about *why* a project is succeed-ing. This is where both a general qualitative analysis of country and sectoral conditions and the participatory techniques we discussed can be invaluable. Those techniques can help us to capture nuances of a situation that might not be evident with a cost-benefit analysis. It could be, for example, that an edu-cation project failed to raise test scores but did increase female participation. Qualitative analysis could reveal important political relationships and interest groups; social customs, practices, and beliefs; and differentiation of groups and identities that could be crucial to both defining and sustaining any suc-cesses of projects. More important, participatory techniques allow us to eval-uate projects from the point of view of the people who matter most, the poor themselves. From this point of view, we see no reason why participatory tech-niques could not be used in a modified way on both a national and a regional scale. Imagine how much more effective the IMF would be if it ever actually took the political context and points of view of the government and the af-fected people into account!

GETTING TO THE HEART OF THE MATTER: THE POLITICAL ECONOMY OF EVALUATION

The Sick Political Cycle of Evaluation

We have demonstrated how the use of a variety of techniques, both system-atic (quantitative) and idiosyncratic (qualitative and participatory) can yield better results in development projects. We also have acknowledged the integral place that evaluation occupies in terms of creating both accountability and learning from development projects. Unfortunately, evaluation is the illegitimate child of development administration: everyone acknowledges its importance and sorry state, but no one is willing to step up to take responsibility for it.[39]

To answer why, we need to do a basic political-economy analysis of the development-agency funding game, which covers most aid agencies, with the exception of the Nordic countries, which we discuss below. As we discussed in Chapter 1, aid agencies were set up with dual purposes: one, to deliver aid as a form of charity; and two, to pursue host country objectives using aid as a tool. Objective two has always been the stronger of these two objectives. We have also seen that this political-economy fact applies not only to development agencies, but also to NGOs, which depend on governments and donors of money.[40] Both the hierarchy of any aid organization itself and this continual need to raise new resources have perverse effects in the aid process. First, donors, whether governments or private backers, want to know that the values they hold dear are the ones guiding the use of their money in development assistance. This means that aid agencies play a game of creating demonstrable results and continual improvements in development deliverance. Thus, we see the questionable situation of agencies that publish their large macro-evaluation reports, such as the World Bank, showing the remarkable overall progress from the previous year, mainly through very difficult-to-pin-down general statistical measures. This makes us wonder what the World Bank will do when the improvement reaches a 99.9% approval rating for projects some year in the future! In the serious downsizing environment of the aid business, most agencies have adopted a "results-based management" (RBM) language. Thus, agencies like USAID want to show their funding agency, the U.S. Congress, that the United States is getting clear benefits for its aid dollars. This led USAID to introduce a whole RBM system, with a mound of new directives. Other agencies, such as CIDA of Canada, have followed suit. It remains to be seen whether RBM will lead to genuine improvements or mostly more window dressing. Our important point here is not about the important aspect of demonstrable results as a part of the evaluation process, but simply the farcical nature of development agencies' attempts to fabricate them.

To be sure, donor agencies are caught in a very difficult situation. They must demonstrate continually improving concrete results in an enterprise that is wrought with complexities in little-understood local contexts, with continually changing and often conflicting directives from their funding agencies. Moreover, as large hierarchies, the central-office directives may be a far cry from the reality experienced in the field. Field personnel will likely need a minimum of five years to really understand a local context for development. For the reasons we discussed in the participatory evaluation section, we want our project directors to be able to navigate the web of political, economic, logistical, and cultural constraints and opportunities within host governments and local projects. In the development business, unfortunately, this almost never happens. Project timelines are often much shorter; there is frequent turnover of personnel; and there are frequent changes in central management and directives. Add to this all the changes happening in the local country and regional environment. Not the least of these is the relationship between the host government and the donor agency. The host government will have its own priorities and engage in rent-seeking behavior in terms of aid flows. It may seek to control and repress the recipient population, rather than helping them develop. As several authors, including Klitgaard and Pincus, point out, the host government actually has a good deal of leverage in aid negotiations. Without the host government, aid organizations cannot operate—they will be out of business. Furthermore, aid organizations have no real leverage, other than threatening to reduce further lending. In practice, this almost never happens, as aid agencies (unlike international finance) do not effectively co-operate to force changes in the accountability of a host government, assuming they could agree on priorities anyway. We have to remember that most of aid is increasingly tied, so that aid agencies' domestic constituencies include not only human-rights and gender-equality organizations, but the aid business as well. Last but not least, aid donors have to compromise with host governments or they will lose access to the very marginalized populations they purport to be helping.[41] Thus, even in the most egregious of circumstances of misman-agement, aid agencies must play ball with host governments—we usually see one renegotiation after another instead of any real change in policy or ac-countability.[42] We might even say that the political environment is in some ways the root cause of the poor distribution of resources, both on the inter-national and the local level, in terms of blocking redistribution or adequate investment in human resources. In many cases, developing countries are strongly divided along class, race, and ethnic lines. Imagine, then, the difficulty of reaping the advantages of participatory techniques in this environment.

Second, evaluation results are largely ignored because they have no impact on funding for new projects.[43] In development agencies, the principal mid-dleman between the budget-authorizing department and the project manager is the loan/grant (or task) officer for a particular area, whether it be a geo-graphic or sectorally focused one. The *loan officer's job is to place the greatest amount of funding into projects as quickly as possible.* Thus, we have set in place a system with very perverse incentives, in which the loan officers who "suc-ceed" best in their jobs are the ones who are able to spend the most money.[44] This creates a natural bias toward the funding of very large infrastructure projects, with high short-term costs and clearly demonstrable results (e.g., a bridge was built), and a haste to fund projects that seem remotely feasible. From the field official's point of view, there is little incentive to give a truly realistic picture of the difficulties, complexities, or obstacles of the projects they propose. More important, while all projects have some monitoring and evaluation in practice, unless the monitoring and evaluation are in the disaster range, they tend to have little, if any, real effect on the funding of the ongoing project and almost none on future projects. What is more important in the lending cycle is developing reliably safe projects with clear rates of return (i.e., no disasters or embarrassments) and developing mutually beneficial close partnerships with host-government personnel that will help one speed through one's project portfolio.[45] In fact, when a project is very poorly executed, it becomes extremely difficult to pull the plug, since there are so many vested interests in reporting the project's success! Thus, the alternative of not funding a project (especially if no particularly attractive ones are available) or cutting off funding midstream when there are warning signs is almost never considered.[46] Last but not least, in the large development agencies, such as the World Bank, loan officers are often rotated to different geographic and sometimes sectoral positions, and thus they have a difficult time accumulating the deep personal expertise in particular types of projects. More important, they do not therefore have a long-term stake or sense of accountability for the projects.

Third, and maybe most nefarious (though it's difficult to say), *evaluation is not conducted with any regard to the independence of the evaluator.* Aid agencies all claim that they have in-house accountability agencies and that they contract out evaluations to independent consultants. What a surprise, then, that projects are routinely evaluated with the same kinds of bureaucratic language, such as better "institutionalization of results" needed, or, more recently, "greater incorporation of stakeholder views" needed. As anyone with experience in the aid game knows, evaluations, even when conducted by outside consultants, are hardly independent. This is because contracting procedures in aid agencies severely curtail access to bidding contractors (this is true for all aspects of the aid business), which thus tends to favor those with inside connections and/or experience of contracting techniques. *Second, why would an outside consultant ever write a damning report if he/she wanted to be hired again by the development agency?*[47] And why would an inside inspector general move against its own colleagues upon whom it relies for information to continue its job? Thus even internal investigations tend to have little authority for enforcement and mollified criticism.[48]

Thus we see that the political economy of the aid game condemns development to make the same mistakes over and over. The bottom line is that, for all the guffawing of the development agencies and NGOs for greater accountability on the part of developing country governments, *neither development agencies nor NGOs have any regard for their own accountability or transparency, let alone genuine participation of the project recipients, particularly in resource allocation decisions.* Moreover, there is little or no incentive for learning or research of projects either before start-up or after project completion.[49] We also see why incorporating genuine participation in the aid game is so very difficult. Our hope is that by pushing the lack of accountability of the aid (NGO and donor) agencies to the front and center, we will make some small contribution to improving action on the evaluation front.[50]

Recent Steps Forward

The development-project community tends to reinvent itself in fits and starts, often adopting the language, though often not the spirit or praxis, of its greatest critics. This has certainly been the case with the newest buzzwords of participation, sustainability, and gender mainstreaming, adopted language-wise wholeheartedly by the major development agencies. In this sense, part of the purpose of this book is to move the reality up to match the rhetoric. However, as our Gramscian analysis from Chapter 1 points out, any rhetoric must have a substantive aspect to be credible. In this sense, there are some positive signs that the development community is taking some steps forward to establish more productive evaluation. The new mantra of the development community seems to be a focus on results.

The first recent initiative to reinvent development evaluation for results was the logical framework approach (LFA), which has been adopted by a number of development agencies. LFA basically seeks to condense project information into comparable data modules, including, for example, goal, purpose, impact, outcome, output, input, and activity. The basic idea behind LFA is to create "objectively verifiable indicators" of the progress of a project. This allows for much easier selection and evaluation of a number of projects in a more thorough fashion. The main problem is that the quality of the information in each module can vary greatly. Impact, for example, might be stated in general terms, such as "income enhancement," for one project, and much more specific terms, such as "creating a viable tourist guide service," for another. Another problem is similar to one that we discussed previously, namely that logframe comparisons may miss important details or nuances, such as circumstances that make one seemingly comparable much more difficult but rewarding. The logical framework, as presently used, will also not be appropriate for programmatic or policy objectives, such as macroeconomic reform or pushing for recognition of civil liberties. However, the spirit of creating a uniform information module for purposes of comparability and learning is a genuine step forward. The European Commission has recently sought to improve learning effects of the logframe analysis by adopting the Project-Cycle Management (PCM) framework. The PCM is an interesting step forward that seeks to create a more uniform information output using LFA at each step of the project cycle, including ex-post evaluation.[51] It is too early to really evaluate the PCM now, but the criticisms we have discussed throughout this chapter in terms of incentive structures for learning still apply.

More recently, the results-based management (RBM) approach seems to have come into vogue among a wide variety of donor agencies, including USAID and CIDA of Canada. The basic idea behind RBM is to increase the sense of accountability by delineating clear and measurable objectives for projects. This means the project managers really must be able to demonstrate project success. This implicitly and happily leads to much more consideration at the project-design stage, when baseline data and consideration of clear outcomes must take place. On the other hand, in those areas where development projects are truly experiments or occur in unpredictable conditions, RBM would obviously not be appropriate. Moreover, RBM does not get at the issues of participation and empowerment that are the focus of this book. Unfortunately, the impression one gets from conversations with project managers is all too often that both the logframe and the RBM are viewed as simply another paper hurdle, not really breaking the cycle of lack of accountability leading to projects that neither maximize resources nor satisfaction.

The Operations Evaluation Department (OED) at the World Bank has acquired a new mandate within the organization. The OED seems to be making some headway in instilling a learning aspect to Bank projects, including emphasizing consideration of sustainability and long-term capacity development. The OED seems to have adopted all the right buzzwords, in short, for meaningful evaluation. More important, the OED reports directly to the Bank's Board of Executive Directors, which oversees evaluation through its Committee on Development Effectiveness. However, the OED's new initiatives, while laudable, are inherently limited. First, results are short-term perspectives on project and country strategies. There is no evidence of long-term (> 5 years) reviews of project sustainability. Second, the OED's reports reflect the economistic and overly quantified culture of the World Bank. There is no real evidence of lessons that would help a project manager for a specific type of project; most results are reported as "average performance," which, not surprisingly, seems to consistently increase over time. Most important, the OED can hardly be considered an independent agency of the World Bank— evidently the unit and its personnel are intimately tied to their ability to work within the World Bank. Obviously, then, their results are going to be reported within acceptable political and organizational parameters. This generally reduces the chances for any improvements to nonthreatening, general ones, rather than holding managers and lending officers accountable for their actions. Indeed, no one is holding the OED accountable!

The best efforts seem to be coming from the Scandinavian development agencies. The Swedish International Development Cooperation Agency (Sida) has a Department for Evaluation and Internal Audit that seems to be grappling with many of the issues we have discussed; a selective list of these publications appears in the Bibliography. For instance, a recent report by Sida looks at ways to create a useful information and project-results dissemination system in the agency. Sida's evaluation department also conducts comprehensive reviews of sets of country, project, and evaluation reports to check on the quality of information and, more impressively, the extent to which policy objectives are both realistic and being attained by projects. These documents thus serve as a prototype for a learning process. Sida tends to rely on the logical framework analysis for its evaluations, with all the advantages and problems mentioned before. More important, the drawback with Sida's efforts is, again, the lack of independence and accountability in evaluations and decision-making, respectively. It is interesting to note, by contrast, that the Auditor General reviews Denmark's development assistance.

CONCLUSION: HOW EVALUATION COULD WORK BETTER, EVEN WITHIN THE POLITICAL CONSTRAINTS[52]

One of the key questions anyone who studies political economy is who allocates resources and how? In the aid game, we have seen that there are a mix of actors with power, including the funding agency, the donor agency, and the host government. The need for demonstrable results in line with values of the funding agency constrains the donor agency and sets up the sick environment of development that we have just described. However, the need for host-government permission and collaboration also gives developing-country governments some, admittedly limited, leverage to impose interests. This leaves the recipients, who have a similar type of leverage in terms of whether or not they participate in the project. There is clear evidence for the effectiveness of participation, and both donor agencies and NGOs have made "participation" the latest buzzword.[53] But let's not exaggerate—the limited leverage of impoverished recipients, historically repressed by host governments, means they will offer very little, if any, resistance to the channeled participation in whatever carrots (or onions) are offered by the development business. As we have noted elsewhere in this book, development agencies purposefully avoid any discussion and thus consideration of politics—thus all development efforts are bound to be conducted with a handicapped view. A true evaluation would have to openly consider political obstacles to genuine participation and sustainability.

We should also be realistic, however, not to reify participation itself. In many developing countries, local areas are also full of repression, frequently marked by hierarchical and repressive relationships, such as the control of a local warlord, land owner, or the male head of a household. These relationships are probably well ingrained in the culture from historical practice, so that the outward show of results of equity in participation through a development project may lead to quite illusory long-term effects. Thus, development practitioners will have to try to work within the local context, in order that resistance to the new techniques will not reach such a level as to end the possibilities for transformation. Thus, in the end, development projects must balance respect for the local context and culture with the longer-term hopes for justice, equity, and humanitarian treatment. Our examples from our chapter on gender in development projects point to just this difficult tightrope.

The same kind of tightrope exists in terms of attempting to create a meaningful evaluation culture in development.[54] There is no way to ignore the
prerogatives and power of the funders, donors, and host governments, in diminishing order, but even within those constraints, we believe improvement is
eminently feasible. Here are a few suggestions that result from our discussion:

- Projects should be the particle in a wave of long-term development planning. Creating coherence and long-term sustainability require meaningful evaluation over the
long term. At present, there is almost no documentation of the long-term effects of
projects! Projects that are sustainable should show results after 5, 10, 15, and 20
years. The long-term evaluation might turn some projects labeled as short-term
failures into long-term successes. This requires a change in the incentive structure
of development organizations away from short-term funding and quick-results dem-
onstrations to longer-term evaluations of sustainability.
- Select projects and allocate resources based on input from the beneficiaries.
- Give genuine power and responsibilities to beneficiaries in project decision-making.
The exact decision-making configuration of the stakeholders—aid donor, host government, beneficiaries—will vary from project to project, but each should understand that the beneficiaries must have a direct influence on development decisions
for the project to be successful. This would be true even where the beneficiaries
seem to be making decisions that other parties consider as suboptimal.
- Tie funding to monitoring and evaluation.
- Monitoring and evaluation must include participatory input. Indicators should include perceptive surveys, as well as more concrete or measurable inputs delineated
in the project document.
- Require background reviews of similar projects as part of the project proposal
process.
- Tie evaluations of agencies and loan officers to improvements in effective use of
funds, including opinions of recipients, not total loan amounts.
- Accept failures and policy experiments as important building blocks for learning.
- Create long-term groups to study sets of projects for lessons, with the power to
change loan, project, and programmatic criteria.
- Create long-term planning and long-term budget cycles.
- Ensure independent evaluation by hiring a variety of evaluators, including academics, retired development practitioners, and local developing-country representatives,
and loosening the bureaucratic contracting filters.
- Build in flags in cases of unexpectedly significant positive or negative results, so that
the lessons from these projects can be incorporated and highlighted for agency-wide
usage.
- Build in occasional audits and evaluations of evaluations by truly independent agencies. Creating a sense of random auditing will reduce the costs of mandatory auditing
that then becomes pro forma for a lack of resources. Auditors monitoring projects
should be able to report directly to an executive decision-maker to pull the plug on
projects that are not working or to recommend a revamping of them. On the other

hand, projects that are going exceptionally well should be publicized and receive additional incentives/funding.

- Keep in mind that no project are "failures," given the heterogeneity of time/space contexts, and, more important, the possibility for learning from them. Even the best project selection tools will not anticipate the myriad complicating factors that come into play once the project is initiated.

- The information system around the project life cycle must take evaluation seriously and be integrated with the decision-making system in a way that sets up incentives for learning from projects. Information should be modular to the extent possible, so that a user-friendly database of case studies is readily available across agencies. The logical-framework approach might be a good start for a more elaborate mold for project information. Unless the proper incentives of the decision-making system are in place, there will be no incentive for either honesty or learning in the decision-making system. For example, an officer's success should be judged on the basis of his/her ability to manage and learn from projects, based on evaluation criteria, not on how much funding was pushed out.

- The culture of the development enterprise must encapsulate the idea that the ultimate evaluation of the project depends as much on the process as on the specific outcomes. Processes that empower and build capacity among beneficiaries are by nature successful, regardless of the technical outcomes. Sustainability in a technical sense over the long term depends on empowerment and capacity.

- NGOs and donor agencies must find a way to cooperate with each other in order to create a learning community in development. Eventually, such a community could fund independent, experienced evaluation teams that could work across agencies, and an information system, including libraries and researchers, learning and spreading lessons from project experience.

- Political sustainability on the national, regional, and local levels must be considered as part of project analysis. While development agencies would like to pretend to be apolitical, every action and policy they take is political. By looking to long-term development of institutional capacity, as discussed in our previous chapter, they can balance out the short-term need to find a political coalition to get the project going.

In terms of general approaches, rather than seeing the CBA (quantitative, modeling) vs. the PRA (participatory, contextual) methodologies of project planning and evaluation as conflicting, we see them as two necessary sides of the same coin. The real trick in terms of methodologies is to arrive at a method for training development managers to be capable in both areas. Achieving an understanding of a local geographic and sectoral context, however, takes years and requires long-term contact with the local community, so this implies not only changes in training but also in the assignment structure of aid organizations. We see no reason why economists, political scientists, and anthropologists should not all get along. In the end, improvements to development projects rely not just on improvement of project and sectoral techniques and evaluation, but upon a fundamental reorientation of development at all levels of activity and thought. Hopefully, we have helped to move the conversation toward that goal.

Notes

CHAPTER 1

1. Because the book is written for a diverse audience, experts may want to skim over sections of material already familiar to them.

2. For a primer on the postmodern critique of development from a theoretical point of view, see Arturo Escobar, *Encountering Development* (Princeton, N.J.: Princeton University Press, 1995). An advanced treatment is found in Trevor Parfitt, *The End of Development: Modernity, Post-Modernity and Development* (Sterling, Va.: Pluto Press, 2002).

3. We should clarify that we are utilizing a pragmatic form of postmodernism, not the extreme relativism that is the subject of rhetorical debates (and a false target).

4. Of course, most of these initiatives would not be considered by their subjects as "postmodern," but we see a nexus between postmodern values and them.

5. There are a growing number of histories of development, many from quite polemical angles. For the ease of use, we rely primarily upon the bibliography at the end of each chapter for references and further reading. By deconstruction, we mean the technique of using a genealogy, or study of the origins of a term, as well as a look at the dialectic between the discourse or language used and the facts of the case. Both of these reveal the power relationships behind both the ideas and the practices of the development culture.

6. We use the term "exemplar" to mean a symbolic node or referent. In this case, the Marshall Plan is constantly evoked as a symbol of clear progress through development assistance, in this case, European postwar recovery. Of course, the Marshall Plan also involved centralized government control and various conditionalities by the U.S. donor, an aspect that is conveniently forgotten when the image (sign) of the Marshall Plan is evoked to legitimize aid.

7. In 1997, only 4 countries—Denmark, Norway, the Netherlands, and Sweden—

exceeded the United Nations' already pathetically low target of giving aid worth 0.7% of GDP. The U.S. rate was 0.09, the lowest of any Development Assistance Committee member. The decline in aid levels is also well documented. See Michel, especially pp. 69 and 93.

8. The European countries (and Japan) together might form a rival bloc, but thus far have not yet been able to do so on a consistent basis. The United Kingdom, for example, has a mode of capitalism and foreign policy much closer to the United States.

9. Alternative measurements of aid would look at aid/GNP, but we do not agree with this orientation. Aid should go to the poorest of the poor, who, *by definition*, are almost always in countries with the lowest GNP.

10. This section on European aid was written with the help of Trevor Parfitt.

11. For a fuller account of Europe as an aid donor, the reader might consult the "Europe Dossier" at http://www.euforic.org/.

12. A more detailed examination of the Euromed can be found in Parfitt, 1997.

13. It is interesting to note that a large proportion of aid to India is through PL 480, agricultural dumping, which hurts the poorest of the poor, for example, rural farmers. Colombia is a major recipient of U.S. aid, the third largest by some estimates, but receives mostly military aid.

14. Though there is recent acknowledgment of this problem, creating coordination, both in terms of organization and information, has been extremely slow and halting. A few new information portals that are definite steps forward in terms of coordinating information are the Eldis system, found at http://www.eldis.org/ and the "Accessible Information on Development Projects" page found at http://www. developmentgateway.org/node/100647.

15. Rather than reviewing the literature here, we try to deconstruct some of the ontology behind the newly in-vogue concepts, and then discuss the implications for development projects.

16. This dovetails nicely, of course, with some of the new institutionalism's conceptions of growth and development. See Anil and Ron Hira, "The New Institutionalism: Contradictory Notions of Change," *The American Journal of Economics and Sociology* (April 2000): pp. 267–82.

17. See especially Michelle Miller-Adams, *The World Bank: New Agendas in a Changing World* (New York: Routledge, 1999) for evidence on this point.

CHAPTER 2

1. J. Price Gittinger, *Economic Analysis of Agricultural Projects*, 2nd ed. (Washington, D.C.: World Bank, 1982), p. 3.

2. Warren C. Baum and Stokes M. Tolbert. *Investing in Development: Lessons of World Bank Experience*. (Washington, D.C.: World Bank, 1985), p. 8.

3. Gittinger, pp. 13–14.

4. Ibid., p. 12.

5. Ibid., p. 35.

6. Dennis A. Rondinelli, *Development Projects as Policy Experiments: An Adaptive Approach to Development Administration* (London: Methuen, 1983), p. 5.

7. Baum and Tolbert, 1985, pp. 335–36.

8. Analyses of the synoptic and other models of decision-making may be found

in Anthony G. McGrew and M. J. Wilson, eds., *Decision Making Approaches and Analysis* (Manchester, U.K.: Manchester University Press, 1982).

9. Rondinelli, 1983, p. 65.

10. Ibid., pp. 72–73.

11. Wayne Parsons, *Public Policy: An Introduction to the theory and Practice of Public Policy* (Cheltenham, U.K.: Edward Elgar, 1995), p. 272.

12. Kathleen Staudt, *Managing Development: State, Society, and International Contexts* (London: Sage Publications, 1991), p. 129.

13. R. K. Merton, "Bureaucratic Structures and Personality," in *Reader in Bureaucracy*, eds. R. K. Merton, with Alisa P. Gray, Barbara Hockey, and Hanan C. Selvin. (Glencoe, Ill.: The Free Press, 1952), pp. 361–71.

14. B. B. Schaffer, "Deadlock in Development Administration," in *Politics and Changes in Developing Countries*, ed. C. Leys (Cambridge: Cambridge University Press, 1969), p. 190.

15. Quoted in Coralie Bryant and Louise G. White, *Managing Development in the Third World* (Boulder, Colo.: Westview Press, 1982), pp. 51–52.

16. Trevor Parfitt, "The Decline of Eurafrica? Lome's Mid-Term Review," *The Review of African Political Economy* 65 (1996): 56.

17. Ibid., pp.58–59.

18. Commission of the European Communities (CEC), *Manual: Project Cycle Management—Integrated Approach and Logical Framework* (Brussels: CEC, 1993), pp. 20–21.

19. United Nations Development Programme (UNDP), *How to Write a Project Document: A Manual for Designers for UNDP Projects* (New York: UNDP, 1991), p. 23.

20. Ibid., pp. 55–56.

21. Ibid., pp. 51–58.

22. Commission of the European Communities, 1993, p. 24.

23. Ibid., p. 36.

24. Rondinelli, 1983, p. 92.

25. Ibid., p. 127.

26. See Mark Turner and David Hulme, *Governance, Administration and Development: Making the State Work* (Basingstoke, Hampshire, U.K.: Palgrave, 1997), p. 146.

27. Baum and Tolbert, 1985, pp. 53–54.

28. Mick Foster, *New Approaches to Development Cooperation: What Can We Learn from Experience with Sector Wide Approaches*, Working Paper 140 (London: Overseas Development Institute, 2000), p. 7.

29. Commission of the European Communities (CEC), *Experience of Sector Wide Approaches in Health: A Simple Guide for the Confused* (Brussels: CEC, 2000), p. 7.

30. Ibid., p. 1.

31. Foster, 2000, p. 35.

32. Ibid., p. 25.

33. Adrienne Brown, Mick Foster, Andy Norton, and Felix Naschold, *The Status of Sector Wide Approaches*, Working Paper 142 (London: Overseas Development Institute, 2000), pp. 9–11.

34. Brown et al., 2000, pp. 14–17.

35. Ibid., p. 22.

36. Ibid., p. 37.

37. Ibid.

38. Ibid., p. 47.

39. Department for International Development (DfID), International Institute for Environment and Development (IIED), and CAPE ODI, *Strategies for Sustainable Development: Can Country-Level Strategic Planning Frameworks Achieve Sustainability and Eliminate Poverty?* (London: DfID, IIED, and CAPE ODI, 2000), pp. 4–5.

40. World Bank, *Comprehensive Development Framework: Progress Report to the World Bank's Executive Board-May 2000* (Washington, D.C.: World Bank 2000), p. 1.

41. World Bank, *Partners in Transforming Development: New Approaches to Developing Country-Owned Poverty Reduction Strategies* (Washington, D.C.: World Bank, 2000), p. 3.

42. World Bank, *Overview of Poverty Reduction Strategies* (Washington, D.C.: World Bank, 2001), p. 1.

43. World Bank, 2001, p. 2.

44. See Neil Thin, Mary Underwood, and Jim Gilling, *Sub-Saharan Africa's Poverty Reduction Strategy Papers from Social Policy and Sustainable Livelihoods Approaches*, (A Report for the Department for International Development) (Oxford: Oxford Policy Management, 2001).

45. Oxfam, *Making PRSPs Work; The Role of Poverty Assessments* (Oxford: Oxfam, 2001), p. 5.

46. Ibid., p. 5.

47. Ibid., p. 5.

CHAPTER 3

1. W. M. Adams, *Green Development: Environment and Sustainability in the Third World*, 2nd ed. (London: Routledge, 2001), pp. 270–72.

2. Ramachandra Guha and Juan Martinez-Alier, *Varieties of Environmentalism: Essays North and South* (London: Earthscan, 1997), pp. xv–xvi.

3. Ibid., p. xiv.

4. Eric Hobsbawm, *Age of Extremes: The Short Twentieth Century, 1914–1991* (London: Michael Joseph, 1994), p. 570.

5. Adams, 2001, p. 247.

6. Ibid., p. 222.

7. Ibid., p. 225.

8. Ibid., p. 226.

9. Catherine Caufield, *Masters of Illusion: The World Bank and the Poverty of Nations* (London: Pan Books, 1996), p. 8; and Jai Sen, "What Kind of Country Do We Want India to Be?" *Mainstream*, 2000, http://www.narmada.org/articles/JAI_SEN/whatkind.html (accessed July 10, 2002), p. 3.

10. Quoted in Caufield, 1996, p. 8.

11. Ibid., p. 20.

12. See Caufield, 1996, chapter 1.

13. Ibid., p. 12.

14. Ibid., pp. 24–28.

15. Adams, 2001, pp. 240–47.

16. Ibid., p. 57.

17. World Commission on Environment and Development (WCED), *Our Common Future* (Oxford: Oxford University Press, 1987), p. 8.

18. Ibid., p. 89.

19. Ibid.

20. Adams, 2001, p. 72.

21. Ibid., p. 88–89.

22. N. Low and B. Gleeson, *Justice, Society and Nature: An Exploration of Political Ecology* (London: Routledge, 1998), p. 81.

23. Wilfred Beckerman, "How Would You Like Your 'Sustainability,' Sir? Weak or Strong? A Reply to My Critics" *Environmental Values* 4 (1995), 169–79.

24. Adams, 2001, p. 105.

25. "Kyoto Protocol to the United Nations Framework Convention on Climate Change, December 10, 1997," in Michael Totten, *Getting It Right: Emerging Markets for Storing Carbon in Forests* (Washington, D.C.: World Resources Institute and Forest Trends, 1999), p. 12.

26. See World Resources Institute, *Evaluating Carbon Sequestration Projects: A First Attempt*, 1994, http://www.wri.org/wri/climate/Guatemala.html (accessed July 14, 2002).

27. See Tim Hisch, "Carbon-Trading in Bolivia," BBC News, November 10, 2000, http://news.bbc.co.uk/hi/English/world/Americas/newsid_1016000/1016598.stm (accessed January 3, 2004).

28. Totten, 1999, p. 10.

29. Ibid., p. 31.

30. See Alex Kirby, "The Bonn Deal: Winners and Losers," BBC News, July 23, 2001, http://news.bbc.co.uk/hi/English/sci/tech/newsid_1452000/1452903.stm (accessed January 4, 2004).

31. See Alex Kirby, "Trees 'Will Not Avert Climate Change,'" BBC News, October 20, 1999, http://news.bbc.co.uk/hi/English/world/Americas/newsid_1016000/1016598.stm (accessed January 4, 2004).

32. See Alex Kirby, "Tree Planting Worries Over Global Worries," BBC News, May 23, 2001, http://news.bbc.co.uk/hi/English/sci/tech/newsid_1347000/1347068.stm (accessed January 4, 2004).

33. Adams, 2001, p. 118.

34. Avijit Gupta and Mukul G. Asher, *Environment and the Developing World: Principles, Policies and Management* (New York: John Wiley & Sons, 1998), p. 28.

35. Harrop and Nixon, *Environmental Assessment in Practice* (London: Routledge, 1999), p. 9.

36. Gupta and Asher, 1998, p. 231.

37. Ibid., p. 231.

38. Harrop and Nixon, 1999, p. 21.

39. Ibid.

40. Harrop and Nixon, 1999, p. 25; and Asit K. Biswas and Qu Geping, eds., *Environmental Impact Assessment for Developing Countries* (London: Tycooly Publishing, 1987), pp. 203–4.

41. Guha and Martinez-Alier, 1997, p. xx.

42. Robert Chambers, "Sustainable Rural Livelihoods: A Key Strategy for People, Environment and Development," in *The Greening of Aid*, eds. Czech Conroy and Miles Litvinoff (London: Earthscan, 1988), p. 3.

43. See Ibid., pp. 8–13.

44. Ibid., p. 10.

45. Ibid., p. 11.

46. See United Nations Development Programme (UNDP), *Sustainable Livelihoods Concept Paper,* 1999, http://www.undp.org/sl/Documents/Strategy_papers/Concept_paper/Concept_of_SL.htm (accessed July 20, 2002), p. 1.

47. Ibid., pp. 1–2.

48. United Nations Development Programme (UNDP), *SLA in Urban Areas,* 1999, http://www.undp.org/sl/Documents/General%20info/Urban_.../sla_and_urban_development.htm (accessed July 20, 2002), p. 3.

49. UNDP, *Sustainable Livelihoods Concept Paper,* p. 2.

50. UNDP (by Samir Wonmali and Novesh Singh), *Sustainable Livelihoods: Lessons Learned from Global Programme Experience,* http://www.undp.org/sl/Documents/Lessons%20Learned/ sl_lessons / sl_lessons.htm (accessed July 20, 2002), p. 7.

51. Ibid., p. 2.

52. Ibid., p. 3.

53. UNDP, *Sustainable Livelihoods Concept Paper,* p. 4.

54. Cathryn Turton, *Sustainable Livelihoods and Project Design in India,* Working Paper 127 (London: Overseas Development Institute, 2000), p. 15.

55. Department for International Development, United Kingdom (DfID), Directorate General for Development, European Commission (EC), United Nations Development Programme (UNDP), and the World Bank, "Linking Poverty Reduction and Environmental Management: Policy Challenges and Opportunities—A Contribution to the World Summit on Sustainable Development Process," consultation draft (2002), p. x.

56. Ibid., p. xi.

57. Alex Kirby, "Summit's Failed Hopes," BBC News, September 4, 2002, http://news.bbc.co.uk/2/hi/africa/2236899.stm (accessed January 10, 2004).

58. BBC News, "World Summit in Quotes," September 4, 2002, http://news.bbc.co.uk/2/low/africa/2231001.stm (accessed January 10, 2004).

CHAPTER 4

1. Anil Hira, *Ideas and Economic Policy in Latin America: Regional, National and Organizational Case Studies* (Westport, Conn.: Greenwood, 1998).

2. Numerous studies have pointed to both the lack of success and the lack of a clear theory or evaluation that could guide civil-service reform. See Robert Klitgaard, "Cleaning Up and Invigorating the Civil Service," *Public Administration and Development* 17 (1997): 487–509; and Haruna Dantaro Dlakwa, "Salient Features of the 1988 Civil Service Reforms in Nigeria," *Public Administration and Development* 12 (1992): 297–311.

3. The World Bank's "Governance and Public Sector" Web site, http://www1.worldbank.org/publicsector, on the page on "Strategies and Sequencing in Public Sector Reform," states, "On average only about one third of (civil service) reforms achieved satisfactory outcomes. Even when desirable, outcomes were often not sustainable. Downsizing and capacity building initiatives often failed to produce permanent reductions in civil service size and to overcome capacity constraints in economic management and service delivery. In later reform programs, there is little evidence

that civil servants began to "own" and adhere to formal rules such as codes of ethics." Then they go on predictably to cite technical problems or failures in implementation. As you will see in the conclusion, I think this is a misdiagnosis. According to the World Bank's *Reforming Public Institutions and Strengthening Governance* (Washington, D.C.: World Bank, 2000), "Despite relatively long operational experience, the Bank has not conducted systematic evaluations of public sector and institutional development operations across LCR (Latin America and Caribbean Region)." See bibliography for http://www1.worldbank.org/publicsector, retrieved May 11, 2001, and for the Girishankar evaluation report, *Civil Service Reform: A Review of World Bank Assistance*, on which it is based.

4. Thanks to James Busumtwi-Sam for reminding me of these.

5. Apparently, a new (2001) legislation seeks to create true decentralization in Indonesia, including local power to tax.

6. See Barbara Ingham and A.K.M. Kalam, "Decentralization and Development: Theory and Evidence from Bangladesh," *Public Administration and Development*, 12 (1992): 373–85 for a similar study of Bangladesh and Kent Eaton, "Political Obstacles to Decentralization: Evidence from Argentina and the Philippines," *Development and Change* 32 (January 2001): 101–27, on Argentina and the Philippines.

7. See also Henry Veltmeyer and Anthony O'Malley, eds., *Transcending Neoliberalism: Community-Based Development in Latin America* (Bloomfield, Conn.: Kumarian Press, 2001) on this aspect of the donor game in decentralization, especially pp. 59–64. They point out that decentralization should be a community-based, not an administratively-based, model.

8. White provides a nice case study showing how, notwithstanding the rhetoric, NGOs are extremely politicized and have interests that are often not coincident with the poor. See Sara H. White, "NGOs, Civil Society, and the State in Bangladesh: The Politics of Representing the Poor," *Development and Change* 30 (1997): 307–26.

9. See Walter Little and Eduardo Posada-Carbo, eds., *Political Corruption in Europe and Latin America* (New York: St. Martin's Press, 1996), for an interesting collection of essays on historical contexts of corruption in Latin America.

10. World Bank employees, for instance, have relatively high salaries, pay no taxes, and have a host of fringe benefits, including child care and foreign travel subsidies.

11. This same emphasis on organizational culture was the conclusion drawn from an extensive six-nation study of civil-service reforms; see Merilee Grindle and Mary Hilderbrand, "Building Sustainable Capacity in the Public Sector: What Can Be Done?" *Public Administration and Development* 15 (1995): 441–63.

CHAPTER 5

1. Quoted in Peter Oakley, Ellen Birtei-Doku, Ole Therlrildsen, David Sanders, Charlotte Harland, Adriana Herrera Garibay, and UNIFEM, *Projects with People* (Geneva: International Labour Organization, 1991), p. 6.

2. Ibid., p. vii.

3. See Barbara Thomas-Slayter, "A Brief History of Participatory Methodologies," in *Power, Process and Participation: Tools for Change*, eds. Rachel Slocum, Lori Wichbert, Dianne Rocheleau, and Barbara Thomas-Slaytes (London: Intermediate Technology Publications, 1995), pp. 9–11.

4. See Robert Chambers, *Rural Development: Putting the Last First* (Harlow, U.K.: Longman, 1983).

5. John Cohen and Norman Uphoff, *Rural Development Participation: Concepts and Measures for Project Design, Implementation and Evaluation* (Ithaca, N.Y.: Cornell University Press, 1977), p. 6.

6. Oakley et al., 1991, p. 9.

7. World Bank, "The World Bank and Participation" (Washington, D.C.: Operations Policy Department, 1998), p. 4.

8. Oakley et al., 1991, p. 175.

9. See Stan Burkey, *People First: A Guide to Self-Reliant, Participatory Rural Development* (London: Zed Books, 1993), and Chapter 3 of this book for a fuller explication of these issues.

10. Oakley et al., 1991, p. 171.

11. Thomas-Slayter, 1995, pp. 12–14.

12. Robert Chambers, *Whose Reality Counts? Putting the First Last* (London: Intermediate Technology Publications, 1997), p. 102.

13. Louise Fortmann, "Women's Renderings of Rights and Space: Reflections on Feminist Research Methods," *Power, Process and Participation: Tools for Change*, eds. Rachel Slocum, Lori Wichbert, Dianne Rocheleau, and Barbara Thomas-Slaytes (London: Intermediate Technology Publications, 1995), pp. 35–37.

14. Fortmann, 1995, p. 37.

15. Chambers, 1997, p. 212.

16. Ibid., p. 212–13

17. Ibid., p. 197.

18. Robert Leurs, "Current Challenges Facing Participatory Rural Appraisal," in *Who Changes? Institutionalizing Participation in Development*, eds. James Blackburn with Jeremy Holland (London: Intermediate Technology Publications, 1998), p. 128.

19. Ibid., p. 125.

20. Andrea Cornwall, Samuel Musyoki, and Garett Pratt, *In Search of a New Impetus: Practitioners' Reflections on PRA and Participation in Kenya*, IDS Working Paper 131 (Sussex, U.K.: Institute of Development Studies, 2001), p. 8.

21. Ibid., p. 7.

22. Ibid., p. 7.

23. Dereje Wordofa, "Internalising and Diffusing the PRA Approach: The Case of Ethiopia," in *Who Changes? Institutionalizing Participation in Development*, eds. James Blackburn with Jeremy Holland (London: Intermediate Technology Publications, 1998), p. 16.

24. Cornwall, Musyoki, and Pratt, 2001, p. 11.

25. Garett Pratt, *Practitioners' Critical Reflections on PRA and Participation in Nepal*, IDS Working Paper 122 (Sussex, U.K.: Institute of Development Studies, 2001), p. 36.

26. Cornwall, Musyoki, and Pratt, 2001, p. 12.

27. Ibid., p. 12.

28. Wordofa, 1998, p. 15.

29. Chambers, 1997, p. 215.

30. Leurs, 1998, p. 125.

31. Chambers, 1997, p. 226.

32. IDS Workshop, "Towards a Learning Organisation—Making Development Agencies More Participatory from the Inside," in *Who Changes? Institutionalizing Par-*

ticipation in Development, eds. James Blackburn with Jeremy Holland (London: Intermediate Technology Publications, 1998), p. 147.

33. Ibid., p. 148.

34. Ibid., p. 149.

35. Ibid., p. 150.

36. Ibid., p. 151.

37. Heinrich Eylers and Reiner Forster, "Taking on the Challenge of Participatory Development at GTZ: Searching for Innovation and Reflecting on the Experience Gained," in *Who Changes? Institutionalizing Participation in Development*, eds. James Blackburn with Jeremy Holland (London: Intermediate Technology Publications, 1998), p. 106.

38. John Thompson, "Participatory Approaches in Government Bureaucracies: Facilitating Institutional Change," in *Who Changes? Institutionalizing Participation in Development*, eds. James Blackburn with Jeremy Holland (London: Intermediate Technology Publications, 1998), pp. 115–16.

39. Cornwall, Musyoki, and Pratt, 2001, pp. 28–29.

40. Burkey, 1993, p. 61.

41. Ibid., p. 62.

42. Quoted in Ibid., 1993, pp. 63–64.

43. See Trevor Parfitt, *The End of Development: Modernity, Post-Modernity and Development* (London: Pluto Press, 2002) for a more complete explanation of these arguments.

CHAPTER 6

Special thanks go to Mónica Escudero, Kathleen Staudt, and Jane Jaquette for helpful comments on this chapter.

1. Most of the authors in the literature, as well as the practitioners with whom I have discussed these issues, are quite skeptical that either international or bilateral development agencies have made a genuine commitment to gender issues.

2. A brief anticipatory disclaimer: I would like to point out that it is not my purpose here to review all feminist theory, or even provide a comprehensive perspective of gender and development. The purpose is to see what postmodernism can add, in a practical way, to current thinking and practices regarding gender and development. Considerably better treatment of other issues can be found elsewhere; some references are provided in the bibliography.

3. As in other academic enterprises, there are innumerable splinters and hybrid theories. Among the most important are the women and development approach, and the dependency-globalization approach. See the bibliography for background readers. See Jane L. Parpart, M. Patrica Connelly, and V. Eudine Barriteau, eds., *Theoretical Perspectives on Gender and Development* (Ottawa: International Development Research Centre, 2000); and Valentine M. Moghadam, ed., *Patriarchy and Economic Development: Women's Positions at the End of the Twentieth Century* (Oxford: Clarendon Press, 1996) for further discussion.

4. Boserup's pioneering 1970 work was a key catalyst in gaining attention to gender issues. Ester Boserup, *Woman's Role in Economic Development*, 2nd ed. (London: Earthscan, 1989).

5. Thanks to Robert Anderson for pointing this out to me.

6. Josette Murphy, *Mainstreaming Gender in World Bank Lending: An Update* (Washington: World Bank, 1997) cites gender as a significant factor in improving project success rates in World Bank projects.

7. See Kathleen Staudt, *Policy, Politics, and Gender: Women Gaining Ground* (West Hartford, Conn.: Kumarian Press, 1998) and *Women, International Development and Politics: The Bureaucratic Mire* (Philadelphia: Temple University Press, 1997). She points out that, as in other areas of operation, there is little coherence or transparency among development agencies in regard to gender.

8. Prudence Woodford-Berger, *Gender Equality and Women's Empowerment: A DAC Review of Agency Experiences 1993–1998*, SIDA Studies in Evaluation 00/1 (Stockholm: SIDA, 2000). Among the different agencies, SIDA seems to be one of the most progressive.

9. See Staudt, 1997 for further discussion.

10. Swedish International Development Cooperation Agency, *Promoting Equality between Women and Men in Partner Countries* (Stockholm: SIDA, 1997).

11. Anne Marie Goetz says that changing NGO discrimination is even harder, because of the "wolf in sheep's clothing" factor of NGO rhetoric. See Anne Marie Goetz, "Dis/Organizing Gender: Women Development Agents in State and NGO Poverty-Reduction Programmes in Bangladesh," in *Women and the State: International Perspectives* eds. Shirin M. Rai and Geraldine Lievesley (Bristol, Penn.: Taylor and Francis, 1996), pp. 118–42, esp. 137–38.

12. See Staudt, 1997, pp. 312–15 for further discussion.

13. Maxine Molyneaux has a nice categorization for this difference between practical and strategic interests. The former refers to the need to deal with immediate problems facing women, such as health and education. The latter refers to the need to create a feminist consciousness. See Maxine Molyneaux, "Mobilization without Emanicipation? Women's Interest, the State and Revolution in Nicaragua," *Feminist Studies* 11, no. 2 (1985): 227–54; Caroline O. N. Moser, *Gender Planning and Development: Theory, Practice and Training* (New York: Routledge, 1993); and Patricia L. Howard, "Beyond the 'Grim Resisters': Towards More Effective Gender Mainstreaming Through Stakeholder Participation," *Development in Practice* 12, no. 2 (2002): 164–76.

14. Ministry of Foreign Affairs (Norway), *WID/Gender Units and the Experience of Gender Mainstreaming in Multilateral Organisations* (Oslo: Ministry of Foreign Affairs, 1999).

15. See Rai and Lievesly, *Women and the State: International Perspectives* for a number of examples, but the case is clear if one looks at the gender advisory board of any international development agencies.

16. See Sue Ellen M. Charlton, *Women in Third World Development* (Boulder, Colo.: Westview Press, 1984), pp. 186–93; and Barbara Wolfe Jancar, *Women under Communism* (Baltimore: Johns Hopkins University Press, 1978).

17. International Fund for Agriculture and Development (IFAD), *Gender and Household Food Security*, found at http://www.ifad.org/gender/thematic/guatemala/guat_e.htm (1998).

18. USAID, *More, But Not Yet Better: An Evaluation of USAID's Programs and Policies to Improve Girls' Education*, Program and Operations Assessment Report No. 25 (Washington: USAID, 1999).

19. Food and Agriculture Organization (FAO) of the United Nations, *Gender and Participation in Agricultural Development Planning: Key Issues from Ten Case Studies* (Rome: FAO, 1997), pp. 4, 5, 6, 9.

20. As stated before, we reject the naïve arguments that all postmodernism must be completely relativistic. We think that a "do-no-harm" standard is perfectly compatible with the core respect that postmodernism requests for all subjects and others.

21. However, one could posit that, at least in the short run, they will have to fall into general historical and social archetypal parameters, à la Jung's psychological archetypes.

22. Sally Baden and Anne Marie Goetz, in "Who Needs [Sex] When You Can Have [Gender]: Conflicting Discourses on Gender at Beijing," call patriarchy "a straw man." Meanwhile, Cecile Jackson's essay, "Rescuing Gender from the Poverty Trap," points out that the equation of gender with poverty is one of the basic problems with the WID approach and a mechanism that aid bureaucracies use to prevent true mainstreaming. Both are in Cecile Jackson and Ruth Pearson, eds., *Feminist Visions of Development: Gender, Analysis and Policy* (New York: Routledge, 1998), pp. 19–38 and 39–64, respectively.

23. Kate Young, "Planning from a Gender Perspective," p. 372, in Nalini Visvanathan, Lynn Duggan, Laurie Nisonoff, and Nan Wiegersma, eds., *The Women, Gender & Development Reader* (London: Zed Books, 1997), pp. 366–73. Embedded quotes are Young's quotes of the Programme of Action of the Government of India National Policy on Education, 1986.

24. It is interesting to note that there is very little difference in the numbers of women in national political office between North and South—the proportions are low everywhere. Data are available from the United Nation's WISTAT database.

25. A USAID evaluation of projects for sub-Saharan African education states, "Schooling girls has deep cultural ramifications. Policy or program decisions that do not take into account local attitudes, beliefs, and conditions, and that are seen as imposed, are likely to fail." See USAID (Karen Tietjen), *Educating Girls in Sub-Saharan Africa: USAID's Approach and Lessons for Donors*, Technical Paper No. 54 (Washington, D.C.: USAID, 1997), 13.

26. See Dorienne Rowan-Campbell, "Development with Women," found at http://www.developmentinpractice.org/readers/women/rowan.htm.

CHAPTER 7

Duncan Knowler and Cindy O'Brien of Simon Fraser University made excellent comments that helped me to significantly improve this chapter.

1. This is a widely cited figure and, in fact, the self-determined failure rate is actually much higher in many aid agencies. For one citation, see Steve Curry and John Weiss, *Project Analysis in Developing Countries* (London: Macmillan, 2000), p. 329.

2. D. W. Pearce and C. A. Nash, *The Social Appraisal of Projects: A Text in Cost-Benefit Analysis* (New York: Halstead Press, 1981), p. 3.

3. I.M.D. Little and J. A. Mirrlees, *Project Appraisal and Planning for Developing Countries* (New York: Basic Books, 1974), p. 147.

4. Pearce and Nash, 1981, pp. 51–52.

5. Lyn Squire and Herman G. Van Der Tak, *Economic Analysis of Projects* (Baltimore, Md.: The Johns Hopkins University Press, 1975), pp. 24–25.

6. The basic aspects of cost-benefit analysis are taken from Harvey S. Rosen, *Public Finance*, 3rd ed. (Homewood, Ill.: Richard D. Irwin, Inc., 1992), pp. 240–66.

7. Ibid., p. 246.

8. Ibid., p. 247.

9. Little and Mirrlees, pp. 29–32.

10. N. Imboden, *A Management Approach to Project Appraisal and Evaluation* (Paris: Development Centre of the OECD, 1978), p. 35.

11. Little and Mirrlees, pp. 224–25.

12. Ibid., pp. 70–71. Thanks to Duncan Knowler for pointing out the importance of trade taxes as well.

13. Ibid., pp. 292–93.

14. A very good discussion on this issue is found in Christer Gunnarsson, *Capacity Building, Institutional Crisis, and the Issue of Recurrent Costs* (Stockholm: Almkvist and Wiksell Intl., 2001).

15. Robert Sugden and Alan Williams, *The Principles of Practical Cost-Benefit Analysis* (Oxford: Oxford University Press, 1978), pp. 212–13.

16. Little and Mirrlees, p. 173.

17. See Duncan Knowler, "Recent Experience with Incorporating Environmental Concerns into Project Appraisals," *Impact Assessment and Project Appraisal*, forthcoming, for a review of the literature. A few other references are included in the bibliography. Unfortunately, we have neither the space nor the expertise to deal adequately with environmental evaluation here.

18. I.M.D. Little and J. A. Mirrlees, "Project Appraisal and Planning Twenty Years On," *Proceedings of the World Bank Annual Conference on Development Economics 1990* (Washington, D.C.: World Bank, 1991), p. 352.

19. Little and Mirrlees, 1974, pp. 340–41.

20. See Patricia Adams, *Odious Debts: Loose Lending Corruption, and the Developing Country's Environmental Legacy* (Toronto: Earthscan Canada, 1991).

21. Little and Mirrlees, 1974, p. 57.

22. Ibid., pp. 242–43.

23. Sugden and Williams, pp. 203–4.

24. Little and Mirrlees, 1974, pp. 254–55.

25. Sugden and Williams, p. 219.

26. Ibid., p. 76.

27. Imboden, p. 38.

28. Little and Mirrlees, 1974, pp. 131–33.

29. Little and Mirrlees, 1991, p. 357.

30. Little and Mirrlees, 1974, pp. 312–13.

31. Imboden, p. 41.

32. Pearce and Nash, pp. 87–88.

33. Little and Mirrlees, 1991, p. 360.

34. Ibid., p. 362.

35. Ibid., p. 364.

36. We use "recipients" here, although the development literature often refers to them as the "primary stakeholders," with other stakeholders possibly including the host government, the development agency, and so on.

37. See Robert Chambers, *Whose Reality Counts? Putting the First Last* (London: IT, 1997) for the seminal book in this movement.

38. This typical hypocritical state of affairs is noted by Robert Chambers in "Relaxed and Participatory Appraisal Notes on Practical Approaches and Methods: Notes for participants in PRA familiarization workshops in the second half of 1999," found on the IDS participation Web site, http://www.ids.ssux.ac.uk.

39. We should not be viewed as radicals in our assessment in this section of the "aid business," as there are any number of damning reports by watchdog committees, observers, and internal reports that back up our analysis. See Elzing, UK International Development Committee, Donecker, Kruse, The CornerHouse, Thin, Robert Chambers's "Notes for Participants," and Graham Hancock's *Lords of Poverty* in the bibliography. Unfortunately, much of this literature, such as Hancock's, borders on the polemical, which is not our intention.

40. See Terje Tvedt, *Angels of Mercy or Development Diplomats? NGOs and Foreign Aid* (Trenton, N.J.: Africa World Press, 1998); and Deepa Narayan, with Raj Patel, Kai Schafft, Anne Rademacher, and Sarah Koch-Schulte, *Voices of the Poor: Can Anyone Hear Us?* (Washington, D.C.: World Bank, 2000). Narayan on the problems and overall ineffectiveness of NGOs, especially pp. 224–30, and pp. 5–7 and 131–42, respectively.

41. An interesting case occurred a few years ago when Oxfam was kicked out of Egypt for crossing the line in terms of gender development projects. It is hard to believe Oxfam did more good with the moral stance than if it had found a way to stay in the country.

42. Where one does not changes, such as finding macroeconomic stability in Brazil in the late 1990s, attempting decentralizing educational reforms in Chile, or developing innovation policy experiments in Malaysia, these always come from domestic political changes that lead to host government self-initiation.

43. No major party in the game is affected by project failure. Host governments continue to receive funding, and the donor agency's loans, in virtually every case, are fully guaranteed by the host government. See Glenn P. Jenkins, "Project Analysis and the World Bank," *The American Economic Review* 87, no. 2 (May 1997): 40.

44. See also Jonathon Pincus, "The Post-Washington Consensus and Lending Operations in Agriculture: New Rhetoric and Old Operations Realities," in *Development Policy in the Twenty-First Century: Beyond the Post-Washington Consensus* eds. Ben Fine, Costas Lapavitsas, and J. Pincus (New York: Routledge, 2001), pp. 182–218.

45. The sick vicious circle of incompetence that this game sometimes takes on is captured somewhat nicely in Klitgaard's famous book, *Tropical Gangsters* (New York: Basic Books, 1990).

46. Thanks to Cindy O'Brien for pointing this out to me.

47. As we have seen with the demise of Arthur Andersen's cooking of Enron's books, this is a problem not unique to development.

48. The number of development consulting agencies that "get the big contracts," is around 3–4 depending on the particular type of project. Not only is there evident collusion between contractors and agencies, but there is obvious collusion among contracting agencies to create a uniform and palatable product. This prevents them from ever criticizing each other. The oldest game in town is seen in any number of well-paid "development expert" jobs advertised in the *Washington Post* classifieds. They call for someone with years of "contract work" experience, thus cementing the golden

parachute for those lucky enough to get a job in USAID's (or any other agency's) contracting office.

49. See Jenkins, p. 40 and World Bank, *Assessing Aid-What Works, What Doesn't, and Why* (Washington, D.C.: World Bank, 1998), for evidence that pre-project analysis results in significantly higher rates of project success. The World Bank's own report assessing aid states, "But serious, rigorous evaluations that generate solid knowledge are expensive, and no one government has the incentive to undertake evaluations that will benefit other countries," (p. 92).

50. Though outside the scope of our present task, it seems clear that both aid and government spending fail to reach the poorest groups, who are rarely politically powerful. Both types of spending, particularly social spending, tend to benefit middle and upper classes disproportionately. See Narayan, et al., especially pp. 83–126.

51. See Erik Kijne, "Project-Cycle Management (PCM): A Tool for Aid Effectiveness," in *Cost-Benefit Analysis and Project Appraisal in Developing Countries* ed. Colin Kirkpatrick and John Weiss (Brookfield, Vt.: Edward Elgar, 1996).

52. While we have limited our political economy analysis here to evaluation, the same collusive, greedy, and dysfunctional relationships exist in regard to contracting out work, which is becoming an increasingly common feature of the aid business. There are the same barriers to entry in these areas as in evaluation, though local contractors, generally wealthy local businesses, sometimes get their fingers in the pie (mainly out of necessity, as no other suppliers are available).

53. See World Bank, *Voices of the Poor: Can Anyone Hear Us?* (Washington, D.C.: World Bank, 2000) for both evidence and popularization of participation, especially pp. 22 and 79–87.

54. A promising start, if mostly lip service for the moment, is found in Asian Development Bank (ADB), *Postevaluation and Feedback: Realities and Challenges in the Asian and Pacific Region* (Manila: ADB, 1995).

Selected Bibliography

GENERAL ISSUES OF DEVELOPMENT AID, DEVELOPMENT PROJECTS, AND POSTMODERNISM (CHAPTERS 1–2)

Albrow, Martin. 1970. *Bureaucracy.* London: Pall Mall Press.

Baron, Stephen, John Field, and Tom Schuller, eds. 2000. *Social Capital: Critical Perspectives.* New York: Oxford University Press.

Baum, Warren C., and Stokes M. Tolbert. 1985. *Investing in Development: Lessons of World Bank Experience.* Washington, D.C.: World Bank.

Beetham, David. 1987. *Bureaucracy.* Buckingham, UK: Open University Press.

Bensabat Kleinberg, Remonda, and Janine A. Clark, eds. 2000. *Economic Liberalization, Democratization and Civil Society in the Developing World.* New York: St. Martin's Press.

Brown, Adrienne, Mick Foster, Andy Norton, and Felix Naschold. 2000. *The Status of Sector Wide Approaches.* Working Paper 142. London: Overseas Development Institute.

Bryant, Coralie, and Louise G. White. 1982. *Managing Development in the Third World.* Boulder, Colo.: Westview Press.

Burnell, Peter. 1997. *Foreign Aid in a Changing World.* Philadelphia: Open University Press.

Busumtwi-Sam, James. 2002. "Rethinking Development: Governance, Participation, and Ownership." In *Turbulence and New Directions in Global Political Economy,* edited by James Busumtwi-Sam and Laurent Dobuzinskis, chapter 5. Houndmills, Basingstoke: Palgrave/Macmillan.

Chabbot, Charlotte. 1999. "Development INGOs." In *Constructing World Culture: International NoNGOvernmental Organizations Since 1875,* edited by John Boli and George M. Thomas, 222–48. Stanford, Calif.: Stanford University Press.

Coleman, James. 1997. "Social Capital in the Creation of Human Capital," In *Education, Culture, Economy and Society*, edited by A. H. Halsey, H. Lauder, P. Brown, and A. Stuart Wells, 80–95. Oxford: Oxford University Press.

Commission of the European Communities (CEC). 1993. *Manual: Project Cycle Management—Integrated Approach and Logical Framework*. Brussels: CEC.

———. 2000. *Experience of Sector Wide Approaches in Health: A Simple Guide for the Confused*. Brussels: European Commission.

Cusworth, John W., and Tom R. Franks, eds. 1993. *Managing Projects in Developing Countries*. Harlow, Essex, England: Longman Scientific & Technical.

Department for International Development (DfID), International Institute for Environment and Development (IIED), and Centre for Aid and Public Expenditure for the Overseas Development Institute (CAPE ODI). 2000. *Strategies for Sustainable Development: Can Country-Level Strategic Planning Frameworks Achieve Sustainability and Eliminate Poverty?* London: DfID, IIED, and CAPE ODI.

Eldis. http://www.eldis.org. (A portal to a wide range of information on development.)

Escobar, Arturo. 1995. *Encountering Development: The Making and Unmaking of the Developing World*. Princeton, N.J.: Princeton University Press.

Euforic. http://www.euforic.org. (Europe's Forum on International Cooperation.)

Foster, Mick. 2000. *New Approaches to Development Cooperation: What Can We Learn from Experience with Sector Wide Approaches*. Working Paper 140. London: Overseas Development Institute.

Foucault, Michel. 2000. *Power*. Edited by James D. Faubionand translated by Robert Hurley et. al. New York: New Press.

Freedman, Jim. 2000. *Transforming Development: Foreign Aid for a Changing World*. Toronto: University of Toronto Press.

Garner, Roberta. 1996. *Contemporary Movements and Ideologies*. San Francisco: McGraw-Hill. A good introduction to social movements theory for undergraduates.

Gittinger, J. Price. 1982. *Economic Analysis of Agricultural Projects*. 2d ed. Baltimore: Johns Hopkins University Press.

Gore, Charles. 2000. "The Rise and Fall of the Washington Consensus as a Paradigm for Developing Countries." *World Development* 28, no. 5: 789–804.

Gramsci, Antonio. 1994. *Letters from Prison*, edited by Frank Rosengarten and translated by Ray Rosenthal. New York: Columbia University Press.

Hira, Anil. 1998. *Ideas and Economic Policy in Latin America: Regional, National, and Organizational Case Studies*. Westport, Conn.: Greenwood.

Hira, Anil, and Ron Hira. 2000. "The New Institutionalism: Contradictory Notions of Change." *The American Journal of Economics and Sociology* 59 no. 2 (April): 267–82.

Honadle, George, and Rudi Klauss. 1979. *International Development Administration: Implementation Analysis for Development Projects*. New York: Praeger.

Hook, Steven W., ed. 1996. *Foreign Aid toward the Millenium*. Boulder, Colo.: Lynne Rienner.

Howell, Jude, and Jenny Pearce. 2001. *Civil Society & Development: A Critical Exploration*. Boulder, Colo.: Lynne Rienner.

Hudock, Ann C. 1999. *NGOs and Civil Society: Democracy by Proxy?* Cambridge, UK: Polity Press.

Institute of Development Studies (IDS). http://www.ids.ac.uk/ids. Web page of the

IDS at Sussex University, UK, with many references on participatory techniques in development.

International Monetary Fund (IMF). http://www.imf.org.

———. 2001. *The IMF's Poverty Reduction and Growth Facility (PRGF).*Washington, D.C.: IMF External Relations Department.

LaPalombara, Joseph, ed. 1963. *Bureaucracy and Political Development*. Princeton, N.J.: Princeton University Press.

McGrew, Anthony G., and M. J. Wilson, eds. 1982. *Decision Making Approaches and Analysis*. Manchester, UK: Manchester University Press.

Meadowcroft, James. 2000. "Sustainable Development: A New(ish) Idea for a New Century?" *Political Studies* 48: 370–87.

Merton, R. K. 1952. 'Bureaucratic Structures and Personality' In *Reader in Bureaucracy*, edited by R. K. Merton, Ailsa P. Gray, Barbara Hockey, and Hanan Charles Selvin, 361–71. Glencoe, Ill.: The Free Press.

Michel, James H. 1998. *Development Co-operation*. Paris: OECD.

Miller-Adams, Michelle. 1999. *The World Bank: New Agendas in a Changing World*. New York: Routledge.

Morrison, David R. 1998. *Aid and Ebb Tide: A History of CIDA and Canadian Development Assistance*. Waterloo, Ontario: Wilfrid Laurier University Press.

Morss, Elliot R., and David D. Gow. 1985. *Implementing Rural Development Projects: Lessons from AID and World Bank Experiences*. Boulder, Colo.: Westview.

Ottaway, Marina, and Thomas Carrothers, eds. 2000. *Funding Virtue: Civil Society Aid and Democracy Promotion*. Washington: Carnegie Endowment for International Peace.

Oxfam. 2001. *Making PRSPs Work: The Role of Poverty Assessments*. Oxford: Oxfam.

Parfitt, Trevor. 1996. "The Decline of Eurafrica? Lome's Mid-Term Review." *The Review of African Political Economy* 67: 53–66.

Parfitt, Trevor. 2002. *The End of Development: Modernity, Post-Modernity and Development*. Sterling, Va.: Pluto Press.

Parfitt, Trevor. 1997. "Europe's Mediterranean Designs: An Analysis of the Euromed Relationship with Special Reference to Egypt." *Third World Quarterly* 18, no. 5: 865–82.

Parsons, Wayne. 1995. *Public Policy: An Introduction to the Theory and Practice of Public Policy*. Cheltenham, UK: Edward Elgar.

Patterson, Rubin. 1997. *Foreign Aid After the Cold War: The Dynamics of Multipolar Economic Competition*. Trenton, N.J.: Africa World Press.

Perrings, Charles, and Alberto Ansuategi. 2000. "Sustainability, Growth and Development." *Journal of Economic Studies* 27, no. 1/2: 19–54.

Putnam, Robert D. 1993. *Making Democracy Work*. Princeton, N.J.: Princeton University Press.

Rondinelli, Dennis A. 1983. *Development Projects as Policy Experiments: An Adaptive Approach to Development Administration*. London: Methuen.

———. 1993. *Development Projects as Policy Experiments: An Adaptive Approach to Development Administration*. New York: Routledge.

Schaffer, B. B. 1969. "Deadlock in Development Administration" In *Politics and Changes in Developing Countries*, edited by C. Leys. Cambridge: Cambridge University Press.

Smillie, Ian, and Henny Helmich, eds. 1999. *Stakeholders: Government-NGO Partner-ships for International Development*. London: Earthscan and OECD.

Smith, Brian H. 1990. *More Than Altruism: The Politics of Private Foreign Aid*. Prince-ton, N.J.: Princeton University Press.

Sogge, David, ed. 1996. *Compassion and Calculation: The Business of Private Foreign Aid*. Chicago: Pluto Press.

Staudt, Kathleen. 1991. *Managing Development: State, Society, and International Contexts*. London: Sage.

Staudt, Kathleen. 1991. *Managing Development: State, Society, and International Contexts*. Thousand Oaks, Calif.: Sage Publications.

Stiles, Kendall, ed. 2000. *Global Institutions and Local Empowerment: Competing Theo-retical Perspectives*. New York: St. Martin's Press.

Theobald, Robin. 1990. *Corruption, Development and Underdevelopment*. Durham, N.C.: Duke University Press.

Thin, Neil, Mary Underwood, and Jim Gilling. 2001. *Sub-Saharan Africa's Poverty Reduction Strategy Papers from Social Policy and Sustainable Livelihoods Approaches*. Report for the Department for International Development. Oxford: Oxford Policy Management.

Thorbecke, Erik. 2000. "The Evolution of the Development Doctrine and the Role of Foreign Aid, 1950–2000." In *Foreign Aid and Development: Lessons Learnt and Directions for the Future*, edited by Fin Tarp, 17–47. New York: Routledge.

Turner, Mark, and David Hulme. 1997. *Governance, Administration and Development: Making the State Work*. Basingstoke, Hampshire: Palgrave.

Tvedt, Terje. 1998. *Angels of Mercy or Development Diplomats? NGOs & Foreign Aid*. Trenton, N.J.: Africa World Press.

United Nations Development Programme (UNDP). 1991. *How to Write a Project Doc-ument: A Manual for Designers for UNDP Projects*. New York: UNDP.

USAID. http://www.usaid.gov.

Wignaraja, Ponna, ed. 1993. *New Social Movements in the South: Empowering the People*. Atlantic Highlands, N.J.: Zed Books.

World Bank. http://www.worldbank.org.

World Bank. 2000. *Comprehensive Development Framework: Progress Report to the World Bank's Executive Board-May 2000*. Washington, D.C.: World Bank.

———. 2001. *Overview of Poverty Reduction Strategies*. Washington, D.C.: World Bank.

———. 2000. *Partners in Transforming Development: New Approaches to Developing Country-Owned Poverty Reduction Strategies*. Washington, D.C.: World Bank.

ENVIRONMENTAL ISSUES (CHAPTER 3)

Adams, W. M. 2001. *Green Development: Environment and Sustainability in the Third World*, 2d ed. London: Routledge.

Barrow, C. J. 1997. *Environmental and Social Impact Assessment: An Introduction*. Lon-don: Arnold.

Baumann, Pari. 2000. *Sustainable Livelihoods and Political Capital: Arguments and Evi-dence from Decentralisation and Natural Resource Management in India*. Working Paper 136. London: Overseas Development Institute.

Biswas, Asit K., and Qu Geping. 1987. *Environmental Impact Assessment for Developing Countries*. London: Tycooly Publishing.

Caufield, Catherine. 1998. *Masters of Illusion: The World Bank and the Poverty of Nations.* London: Pan Books.

Chambers, Robert. 1988. "Sustainable Rural Livelihoods: A Key Strategy for People, Environment and Development." In *The Greening of Aid*, edited by Czech Conroy and Miles Litvinoff. London: Earthscan.

Conroy, Czech, and Miles Litvinoff, eds. 1988. *The Greening of Aid: Sustainable Livelihoods in Practice.* London: Earthscan.

Department for International Development, United Kingdom (DfID), Directorate General for Development, European Commission (EC), United Nations Development Programme (UNDP), and the World Bank. 2002. "Linking Poverty Reduction and Environmental Management: Policy Challenges and Opportunities—A Contribution to the World Summit on Sustainable Development Process," consultation draft, accessible at http://www.eldis.org/static/DOC2619.htm.

Guha, Ramachandra, and Juan Martinez-Alier. 1997. *Varieties of Environmentalism: Essays North and South.* London: Earthscan.

Gupta, Avijit, and Mukul G. Asher. 1998. *Environment and the Developing World: Principles, Policies and Management.* New York: John Wiley & Sons.

Harrop, D. Owen, and J. Ashley Nixon. 1999. *Environmental Assessment in Practice.* London: Routledge.

Hobsbawm, Eric. 1994. *Age of Extremes: The Short Twentieth Century, 1914–1991.* London: Michael Joseph.

Low, N., and B. Gleeson. 1998. *Justice, Society and Nature: An Exploration of Political Ecology.* London: Routledge.

Norton, Andy, and Mick Foster. 2001. *The Potential of Using Sustainable Livelihoods Approaches in Poverty Reduction Strategy Papers.* Working Paper 148. London: Overseas Development Institute.

Sen, Jai. 2000. "What Kind of Country Do We Want India to Be?" *Mainstream.* http://www.narmada.org/articles/JAI_SEN/whatkind.html.

SLA in Urban Areas. United Nations Development Programme, http://www.undp.org/sl/Documents/General%20info/Urban_ . . . /sla_and_urban_development.htm, 1999.

Totten, Michael. 1999. *Getting It Right: Emerging Markets for Storing Carbon in Forests.* Washington, D.C.: World Resources Institute and Forest Trends.

Turton, Cathryn. 2000. *Sustainable Livelihoods and Project Design in India.* Working Paper 127. London: Overseas Development Institute.

United Nations Development Programme (UNDP). 1999. *Sustainable Livelihoods Concept Paper.* http://www.undp.org/sl/Documents/Strategy_papers/Concept_paper/Concept_of_SL.htm.

Wonmali, Samir, and Novesh Singh. "Sustainable Livelihoods: Lessons Learned from Global Programme Experience." United Nations Development Programme. http://www.undp.org/sl/Documents/Lessons%20Learned/ sl_lessons / sl_lessons.htm, 1999.

World Commission on Environment and Development. 1987. *Our Common Future.* Oxford: Oxford University Press.

World Health Organisation (WHO) and Centre for Environmental Management and Planning (CEMP). 1992. *Environmental and Health Impact Assessment of Devel-*

opment Projects: A Handbook for Practitioners. London and New York: Elsevier Applied Science.

World Resources Institute. 1994. *Evaluating Carbon Sequestration Projects: A First Attempt.* http://www.wri.org/wri/climate/Guatemala.html.

DEVELOPMENT ORGANIZATIONS, GOVERNANCE, AND DECENTRALIZATION (CHAPTER 4)

Dlakwa, Haruna Dantaro. 1992. "Salient Features of the 1988 Civil Service Reforms in Nigeria." *Public Administration and Development* 12: 297–311.

Eaton, Kent. 2001. "Political Obstacles to Decentralization: Evidence from Argentina and the Philippines." *Development and Change* 32: 101–27.

Foucault, Michel. 1972. *The Archaeology of Knowledge.* New York: Pantheon Books.

Girishankar, Navin. 1999. *Civil Service Reform: A Review of World Bank Assistance.* OED Report No. 19599. Washington, D.C.: World Bank.

Gramsci, Antonio. 1968. *The Modern Prince and Other Writings.* New York: International Publishers.

Grindle, Merilee, and Mary Hilderbrand. 1995. "Building Sustainable Capacity in the Public Sector: What Can Be Done?" *Public Administration and Development* 15: 441–63.

Hira, Anil. 1998. *Ideas and Economic Policy in Latin America: Regional, National, and Organizational Case Studies.* Westport, Conn.: Greenwood.

Ingham, Barbara, and A. K. M. Kalam. 1992. "Decentralization and Development: Theory and Evidence from Bangladesh." *Public Administration and Development* 12: 373–85.

Klitgaard, Robert. 1997. "Cleaning Up and Invigorating the Civil Service." *Public Administration and Development* 17: 487–509.

Little, Walter, and Eduardo Posada-Carbo, eds. 1996. *Political Corruption in Europe and Latin America.* New York: St. Martin's Press.

McCourt, Willy, and Martin Minogue. 2001. *The Internationalization of Public Management: Reinventing the Developing State.* Northampton, Mass.: Edward Elgar.

Minogue, Martin, Charles Polidano, and David Hulme, eds. 1998. *Beyond the New Public Management: Changing Ideas and Practices in Governance.* Northampton, Mass.: Edward Elgar.

Picciotto, Robert, and Eduardo Wiesner, eds. 1998. *Evaluation and Development: The Institutional Development.* New Brunswick: Transaction Publishers (for the World Bank).

Tendler, Judith. 1997. *Good Government in the Tropics.* Baltimore: Johns Hopkins University Press.

World Bank, Governance and Public Sector Reform. World Bank. http://www1.worldbank.org/publicsector

World Bank. 2000. *Reforming Public Institutions and Strengthening Governance.* Washington, D.C.: World Bank.

Specifically on Decentralization

Angell, Alan, Pamela Lowden, and Rosemary Thorp. 2001. *Decentralizing Development: The Political Economy of Institutional Change in Colombia and Chile.* New York: Oxford University Press.

Bird, Richard M., and Francois Vaillancourt, eds. 1998. *Fiscal Decentralization in Developing Countries.* New York: Cambridge University Press.

Cohen, John M., and Stephen B. Peterson. 1999. *Administrative Decentralization: Strategies for Developing Countries.* West Hartford, Conn.: Kumarian Press.

Manor, James. 1999. *The Political Economy of Decentralization.* Washington, D.C.: World Bank.

Prud'homme, Remy. 1995. "The Dangers of Decentralization." *The World Bank Research Observer* 10, no. 2: 210–26.

Tanzi, Vito. 1995. "Fiscal Federalism and Decentralization: A Review of Some Efficiency and Macroeconomic Aspects." In *Annual World Bank Conference on Development Economics 1995.* Washington, D.C.: World Bank.

Veltmeyer, Henry, and Anthony O'Malley, eds. 2001. *Transcending Neoliberalism: Community-Based Development in Latin America.* Bloomfield, Conn.: Kumarian Press.

White, Sara H. 1997. "NGOs, Civil Society, and the State in Bangladesh: The Politics of Representing the Poor." *Development and Change* 30: 307–26.

World Bank. 2000. "Chapter 5: Decentralization: Rethinking Government." In *World Development Report 1999/2000.* Washington, D.C.: World Bank.

Wunsch, James S., and Dele Olowu, eds. 1990. *The Failure of the Centralized State: Institutions and Self-Governance in Africa.* Boulder, Colo.: Westview.

Journals

Administration and Society

PARTICIPATION (CHAPTER 5)

Archer, David, and Sarah Cottingham. 1996. *The REFLECT Mother Manual: Regenerated Freirean Literacy through Empowering Community Techniques.* London: Actionaid.

Blackburn, James, with Jeremy Holland, eds. 1998. *Who Changes? Institutionalizing Participation in Development.* London: Intermediate Technology Publications.

Booth, David, John Milimo, Ginny Bond, Silverio Chimuka, Mulako Nabanda, Kwibisa Liywalii, Monde Mwalusi, Mulako Mwanamwalye, Edward Mwanza, Lizzie Peme, and Agatha Zulu. 1995. Coping with Cost Recovery: A Study of the Social Impact of and Responses to Cost Recovery in Poor Communities in Zambia, Report to SIDA, commissioned through the Development Studies Unit, Department of Social Anthropology, Stockholm University.

Burkey, Stan. 1993. *People First: A Guide to Self-Reliant, Participatory Rural Development.* London: Zed Books.

Chambers, Robert. 1983. *Rural Development: Putting the Last First.* London: Longman.

———. 1997. *Whose Reality Counts? Putting the First Last.* London: Intermediate Technology Publications.

Cohen, John, and Norman Uphoff. 1977. *Rural Development Participation: Concepts and Measures for Project Design, Implementation and Evaluation.* Ithaca, N.Y.: Cornell University Press.

Cooke, Bill, and Uma Kothari, eds. 2001. *Participation: The New Tyranny.* London: Zed Books.

Cornwall, Andrea, Samuel Musyoki, and Garett Pratt. 2001. *In Search of a New Impetus: Practitioners' Reflections on PRA and Participation in Kenya.* IDS Working Paper 131. Sussex: Institute of Development Studies.

Dewees, Peter. 1989. "Aerial Photography and Household Studies in Kenya." *RRA Notes* 7, 9–12.

Drinkwater, Michael. 1993. "Sorting Fact from Opinion: The Use of a Direct Matrix to Evaluate Finger Millet Varieties." *RRA Notes* 17: 24–28.

Economic Commission for Latin America. 1973. "Popular Participation in Development." *Community Development Journal* 8, no.2: 77–93.

Eylers, Heinrich, and Reiner Forster. 1998. "Taking on the Challenge of Participatory Development at GTZ: Searching for Innovation and Reflecting on the Experience Gained." In *Who Changes? Institutionalizing Participation in Development,* edited by James Blackburn, with Jeremy Holland. London: Intermediate Technology Publications.

Fortmann, Louise. 1995. "Women's Renderings of Rights and Space: Reflections on Feminist Research Methods." In *Power, Process and Participation: Tools for Change,* edited by Rachel Slocum et al. London: Intermediate Technology Publications.

Freudenberger, Karen Schoonmaker. 1995. "The Historical Matrix—Breaking Away from Static Analysis." *Forests, Trees and People Newsletter* 26/27.

Grandin, Barbara. 1988. *Wealth Ranking in Smallholder Communities: A Field Manual.* London: Intermediate Technology Publications.

Guijt, Irene, and Jules N. Pretty, eds. 1992. *Participatory Rural Appraisal for Farmer Participatory Research in Punjab, Pakistan.* London: International Institute for Environment and Development.

IDS Workshop. 1998. "Towards a Learning Organisation—Making Development Agencies More Participatory from the Inside." In *Who Changes? Institutionalizing Participation in Development,* edited by James Blackburn, with Jeremy Holland. London: Intermediate Technology Publications.

Leurs, Robert. 1998. "Current Challenges Facing Participatory Rural Appraisal." In *Who Changes? Institutionalizing Participation in Development,* edited by James Blackburn, with Jeremy Holland. London: Intermediate Technology Publications.

Manoharan, M., et al. 1993. "PRA: An Approach to Find Felt Needs of Crop Varieties." *RRA Notes* 18: 66–68.

Mascarenhas, J., and P. D. Prem Kumar. 1991. "Participatory Mapping and Modelling: User's Notes." *RRA Notes* 12: 9–20.

Maxwell, Simon, and Bart Duff. 1995. "Beyond Ranking: Exploring Relative Preferences in P/RRA." *PLA Notes* 22: 28–35.

Mearns, R. 1989. "Aerial Photographs in Rapid Land Resource Appraisal, Papua New Guinea." *RRA Notes* 7: 12–14A.

Mearns, Robin, D. Shombodon, G. Narangerel, U. Turul, A. Enkhamgalan, B. Myagmarzhav, A. Baynjargal, and B. Bekhsuren. 1992. "Direct and Indirect Uses of Wealth Ranking in Mongolia." *RRA Notes* 15: 29–38.

Oakley, Peter, Ellen Birtei-Doku, Ole Therlrildsen, David Sanders, Charlotte Harland, Adriana Herrera Garibay, and UNIFEM. 1991. *Projects with People.* Geneva: International Labour Organization.

Parfitt, Trevor. 2002. *The End of Development: Modernity, Post-Modernity and Development.* London: Pluto Press.

Paul, S. 1987. *Community Participation in Development Projects*. Discussion Paper No. 6. Washington, D.C.: World Bank.

Pearse, A., and M. Stiefel. 1979. *Inquiry into Participation*. Geneva: United Nations Research Institute for Social Development.

Posadas, Adora. 1995. "Participatory Evaluation of Rice." *Organic Matters, Journal on Phillipine Low External Input Sustainable Agriculture* 18: 40–45.

Pratt, Garett. 2001. *Practitioners' Critical Reflections on PRA and Participation in Nepal*. IDS Working Paper 122. Sussex: Institute of Development Studies.

Rahman, Md., Anisur. 1993. *People's Self Development*. London: Zed Books.

Rondinelli, Dennis. 1983. *Development Projects as Policy Experiments: An Adaptive Approach to Development Administration*. London: Methuen.

RRA Notes 1–21, subsequently *PLA Notes* 22 onwards, Sustainable Agriculture Programme, International Institute for Environment and Development, 3 Endsleigh Street, London, WC1H 0DD.

Sadomba, Wilbert Z. 1996. "Retrospective Community Mapping: A Tool for Community Education. *PLA Notes* 25: 9–13.

Sandford, Dick. 1989. "A Note on the Use of Aerial Photographs for Land Use Planning on a Settlement Site in Ethiopia." *RRA Notes* 6: 18–19.

Slocum, Rachel, Lori Wichhart, Dianne Rocheleau, and Barbara Thomas-Slayter, eds. 1995. *Power, Process and Participation: Tools for Change*. London: Intermediate Technology Publications.

Swift, Jeremy, and Abdi Noor Umar. 1991. "Participatory Pastoral Development in Isiolo District." *Final Report, Isiolo Livestock Development Project, EMI ASAL Programme*, Kenya.

Thomas-Slayter, Barbara. 1995. "A Brief History of Participatory Methodologies." In *Power, Process and Participation: Tools for Change*, edited by Rachel Slocum et al. London: Intermediate Technology Publications.

Thompson, John. 1998. "Participatory Approaches in Government Bureaucracies: Facilitating Institutional Change." In *Who Changes? Institutionalizing Participation in Development*, edited by James Blackburn, with Jeremy Holland. London: Intermediate Technology Publications.

Turk, Carrie. 1995. "Identifying and Tackling Poverty: Actionaid's Experiences in Vietnam." *PLA Notes* 23: 37–41.

Welbourn, Alice. 1991. "The Analysis of Difference." *RRA Notes* 14: 14–23.

Wordofa, Dereje. 1998. "Internalising and Diffusing the PRA Approach: The Case of Ethiopia." In *Who Changes? Institutionalizing Participation in Development*, edited by James Blackburn, with Jeremy Holland. London: Intermediate Technology Publications.

World Bank. 1998. *The World Bank and Participation*. Washington, D.C.: Operations Policy Department, World Bank.

WOMEN AND DEVELOPMENT PROJECTS (CHAPTER 6)

Bose, Christine E., and Edna Acosta-Belen. 1995. *Women in the Latin American Development Process*. Philadelphia, Pa.: Temple University Press.

Boserup, Ester. 1989. *Woman's Role in Economic Development*, 2d ed. London: Earthscan.

Braidotti, Rosi, Ewa Charkiewicz, Sabine Häusler, and Saskia Wieringa. 1994. *Women,*

Environment and Sustainable Development: Towards a Theoretical Synthesis. London: Zed Books.

BRIDGE (Briefings on Development and Gender). http://www.ids.ac.uk/bridge.

Carletto, C. 1998. "Gender and Household Food Security." International Fund for Agriculture and Development (IFAD). http://www.ifad.org/gender/thematic/guatemala/guat_e.htm.

Charlton, Sue Ellen M. 1984. *Women in Third World Development.* Boulder, Colo.: Westview Press.

Cummings, Sarah, Henk van Dam, and Mike Valk, eds. 1998. *Gender Training: The Source Book.* Oxford: Oxfam; Amsterdam: KIT Press.

Datta, Rekha, and Judith Kornberg. 2002. *Women in Developing Countries: Assessing Strategies for Empowerment.* Boulder, Colo.: Lynne Rienner.

Food and Agriculture Organization (FAO) of the United Nations. 1997. *Gender and Participation in Agricultural Development Planning: Key Issues from Ten Case Studies.* Rome: FAO.

Gendered Poverty and Well-Being. 1999. Special issue of *Development and Change,* 30.

Goetz, Anne Marie, ed. 1997. *Getting Institutions Right for Women in Development.* London: Zed.

Guijit, Irene, and Meera Kaul Shah, eds. 1998. *The Myth of Community: Gender Issues in Participatory Development.* London: IT Publications.

Harcourt, Wendy, ed. 1997. *Feminist Perspectives on Sustainable Development.* London: Zed. A good example of the WED approach.

Howard, Patricia L. 2002. "Beyond the 'Grim Resisters': Towards More Effective Gender Mainstreaming through Stakeholder Participation." *Development in Practice* 12 no. 2: 164–76.

Inter-American Development Bank (IDB). 1995. *Women in the Americas: Bridging the Gender Gap.* Washington, D.C.: IDB.

International Center for Research on Women. http://www.icrw.org.

Jackson, Cecile, and Ruth Pearson, eds. 1998. *Feminist Visions of Development: Gender, Analysis and Policy.* New York: Routledge.

Jahan, Rounaq. 1995. *The Elusive Agenda: Mainstreaming Women in Development.* London: Zed.

Jancar, Barbara Wolfe. 1978. *Women under Communism.* Baltimore: Johns Hopkins University Press.

Jaquette, Jane. 1994. *The Women's Movement in Latin America: Participation and Democracy.* Boulder, Colo.: Westview Press.

Kabeer, Naila. 1994. *Reversed Realities: Gender Hierarchies in Development Thought.* London: Verso.

Kardam, Nüket. 1991. *Bringing Women In: Women's Issues in International Development Programs.* Boulder, Colo.: Lynne Rienner.

Marchand, Marianne H., and Jane L. Parpart, eds. 1995. *Feminism/Postmodernism/Development.* New York: Routledge.

Markowitz, Lisa, and Karen W. Tice. 2001. "The Precarious Balance of 'Scaling Up': Women's Organizations in the Americas." Working Paper 271, Women and International Development, Michigan State University.

Ministry of Foreign Affairs (Norway). 1999. *WID/Gender Units and the Experience of Gender Mainstreaming in Multilateral Organisations.* Oslo: Ministry of Foreign Affairs.

Moghadam, Valentine M., ed. 1996. *Patriarchy and Economic Development: Women's Positions at the End of the Twentieth Century.* Oxford: Clarendon Press.

Molyneaux, Maxine. 1985. "Mobilization without Emanicipation? Women's Interest, the State and Revolution in Nicaragua." *Feminist Studies* 11, no. 2: 227–54.

Moser, Caroline O. N. 1993. *Gender Planning and Development: Theory, Practice and Training.* New York: Routledge.

Murphy, Josette. 1997. *Mainstreaming Gender in World Bank Lending: An Update.* Washington, D.C.: World Bank.

Ostergaard, Lise, ed. 1992. *Gender and Development: A Practical Guide.* New York: Routledge.

Parpart, Jane L., M. Patrica Connelly, and V. Eudine Barriteau, eds. 2000. *Theoretical Perspectives on Gender and Development.* Ottawa: International Development Research Centre.

Porter, Fenella, Ines Smyth, and Caroline Sweetman, eds. 1999. *Gender Works: Oxfam Experience in Policy and Practice.* Oxford: Oxfam.

Rai, Shirin M., and Geraldine Lievesley, eds. 1996. *Women and the State: International Perspectives.* Bristol, Pa.: Taylor and Francis.

Rowan-Campbell, Dorienne. n.d. "Development with Women." http://www.developmentinpractice.org/readers/women/rowan.htm.

Scott, Gloria. 1979. *Recognizing the "Invisible" Woman in Development: The World Bank's Experience.* Washington, D.C.: World Bank.

Staudt, Kathleen. 1998. *Policy, Politics, and Gender: Women Gaining Ground.* West Hartford, Conn.: Kumarian Press.

———. 1997. *Women, International Development and Politics: The Bureaucratic Mire.* Philadelphia, Pa.: Temple University Press.

Swedish International Development Cooperation Agency (SIDA). 1997. *Promoting Equality between Women and Men in Partner Countries.* Stockholm: SIDA.

Sweetman, Caroline, ed. 2001. *Men's Involvement in Gender and Development Policy and Practice: Beyond Rhetoric.* Oxford: Oxfam.

Tietjen, Karen. 1997. *Educating Girls in Sub-Saharan Africa: USAID's Approach and Lessons for Donors.* Technical Paper No. 54. Washington, D.C.: USAID.

Tinker, Irene, ed. 1990. *Persistent Inequalities: Women and World Development.* Oxford: Oxford University Press.

United Nations. WISTAT database.

USAID. 1999. *More, But Not Yet Better: An Evaluation of USAID's Programs and Policies to Improve Girls' Education.* Program and Operations Assessment Report No. 25. Washington, D.C.: USAID.

Van Dam, Henk, Angela Khadar, and Minke Valk. 2000. *Institutionalizing Gender Equality: Commitment, Policy and Practice: A Global Source Book.* Amsterdam: Royal Tropical Institute, KIT Publishers, and Oxfam.

Visvanathan, Nalini, Lynn Duggan, Laurie Nisonoff, and Nan Wiegersma, eds. 1997. *The Women, Gender & Development Reader.* London: Zed.

Waylen, Georgina. 1996. *Gender in Third World Politics.* Buckingham, UK: Open University Press.

WomenAction. http://www.womenaction.org/.

Wood, Cynthia A. 2001. "Authorizing Gender and Development: 'Third World

Women,' Native Informants, and Speaking Nearby." *Nepantla: Views from the South* 2, no. 3: 429–38.

Woodford-Berger, Prudence. 2000. *Gender Equality and Women's Empowerment: A DAC Review of Agency Experiences 1993–1998.* Sida Studies in Evaluation. Stockholm: SIDA.

Journals

Development in Practice
Gender and Development

EVALUATION (CHAPTER 7)

Abelson, Peter. 1996. *Project Appraisal and Valuation of the Environment: General Principles and Six Case-Studies in Developing Countries.* New York: St. Martin's Press.

Active Learning Network for Accountability and Performance in Humanitarian Action. http://www.odi.org.uk/alnap.

Adams, Patricia. 1991. *Odious Debts: Loose Lending Corruption, and the Developing Country's Environmental Legacy.* Toronto: Earthscan Canada.

Asian Development Bank (ADB). 1995. *Postevaluation and Feedback: Realities and Challenges in the Asian and Pacific Region.* Manila: ADB.

Boardman, Anthony E., David H. Greenberg, Aidan R. Vining, and David L. Weimer. 2001. *Cost-Benefit Analysis: Concepts and Practice*, 2d ed. Upper Saddle River, N.J.: Prentice-Hall.

Brent, Robert J. 1998. *Cost-Benefit Analysis for Developing Countries.* Northampton, Mass.: Edward Elgar.

Chambers, Robert. 1997. *Whose Reality Counts? Putting the First Last.* London: Intermediate Technology Development Group.

The Corner House. "Dams Incorporated: The Record of Twelve European Dam Building Companies." The Swedish Society for Nature Conservation. http://cornerhouse.icaap.org/, February 2000.

Curry, Steve, and John Weiss. 2000. *Project Analysis in Developing Countries.* London: Macmillan.

DAC Evaluation Group. http://www.oecd.org/dac/Evaluation.

Devarajan, Shantayanan, Lyn Squire, and Sethaput Suthiwart-Narueput. 1997. "Beyond Rate of Return: Reorienting Project Appraisal." *The World Bank Research Observer* 12, no. 1: 35–46.

Dixon, John A., Louise Fallon Scura, Richard A. Carpenter, and Paul B. Sherman. 1994. *Economic Analysis of Environmental Impacts*, 2d ed. London: Earthscan.

Donecker, Jane, and Michael Green. 1998. *Impact Assessment in Multilateral Development Institutions.* London: Department for International Development.

Elzing, Aant. 1981. *Evaluating the Evaluation Game: On the Methodology of Project Evaluation, with Special Reference to Development Cooperation.* Report. Stockholm, Sweden: Swedish Agency for Research Cooperation with Developing Countries.

Estrella, Marisol, ed. 2000. *Learning from Change: Issues and Experiences in Participatory Monitoring and Evaluation.* London: Intermediate Technology Publications.

Gunnarsson, Christer. 2001. *Capacity Building, Institutional Crisis, and the Issue of Recurrent Costs.* Stockholm: Almkvist and Wiksell Intl.

Hancock, Graham. 1989. *Lords of Poverty: The Power, Prestige, and Corruption of the International Aid Business*. New York: Atlantic Monthly Press.

Hanley, Nick, and Clive L. Spash. 1993. *Cost-Benefit Analysis and the Environment*. Brookfield, Vt.: Edward Elgar.

Harberger, Arnold. 1997. "New Frontiers in Project Evaluation? A Comment on Devarajan, Squire, and Suthiwart-Narueput." *The World Bank Research Observer* 12, no. 1: 73–79.

Harvey, Charles. 1998. "Cost-Benefit Analysis and Project Appraisal in Developing Countries." *The Journal of Development Studies* 34, no. 4: 149–53.

Hulme, David. "Impact Assessment Methodologies for Microfinance: Theory, Experience and Better Practice." http://idpm.man.ac.uk, n.d.

Imboden, N. 1978. *A Management Approach to Project Appraisal and Evaluation*. Paris: Development Centre of the OECD.

Institute of Development Studies (IDS), University of Sussex, England. http://www.ids.ssux.ac.uk.

Jenkins, Glenn P. 1997. "Project Analysis and the World Bank." *The American Economic Review* 87, no. 2: 38–42.

Kirkpatrick, Colin, and John Weiss. 1996. *Cost-Benefit Analysis and Project Appraisal in Developing Countries*. Brookfield, Vt.: Edward Elgar. An excellent discussion text on CBA practice.

Klitgaard, Robert. 1990. *Tropical Gangsters*. New York: Basic Books.

Knowler, Duncan. "Recent Experience with Incorporating Environmental Concerns into Project Appraisals." Burnaby, BC, Canada: Simon Fraser University, Department of Resources and Environmental Management. Mimeographed.

Kruse, Stein-Erik, Timo Kyllonen, Satu Ojanpera, Roger C. Riddell, and Jean-Louis Vielajus. 1997. "Searching for Impact and Methods: NGO Evaluation Synthesis Study." Institute of Development Studies, University of Helsinki, http://www.valt.helsinki.fi/ids/ngo/.

Little, I. M. D., and J. A. Mirrlees. 1991. *Project Appraisal and Planning for Developing Countries*. New York: Basic Books.

———. 1991. "Project Appraisal and Planning Twenty Years On." *Proceedings of the World Bank Annual Conference on Development Economics 1990*. Washington, D.C.: World Bank.

Maren, Michael. 1997. *The Road to Hell: The Ravaging Effects of Foreign Aid and International Charity*. New York: Free Press.

Monitoring and Evaluation News. http://www.mande.co.uk.

Narayan, Deepa, with Raj Patel, Kai Schafft, Anne Rademacher, and Sarah Koch-Schulte. 2000. *Voices of the Poor: Can Anyone Hear Us?* Washington, D.C.: World Bank.

OECD. 1994. *Project and Policy Appraisal: Integrating Economics and Environment*. Paris: OECD.

Operations Evaluation Department. http://www.worldbank.org/oed.

Pearce, D. W., and C. A. Nash. 1981. *The Social Appraisal of Projects: A Text in Cost-Benefit Analysis*. New York: Halstead Press.

Pearce, David W., and R. Kerry Turner. 1990. *Economics of Natural Resources and the Environment*. Toronto: Harvester Wheatsheaf.

Pearson, Charles S. 2000. *Economics and the Global Environment*. New York: Cambridge University Press.

Peck, Lennart, and Charlotta Widmark. 2000. "Sida Documents in a Poverty Per-
    spective." *Sida Studies in Evaluation*, Vol. 00, no. 2.
Perkins, Frances C. 1994. *Practical Cost Benefit Analysis: Basic Concepts and Applications.*
    Melbourne: Macmillan.
Pincus, Jonathon. 2001. "The Post-Washington Consensus and Lending Operations
    in Agriculture: New Rhetoric and Old Operations Realities." In *Development
    Policy in the Twenty-First Century: Beyond the Post-Washington Consensus*, edited
    by Ben Fine, Costas Lapavitsas, and J. Pincus, 182–218. New York: Routledge.
Poate, Derek, Roger Riddle, Nick Chapman, and Tony Curran. 2000. "The Evalu-
    ability of Democracy and Human Rights Projects." *Sida Studies in Evaluation*,
    Vol. 00, no. 3.
"Relaxed and Participatory Appraisal Notes on Practical Approaches and Methods:
    Notes for Participants in PRA Familiarisation Workshops in the Second Half
    of 1999." http://www.ids.ac.uk/ids.
Roche, Chris. 1999. *Impact Assessment for Development Agencies: Learning to Value
    Change.* London: Oxfam.
Rosen, Harvey S. 1992. *Public Finance*, 3d ed., Homewood, Ill.: Richard D. Irwin.
Rudquist, Anders, Ian Christoplos, and Anna Liljelund. 2000. "Poverty Reduction,
    Sustainability and Learning." *Sida Studies in Evaluation*, Vol. 00, no. 4.
Sang, Heng-Kang. 1995. *Project Evaluation: Techniques and Practices for Developing Coun-
    tries.* Brookfield, Vt.: Avebury.
Schill, Göran. 2001. "The Management of Results Information at Sida: Proposal for
    Agency Routines and Priorities in the Information Age." *Sida Studies in Eval-
    uation*, Vol. 01, no. 01.
Squire, Lyn, and Herman G. Van der Tak. 1975. *Economic Analysis of Projects.* Baltimore:
    World Bank.
Sugden, Robert, and Alan Williams. 1978. *The Principles of Practical Cost-Benefit Anal-
    ysis.* Oxford: Oxford University Press.
Swedish International Development Agency (SIDA). http://www.sida.se.
Thin, Neil, with Tony Good, and Rebecca Hodgson. "Social Development Policies,
    Results and Learning: A Multi-Agency Review." Department for International
    Development, accessible at http://www.dfid.gov.uk.
Tvedt, Terje. 1998. *Angels of Mercy or Development Diplomats? NGOs and Foreign Aid.*
    Trenton, N.J.: Africa World Press.
UK International Development Committee. 2000. "The Effectiveness of European
    Aid: Exasperation at the Failure of the Commission to Reform Its Development
    Activity Effectively." U.K: International Development Committee.
Walters, Carl. 1986. *Adaptive Management of Renewable Resources.* New York: Macmillan.
World Bank. 1998. *Assessing Aid—What Works, What Doesn't, and Why.* Washington,
    D.C.: World Bank.

Index

Sexuality, conflicting meanings of for women, 129

Shadow indicators, in cost-benefit analysis, 144–46

Sida (Swedish International Development Cooperation Agency), project evaluation by, 157–58

Sierra Leone, effects of corruption on government of, 39

Social benefits, consideration of in cost-benefit analysis, 144

Social capital, concept of, 22–23

Social construction: of gender and power, 129; of values, 27–28

Social differentiation, as barrier to participation, 108

Social equity, as element of sustainable development, 86–87

Social movements, and development aid, 24–25

Soil and Water Conservation Branch, of Kenya, 121–22

Soil conservation, in Africa, 86

Sovereignty, and political sustainability of development projects, 18

Soviet Union, foreign policy of in Cold War era, 3–4

Spontaneity, necessity of in participatory practice, 117

Sri Lanka, participatory development projects in, 121–22

Stabex Fund, impact of corruption on operation of, 40–41

Stakeholders: need to include in SWAPs, 59; need to involve in sustainable-livelihoods approach, 88; roles in decision-making, 159. See also Recipients

Stockholm Conference: and idea of sustainable development, 73; reaction of developing nations to, 69–70

Structural-adjustment programs: and development aid, 4, 59; effect on impoverished people, 60; impact on women, 131; reactions to criticisms of, 23. See also Debt relief

Structure, need for in participatory practice, 117

Success: criteria for in project design, 45; demonstration of in results-based management, 157; environmental awareness and, 73; evaluation methods and explaining, 152; incentives to report, 155; measurement of in public sector, 92–93

Sudan, health impacts of irrigation projects in, 72

Sustainability: of changes in gender relations, 137, 139; defined, 17, 86–87; environmental, 17–18; and evaluation process, 149, 157; lack of in NGO projects, 21; organizational, 19–20; participation as means of enhancing, 105; political, 18; and project design, 35; of projects, 32

Sustainable development: components of, 68; development of idea of, 70–71, 73–75; world summit on in 2002, 89–90. See also Environment

Sustainable-livelihoods approach: benefits of, 88–89; defined, 68; elements of, 85–86; UNDP methodology for, 87–88. See also Livelihoods

SWAPs (Sector Wide Approaches): benefits and drawbacks of, 65; control of by aid agencies, 59–60; and coordination of aid projects, 57; defining features of, 57–58; effectiveness of, 60; leadership in, 58–59

Swedish International Development Cooperation Agency (Sida), project evaluation by, 157–58

Synoptic model, of rational decision-making in project design, 35

Tanzania, SWAPs in, 58–59

Target population. See Local community; Recipients

Tax base, in developing nations, 96–98

Technical Cooperation Agency (GTZ), and participatory approaches, 121

Technological change, impact on sustainability, 73–75

Temporary interventions, emphasis on projects as, 35

About the Authors

ANIL HIRA is Assistant Professor in the Department of Political Science and Latin American Studies at Simon Fraser University. After working in a variety of public administration posts, Professor Hira taught development courses at the American University in Cairo, Tulane University, and Simon Fraser. Among his earlier publications are *Ideas and Economic Policy in Latin America* (Praeger, 1998) and *Political Economy of Energy in the Southern Cone* (Praeger, 2003).

TREVOR PARFITT is Director of the Master's Program in Development at the American University in Cairo. Professor Parfitt has worked as a consultant for a variety of development organizations, including the United Nations' Development Programme and the United States Agency for International Development. Among his publications is the forthcoming *Towards Postmodern Ethics for Development*.